PRAISE FOR *THE UNWRITTEN BOOK*

"Intense . . . Hunt gazes into [the] darkness, but she never stops looking for the cracks." —Jake Cline, *The Washington Post*

"A polestar for writers in years to come . . . It offers us permission to use the oddest, unlikeliest pieces of ourselves as object lessons in mortality. And it's an example of how to write about the subject with verve and openness."
—Mark Athitakis, *Star Tribune* (Minneapolis)

"Brilliant . . . I can't stop reading this book."
—Jeff VanderMeer, on Twitter

"Part literary criticism, part memoir, part family history, [*The Unwritten Book*] explores the things that have a hold on us. I, for one, am ready to be haunted by Samantha Hunt once again."
—Katie Yee, *Literary Hub*

"Like a trunk in the attic, *The Unwritten Book* offers up the most extraordinary, eclectic, and heart-wrenching insights, historical facts, stories, and advice on how to live closer to the dead. This book within a book is a tonic to our efficiency-addled present. I feel more alive and wiser for having read it."
—Cathy Park Hong, author of *Minor Feelings*

"A thrilling meta-detective novel . . . A treatise on fiction disguised as a work of fiction . . . or a work of fiction cleverly hidden in a nonfiction book."
—Patrick Brennan, *Chicago Review of Books*

"A very necessary addition to the haunted nonfiction library."
—Bruce Owens Grimm, *Newcity Lit*

"A bracing chat with a wise woman about the harsh beauty of life on earth." —Anne Pyburn Craig, *Chronogram*

"An ardent investigation into life, love, death, and creativity . . . Rendered in exceptionally honed, often ravishing prose spiked with hilarious or stunning candor . . . A literary performance of uncommon perception, vitality, daring, and heart."
—Donna Seaman, *Booklist* (starred review)

"Hunt writes in touching detail and with heartfelt prose . . . Both intimate and incisive, this genre-melding collection will make readers want to hold their loved ones close."
—*Publishers Weekly*

"A vulnerable, wide-ranging, and at times deeply affecting patchwork of ruminations on the unknown." —*Kirkus Reviews*

"A moving exploration of the concept of haunting and a powerful reverie." —Tobias Carroll, *InsideHook*

"Samantha Hunt's writing is always precise, elliptical, and magical, whether she's weaving a fictional tale or, as in *The Unwritten Book*, delving into the mysteries of life, family, and especially the power of books, both real and imagined. The result is mesmerizing and truly marvelous." —Susan Orlean, author of *On Animals*

"*The Unwritten Book* is a disobedient work—not quite memoir (even as the author interrogates her own life), not quite philosophy (though with much to say on art, faith, ethics, and more), not quite classifiable. Samantha Hunt's readers already know she is one of the best American writers of fiction of her generation; it's little surprise her nonfiction would be this thrilling, this haunting, this smart."

—Rumaan Alam, author of *Leave the World Behind*

"I'm utterly entranced, educated, and vitalized by Samantha Hunt's *The Unwritten Book*, a beautiful, inventive collection shot through with wildness and grace. I can't remember the last time I read something so heavy with grief and darkness that made me feel so accompanied in the human condition, so inspired to return to my life with more curiosity, love, and wonder."

—Maggie Nelson, author of *On Freedom*

Joe Hagan

SAMANTHA HUNT

The Unwritten Book

Samantha Hunt is the author of the story collection *The Dark Dark* and the novels *Mr. Splitfoot*, *The Invention of Everything Else*, and *The Seas*. Hunt is the recipient of a Guggenheim Fellowship, the Bard Fiction Prize, the National Book Foundation's 5 Under 35 prize, and the St. Francis College Literary Prize, and she was a finalist for the Orange Prize and the PEN/Faulkner Award. She lives in upstate New York.

ALSO BY SAMANTHA HUNT

The Dark Dark

Mr. Splitfoot

The Invention of Everything Else

The Seas

The Unwritten Book

The Unwritten Book

An Investigation

SAMANTHA HUNT

PICADOR * FARRAR, STRAUS AND GIROUX * NEW YORK

Picador
120 Broadway, New York 10271

Copyright © 2022 by Samantha Hunt
All rights reserved
Printed in the United States of America
Originally published in 2022 by Farrar, Straus and Giroux
First paperback edition, 2023

The Library of Congress has cataloged the Farrar, Straus and Giroux
hardcover edition as follows:
Names: Hunt, Samantha, author.
Title: The unwritten book : an investigation / Samantha Hunt.
Description: First edition. | New York : Farrar, Straus and Giroux, 2022. |
    Includes bibliographical references.
Identifiers: LCCN 2021053947 | ISBN 9780374604912 (hardback)
Subjects: LCSH: Parapsychology. | Ghosts. | Haunted places. | Hunt, Samantha. |
    Hunt, Samantha—Homes and haunts.
Classification: LCC BF1040 .H86 2022 | DDC 130—dc23/eng/20211220
LC record available at https://lccn.loc.gov/2021053947

Paperback ISBN: 978-1-250-86308-9

Designed by Gretchen Achilles

Our books may be purchased in bulk for promotional, educational, or business
use. Please contact your local bookseller or the Macmillan Corporate and
Premium Sales Department at 1-800-221-7945, extension 5442, or by
email at MacmillanSpecialMarkets@macmillan.com.

Picador® is a U.S. registered trademark and is used by Macmillan Publishing
Group, LLC, under license from Pan Books Limited.

For book club information, please visit facebook.com/picadorbookclub or
email marketing@picadorusa.com.

picadorusa.com • instagram.com/picador
twitter.com/picadorusa • facebook.com/picadorusa

10 9 8 7 6 5 4 3 2 1

for

Diane, Amy, Charley
Lizzie, Katy, Andy

There was a man dwelt by a churchyard.

Well, no, okay, it wasn't always a man, in this particular case it was a woman dwelt by a churchyard. Though, to be honest, nobody really uses that word nowadays. Everybody says cemetery. And nobody says dwelt anymore. In other words:

There was once a woman who lived by a cemetery.

Every morning when she woke up she looked out her back window and saw—

Actually, no. There was once a woman who lived by—no, in—a secondhand bookshop.

—ALI SMITH, "The Universal Story"

The Unwritten Book

Circulation Desk

The sun will set soon. Birds come to the feeder. Each bird is magnificent. Each bird is weird. How did the birds get so weird? A bright red head, spiky tufts, yellow eyes, pink feet, hidden fluorescence, the ability to fly. How did the word "weird" get so weird? And my hands, they are also weird. I'm watching the weird world, the weird birds when a thought arrives from nowhere. What if I've been dead for a long time? What if I've been dead my whole life?

If I am dead, the strangeness of existence is momentarily comprehensible. I catch a glimpse or scent of our dispersed worlds, this place without border, boundary, pain, or punctuation. This place where we are all intimately mixed up with one another. My branch, your book. His leg, her light. All the elements my body and your body have known: a mountain boulder, sediment in the sea, an underground pebble, sand. Everything is ancient, small, and eternal. More birds arrive. More birds leave. My children are playing in the yard. They jump, shriek, and pretend to be something other than their current forms. I hear them speak and, as if waking, my specifics come to collect my body back into being a mother, sister, daughter, wife, friend, a woman who is alive, reading a book outside before dusk. In the yard, I shake off enough deadness to go make dinner. My arms feel stronger with the memory of the rocks that make me.

But we have been dead a long time. "Of bodies chang'd to various forms, I sing." Our repurposed parts, like Frankenstein's creature, are calcium, potassium, phosphorus, sodium, magnesium remixed into bodies. Everything is forever. No one's going anywhere. Toni Morrison writes, "It's hard to make yourself die forever." Thich Nhat Hanh says, "I have been a cloud, a river and the air." Cristina Rivera Garza tells us, "I know you from when you were a tree. From those times."

Being a human is extraordinary. Being a tree or chickadee or pile of ash is also, no doubt, extraordinary. I just don't often remember having been those things. Though I studied geology, the long view of existence—our lives as minerals—is not the story I most often focus on. Rather, I look for and love the drama in the small details particular to one person, the crooked tooth, the bitten nails, the hidden suffering. We mourn the loss of one extraordinary human life: a grandmother, a cousin, a father, a friend. There is exquisite beauty and storytelling in the smallness. Reading life and death like a book. Start here. Finish here. These things that end (humans, winters, childhoods, love affairs, books) have sharp edges, painful as desire and packed with grief. Their hurt is precious and rich with meaning. It speaks to the work our bodies are really made for: feeling.

How do you feel? I feel like a teenage girl. By that I mean I experience torrential emotions, trying to stay as awake to feeling as a teenage girl might be. In her poem "Some Girls," Alison Luterman writes, "I have learned that some girls are boys; some are

birds / some are oases ringed with stalking lions." Girls are brave
in the ways they feel things. I want to have their courage, to be
someone who feels always. I want our world to be led by people
who feel things deeply. Then, some days, I am wrecked by feeling.
Grief and desperation, anger and anxiety tear a hole in my being.
Other days, I feel nothing. Those are the worst days.

My grandma Norma Stallings Nolan Santangelo had an ac-
creted name that marks waves of twentieth-century immigration
in New York. She lived to be 101. She loved Jesus. Her condo
was filled with sexy pictures of him: damp eyes, bare chest, cuts
in his body like small vulvas. His flesh broken and open to the
world. My grandmother loved people. When I introduced her to
the man who became my husband, she flirted with him, danced
with him. I teased her. "Nan, that's my boyfriend." And she said,
"I know, honey. He's so cute." She had little of material value, but
maintained a deep generosity. She was money poor but she'd wink
and say, "I have a rich father," a statement I didn't understand as a
girl. She and her sisters created their own language. "Buz," "Zan,"
"snicky," "Nomy," "jubby." My grandma played with words, dis-
carding definitions she didn't care for. It made her powerful. She
was a pool shark, and a great one because no one ever believed this
small woman could beat them at billiards until she did. She told
me, "If you have a problem with the word 'god,' replace it with the
word 'love.'" The cosmos she described is flexible, kind, and commodious. Now God often looks like her, a tiny feather of a woman
dressed in bright colors and costume jewelry, a god who knows
the names of small flowers and birds even if she created the words
herself, a god who is insecure not from lack of loving but because
she is full of mistakes, broken and open to all. She is without protection, feeling everything, fear, sorrow, and love. My God.

After the word "god" became the word "love," rocks became books, and books rocks. It makes sense to me. The longer I live with books and words, the more I enjoy their erosion. I break them open. I make beaches. And, as my grandma did, I reinterpret meanings. The older I get, the solid rock books of my youth make room for a literature that's more like the trees, so much greenery and decomposition. I confuse which book is which and what chapters belong where. Books composed in the hope of also one day being decomposed. Life and death in the library of trees. Death as a library. Library as a forest.

My friend Annie sent me a quote from Matisse. "Do I believe in God? Yes, when I work." I keep this card on my wall beside a photo of Mr. Morgan's bloodred library in New York City, beside a photo of the long-gone geodesic dome built on the edge of the woods in Vermont where I spent my twenties with an exceptionally open family who allowed me to live in the forest with them, who took me in as one of their own when I was eighteen. These three photos on my wall: art, library, forest. Lately, my library does look more like a forest. Some books grow in memory or importance, some decay. Books, like trees, live longer than people. I make them into my natural history. Books as birds, rocks, trees, bees, moss. I read and write stories that have already been written, of how the dead are ever returning to us, how the dead never left.

In *Swimming to America* Patricia Spears Jones writes about a dream of Borges. "He built a library near a fjord." Then: "When they search for the library, they find mist." Where are those misty volumes?

Many people are dying these days. I've lost four friends in the time I've written this essay. One of them died only yesterday. And revising now, a different time, another friend has died. It doesn't feel like a tremendous leap to connect death, the library, and the forest. They are bounded spaces without a boundary, full of dust and ghosts. Dust that never leaves us. Not creepy or stagnant, but dust, Ms. Jones's mist, and ghosts who are golden with possibility, fermentation, and growth. "Growth" is another word I like to smash open.

Growth surrounds itself with flattering companions like evolution and progress but it can quickly turn to something worse. People get stuck on the accumulation of wealth, piling up hills of money and ownership. Once our basic needs are met, the idea of more is a growth that can be cancerous, murderous. Growth imagines its opposite is decay. As if to grow is to stay alive, and other delusions taught by capitalism. In reality, most of our lives are spent shrinking, eroding into bits and decaying. What if we celebrated that decay and championed the infinitesimal? I look for the bright colors and beauty of rot. Etymologically, there's decadence in decay. Non-etymologically too. Like a gorgeous mushroom, I hope to become brilliantly colored as I age, golden, pink, green, and blue.

When I was a girl I was given a set of tiny green lemonade glasses for my dollhouse. My attraction to these miniatures was so strong, their perfection so overwhelming, that I swallowed a handful of the glasses. Tiny is powerful.

The miniature is having a large moment. A virus has mobilized (and immobilized) our planet with unimaginable swiftness, changing our behaviors of consumption, climate care, equity, access, and ideas of societal control. If I were writing a story (I am always writing a story whether I like it or not) I'd say this virus is a tiny intelligent god, a miniature, complicated hero going into battle against an even more complicated and conflicted species:

humans. Maybe the narrative Covid-19 tells itself is one of hero-ism, David and Goliath, a microscopically small virus trying to fight and sometimes kill the only species that actively, wantonly tries to destroy planet Earth—us.

The New York Public Library perches on Bryant Park. Blood flowed there in the Draft Riots. The park is also a potter's field of bodies. The library was built on the site of the Croton Aqueduct, an edifice whose fifty-foot-tall walls once held the city's water sup-ply. Standing in the library foyer, I remember the water. I swim. I feel fluid in this library. I feel fluid in all libraries because I know how words change. I am devoted to the paper archive because paper is not permanent. It will decay. It will flow. The papyrus Sappho wrote her poems on has crumbled. The brackets below are the translator Anne Carson's way to mark what's missing from Sappho, the holes in the page.

Go [
so we may see [
]
lady

of gold arms [
]
]
doom
]

Time and decay give Sappho's words meanings she might never have imagined, a real fermentation. A real growth.

Loving libraries, tabernacles of impermanence, is like deliriously trying to preserve the most delicate and ephemeral things: the dead katydid on my windowsill, or people, or snowflake crystals, or love.

When I was very young I had a dream about a small door. Crouching through the door, I passed into a series of scarlet, velvety rooms, small getting smaller, a birth canal in reverse. I know a number of people who have had a similar dream. It gave me terrific comfort. I knew the tunnel contained mystery. In the dream, I never pressed through the tunnel all the way, but rather sat in the small passage, content in the unknowing, hidden. The first time I saw Mr. Morgan's red library I was reminded of the dream tunnel and thought, This must be the place where that tunnel led. The Morgan, or a golden bookstore, some uncanny, cranny-filled athenaeum. I am a very slow reader, so a vision of death as a place where I'll finally get some reading done is heaven indeed. In death, might we have access to the infinite stacks of books we never got around to in life, books written by insects, trees, bacteria, and rocks? In death, might we have access to the books that never had a chance to get written? Those books stored in a place whose system of classification escapes recognizable logic, much like the system in the narrow frame of my own body where *Les Fleurs du mal* rubs up against *Flowers in the Attic* rubs up against my undergraduate geology textbook, Willard Bascom's *Waves and Beaches*. Bascom made me realize that our very human attempts to make language, to label waves in the sea, matter little to said waves. Language making is fascinating but also absurd since classification is fleeting. Bascom wrote that in a storm "concepts of wave period and length tend to lose their meaning." Where I live, storms approach out of the mountains and across a wide river. I see them coming from a long way off. The terror they bring is a welcome feeling for me, the possibility of stopping, of newness and chaos, though climate change complicates my love of storms by adding fear and regret. Georges Perec writes that Rabbi Simeon finds seventy different meanings for *Bereshit*, in the beginning, the first word of the Torah. Loss of meaning is only a loss if you have only one narrow meaning.

In this afterlife library we'll dissolve back into the many, the microscopic. I'll browse. I'll read. I'll lose concepts of period and length. I'll lose bits of myself in books, in soil. Alphabet as molecule. Page as ecosystem. Here's the Natural Science section. Here's Poetry. Here's the Universe. Skin cells will become dust; flesh, food; bone to stone. Along with every book we never had the chance to read in life we might find the ghost books too, texts that were never written or never finished, phantom books with invisible and unverifiable Dewey Decimal numbers.

W. G. Sebald's *The Rings of Saturn* is a book that *does* exist and I have read it a few times. It concerns a long walk through a region of Great Britain riddled with buried archeological treasures, an excursion over the lives underground, as all our excursions are. The walk happens in August, "when the dog days were drawing to an end," dog days because they unfold under Sirius, the Dog Star. *The Rings of Saturn* seems to be a book about everything because it maps thought and memory. It moves the way a mind moves, fluently from part to part, node to node. It allows multiple moments in history to rest on top of one another, procreating, generating, electrifying. It allows for large gaps so that a reader might travel independently. Sebald draws our attention to a tremendous number of histories and small stories. While there is a finality to knowledge, there is an infinity to what we don't know. He references so many books, people, and histories

I've never heard of before that the question of what is fiction or nonfiction, though always present, becomes in some way unimportant, or falls into the realm of the fussy. In a 1997 interview with James Wood, Sebald says he is trying "to precisely point up that sense of uncertainty between fact and fiction, because I do think that we largely delude ourselves with the knowledge that we think we possess, that we make it up as we go along, that we make it fit our desires and anxieties and that we invent a straight line of a trail in order to calm ourselves down." *The Rings of Saturn* is a microcosm of an entire library, or an entire brain. I begin to wonder, Do I really want to read all the books? Maybe a better life would be spent rereading the handful of books—different for each reader—that reveal the universe's patterns, eternal, ever-shifting, and wise?

Sebald's book begins with two epigraphs. I've repurposed one.

The rings of Saturn consist of ice crystals and probably meteorite particles describing circular orbits around the planet's equator. In all likelihood these are fragments of a former moon that was too close to the planet and was destroyed by its tidal effect (—> Roche limit).

—*BROCKHAUS ENZYKLOPÄDIE*

You've already encountered one epigraph in this book that has barely even begun, yet here is a second one. In *After the Quake*, Haruki Murakami creates a character who loves salmon skin so much, she dreams of a salmon made up of only skin. Maybe right now you are imagining an entire book made up only of epigraphs. *Bereshit*. This is not that book. Maybe you are writing that book. If so, I look forward to reading it. I love the potential of beginnings.

How many books I have started—reading them, writing them, never finishing. I enjoy the idea of having no end even while I'm arrogant enough to imagine a day when someone might read these words and be extra haunted because at the time of their reading, I'll be dead. This is not a book of epigraphs, or epitaphs, but it is a book of books. *See* The Forest: A Bibliography.

Poems and stories that try to contain the many are my favorite sort of books. Multiple narrators, impossible texts that might have no end, no author, or feel like a house of mirrors: *The Thousand and One Nights*, Ryunosuke Akutagawa's "In a Grove," Ali Smith's "The Universal Story," Faulkner's *As I Lay Dying*, Farid ud-Din Attar's *The Conference of the Birds*. The last, a twelfth-century Persian poem, tells how the birds of the world set out to find their leader. Many birds offer excuses. The hawk can't leave the royal king he serves. The heron cannot go either, as her misery keeps her staring out to sea. "My love is for the ocean, but since I—a bird—must be excluded from the deep, I haunt the solitary shore and weep." Only thirty birds make the journey to find the benevolent, female, mythic Simorgh, a name that means "thirty birds" in Persian. A name that also sounds like someone saying "see more" in English, on a perfect day for bananafish. On their journey the ragtag bunch of birds passes through seven valleys. Each valley has its own story. The poem's title comes from the Quran. "O people! We have been taught the language of birds, and on us have been bestowed all things. This is indeed, grace." I am trying to learn the language of the birds. I'm looking for that grace.

Kites were simultaneously, independently invented in Korea and Guatemala. When Chaucer wrote *A Parliament of Fowls*, he did not know of Attar's *The Conference of the Birds*. Then Chaucer's *Canterbury Tales* and *The Conference of the Birds* share moments of eerie harmony. Like Attar's thirty birds, Chaucer's thirty-one pilgrims are on a journey, traveling to the shrine of Thomas à Becket while engaged in a storytelling contest. Much of *The Canterbury Tales's* magic is in those parts that remain unwritten. Chaucer died before his pilgrims finished telling their stories, or at least before they finished telling their stories in a language the living can read.

The rings of Saturn are far away, 1.2 billion kilometers at their closest. Still, their structure—tiny individual crystals held loosely together in a circular orbit—feels deeply familiar and intimate. Dots and leaps, holes and collisions, bleeding, mingling, messy birth, bumbling, multiverse, stumbling. The rings of Saturn are like the scattered, dusty house I live in, my body. They feel true to the way I've shelved Carl Sagan's *Cosmos* between my other grandma, Marcella's, diary of 1983, "Oct 20 Permanent wave—2:30," and a copy of *Reader's Digest* that features a disaster narrative my dad edited, "Adrift in the South Pacific."

Once I wrote a love letter to an artist who builds tremendous spheres. In the letter, I told him everything I thought about Saturn's rings, how distance between our particles of dust and ice might not signify alienation but rather a kinder plan that allows space for current and mystery to exist between points, between people, between ideas. The nature of longing and tolerance. He never wrote back. I suppose there's a certain mystery to that, and a perfect model for unrequited desire, but afterward, when considering his chilly attitude toward our sixth planet, it was easy not to be in love with him anymore. The desire for bodies is rooted in our mortality. The desire for books shares a similar fevered passion with our decomposition. We will never be able to read all the books or love all the bodies. We feel the comfort of our smallness, our minerals, our parts.

As with the dust of Saturn's rings, our eyeballs also reside in orbits. Rods and cones perceive partial information. Our brains concoct the rest to create vision. Sight contains so much imagination, one wonders if the view of a mountain is fiction or nonfiction.

Thoughts take leaps. Chemistry to minerals to vitamins to living to dying to reading to paper to trees to nature, biology to chemistry. Or, maybe less logical. Maybe chemistry leads to thoughts of nail polish, yeasted breads, high school, or quilts. Either way, collected ideas bounce off one another like some percussive instrument and the sound of one thought striking another thought is a beautiful sound.

All this to ask, where should I begin when writing a book about birds, words, books, death, hormones, collections, desire, letters, booze, family, birds? A circle starts where? Or more to the point, a circle ends where?

Sebald's ring of ice crystals collects the Western canon, those books Sebald ingested in his life and the people he met. *The Rings of Saturn's* first chapter starts with a photo and a description of a hospital window "which for some strange reason has been draped with black netting." The narrator's view is sliced into a grid. A reader sees the sky through this grid, the eternal past the x and y axes of an institution, past the Cartesian plane into the realm of imaginary numbers. Farewell to Melvil Dewey's narrow classifications. Imagine the library shaken like a snow globe, discrete ideas fall gently on a reader within a contained space. Sebald's first chapter moves through Flaubert's walks; the deaths of two colleagues and scholars; the Swiss author Charles-Ferdinand Ramuz; Rembrandt's *Anatomy Lesson*; Descartes's anatomy experiments; the diamond-like quincunx patterns of starfish, crystals, vertebrae, silkworms, water ferns, and horsetail; Borges's (paradise *is* a library) *Book of Imaginary Beings*; and Thomas Browne's *Urn Burial*, his 1658 discourse on fifty Bronze Age sepulchral urns unearthed in Norfolk, near the small locality where Sebald lived. "Browne scrutinizes that which escaped annihilation for any sign of the mysterious capacity for transmigration he has so often observed in caterpillars and moths." The chapter ends wondering what meaning we find in objects left behind by the dead. *Musaeum Clausum* (the hidden library), Browne's posthumously published tract, also considers the books and objects that were *not* left behind by the dead, a catalog of the disappeared and nonexistent. Sebald looks for patterns and leaves enough space between parts that patterns indeed emerge. Orders, ghosts, and mysteries peek though these blanks. We understand Descartes's grid even as we leave the mappable world behind for one that permits silence, mystery, memory, the dead. Because where we're going, you know, we don't need *des cartes*.

I have lost my mind to books. That is also true. I sometimes study a book to the point of obsession. I paw at it until I've worn through the very fabric of sanity. Sometimes it's fun, like being addicted to crosswords. The universe is filled with clues. Even if it's not. Sebald and my dad died the same year, 2001. A good year for death around these parts. Sebald and my dad mingle into one story. What I mean is, there's an owl outside my house at 3:00 a.m. talking to another owl. I imagine the nature of their conversation. I bet I'm wrong. I haven't yet learned the language of the birds. That's okay. Delusion can be close to revelation. Birding delights me. Believing delights me. It's a game. It's artifice. It's art. Barry Holstun Lopez writes of the great blue heron, "If you will not speak I will have to consider making you up."

Octavia E. Butler's *Parable of the Sower* and *Parable of the*

Talents, published in the 1990s, are set in Los Angeles, 2024–2032. The city suffers under climate change and drought. Its gated communities are rife with guns and fear. Slavery is common; women are silenced; white violence rages. Police and education have been privatized. News is delivered in "bullets." The government does not believe in science. There's even a presidential candidate running on the slogan "Make America Great Again." Citizens cope by ingesting "smart drugs" (which we should, in pursuit of honesty, now call our phones) or pills that turn arson's destruction into an erotic sensation. Burn it all down. Or, people cope by wearing "dream masks" that plunge a person into virtual, simpler times. A deadened world tries to feel again though acts of annihilation or nostalgia. Butler's work is so prescient, I experience it as divination, observation of the highest order. Her science fiction reads to me as realism. Thirty years ago, Butler read patterns and made deductions as to where we were heading. Her fifteen-year-old narrator, Lauren, "suffers" from a condition known as hyperempathy. Lauren feels the emotions of other people. Lauren feels a lot. In the world of the *Parables*, feeling and empathy are dangerous. Lauren is often crippled by the pain she experiences. In a talk called "'Devil Girl from Mars': Why I Write Science Fiction," delivered at MIT in 1998, Butler said of the *Parables*, "This was a cautionary tale, although people have told me it was prophecy. All I have to say to that is: I certainly hope not." At the age of fifty-eight, Butler fell, hit her head, and died suddenly. She was young, with so many books still unwritten. The story I make around Butler's premature death is one of limits, one that links her to Lauren and the dangers of feeling, a seer who saw too much, felt too deeply, was changed by the seeing and transformed into an entity I am not yet able to understand, though that doesn't stop me from trying.

In *The Body Keeps the Score*, Bessel van der Kolk writes, "Imagination is critical to recovery."

There's a *re* in the word "read," suggesting that an obsessive return, rereading, or repeating cycle is built into the word. The same book read at the age of eighteen, twenty-seven, fifty-three, ninety-one is a different body of water. "Read," from *rædon*, is etymologically related to the words "riddle," "discuss," "to make out." Which is the first time I've thought about making out as a way of reading or process of unpacking meaning, a wet, sloppy kiss between author and reader. We let words come inside our bodies. Reading is deeply intimate, generative procreation. There's breath in that inspiration. I read Toni Morrison's *The Bluest Eye* for a college course on contemporary literature. Twenty-five years later I cracked it open again to teach a class on Blueness and was alarmed to re-find things inside that book I thought were my own guts. I had devoured Morrison's book and made it into me. Morrison's cells had divided and multiplied in my body. And not just Morrison's, but every book I've loved. Every book she loved.

Like wine, the notes get complicated and delicious. In Morrison, I taste hints of Faulkner. In Faulkner, I taste the King James. In the King James, the fabulist works of Aesop, a storyteller who dissolved into a fiction. One version of Aesop's history says he was a slave who told stories to win his freedom. Who was Aesop's mother? What stories did she tell him? In each book we discover flavors we don't recognize, bits from books so hidden and lost to us, they are now soil. In reading, I taste the dirt.

In the early 1980s my family lost our collective mind over Kit Williams's *Masquerade*, a gloriously illustrated picture book my father brought home from work one day. Williams hid a riddle inside its pages. Solve the riddle and you might find the golden,

jewel-encrusted hare Williams had smithed and buried somewhere in England.

One *Masquerade* buff, Ron Fletcher, became so wrapped up
in the treasure hunt that seemingly unconnected events, objects,
and phenomena—a whiskey bottle label, a blue ribbon pinned
to a tree, a found love letter, his own last name—were read as
signals and secret messages there to help Fletcher solve Williams's
riddle. Some people might consider what happened to Fletcher to
be mental illness. Some people are narrow-minded. Jess Zimmerman writes beautifully about Fletcher in her essay "'This Goes All
the Way to the Queen': The Puzzle Book That Drove England to
Madness."

In 1958, German neurologist Klaus Conrad coined the
term *Apophänie* to describe schizophrenic patients' tendency to imbue random events with personal meaning.
An apophany has the form factor of an epiphany—the
sense of breakthrough, of events finally coming together
and making sense—but without any relationship to real
explanations. But though Conrad focused on instances of
apophany occurring with psychosis, the phenomenon he
described applies to the ill and the well alike. Now called
"apophenia," the instinct to pick out patterns from mean-
ingless information is essentially universal.

How might we use this universal tendency to notice patterns,
and see our connectedness, rather than finding divisions and para-
noia? Apophenia as conjunction. Hold two unrelated objects in
your hands. An apple and a tornado. A baby chick and your fearful uncle. Wild rice and snow. You and the stranger approaching

you on the street. To make these leaps, to pull together the seemingly unconnected—words across the blank spaces that hold
them—is how we read. It is to make peace, to make out, to make
abnormal meaningfulness.

My family spent years puzzling over the *Masquerade* treasure's
whereabouts. We were disappointed when the jewel was finally
found. Not that we thought we would find it. We didn't even live
on the same continent as the prize, but we were disappointed because it meant the game was over. We would have preferred for
the hare to remain lost. Having treasure is less fun than wanting
treasure, searching for treasure in misty fjords.

On the topic of our wanting, the classics scholar and poet
Anne Carson asks us to consider the word "eros" as "deferred, de-
fied, obstructed, hungry, organized around a radiant absence—to
represent eros as lack." Desire as lack, rather than love, a hole un-
filled. "Eros is an issue of boundaries . . . Who is the real subject
of most love poems? Not the beloved. It is that hole."

Ross Gay, in an essay titled after a line from Zadie Smith, "'Joy
Is Such a Human Madness,'" writes:

> Here's the ridiculous part. Is it possible that people come
> to us—I do not here aspire exactly to a metaphysical argu-
> ment, and certainly not one about fate or god, but rather
> just a simple, spiritual question—and then go away from
> us—
>
> I don't even want to write it.
>
> Rather this: And what comes through the hole?

Gay asks, do people come and go from our lives so that we
might begin to understand what the hole contains? Holes in our

bodies, in the earth, in our understanding? What better site of desire than the hole left by the dead? What better way to know ourselves than to look into that place, to dig into the place where the dead went? Yes. Where is that place again?

My mom lost her wedding ring. She does that regularly, as her house is complicated by an abundance of stuff. She is an artist. Some people might use an ugly word to describe my mother's home, but it's a bad word. She hates the word and I won't use it here. Imagine instead the hole that swallowed that word. My mom says, "I know I shouldn't be so attached to objects." Then, "Can you look in your house? Maybe I left my ring at your house." I have my own problematic attachment to objects, especially books. She asks my dad to help her find the ring also. He's been dead for decades. But, after she asks him, she finds the ring in a coin purse under a bag of hangers in her hall. "I have no idea how it got there," she says.

Nick Cave, the artist, created his first Soundsuit in 1992 after Rodney King was beaten by members of the Los Angeles Police Department. Cave's suits are assemblages of twigs, toys, sweaters, buttons, beads, pot holders, globes, stuffed animals, afghans, cookie tins, ceramic birds, sock monkeys, baskets. Cave's care-full constructions translate these objects into something more meaning-full than their original purpose. More meaning-full because the bits that make up his Soundsuits are now in relation with other objects. These objects are now family, stuck together whether they like it or not. I read the objects and the space between his objects. Cave calls his suits "alternative relics that contain or hold a spirit." Wearing a Soundsuit shields or dissolves identity so that one can exist without so much classification. What happens once we have loosened identity? In an interview with Diana Sette, Cave asks, "How do you step into the unknown?"

Nick Cave, the singer, a different Nick Cave (if we believe in the boundaries between bodies), in reference to the death of his child, writes:

> I feel the presence of my son, all around, but he may not be there. I hear him talk to me, parent me, guide me, though he may not be there . . . Dread grief trails bright phantoms in its wake. These spirits are ideas, essentially. They are our stunned imaginations reawakening after the calamity.

One daughter asks me, "Where is your dad?"

"He is a cardinal now." A story my siblings and I came up with after he died, something to make death bearable and visible.

"Like a bird?"

"Yes." And then sometimes we have four or five cardinals in our yard at the same time. It's not a magical deduction. It's not supernatural. It's reading.

A magazine asks me, "What does your writing space look like? What objects, photographs, texts or talismans do you keep there?" Dori's rocking chair, Peter's futon, Uncle Zeke's dollhouse, Nanny's bookcase, Matthew's photos, Patchen's photos, Grandpa Nolan's painting, Grandpa Hunt's tissue box, Grandma Hunt's diaries, my father's manuscripts, typewriter, pencil nubs, and the dirty socks I found in his suitcase after he died. I am surrounded by dead people's things.

I inherited my neighbor's end table when she died. I put it in my studio. I found a disposable camera in one of its drawers. I had no way of knowing how long the camera had sat in that drawer. It looked old, eighties design. I sent the camera out for processing, hoping to find my neighbor or some other deep past in the film.

Gillian Welch sings about dreaming a highway back to people and times that are lost. She describes the roads we sometimes walk back to the dead. Time had really turned up the violet, blue, and green in my neighbor's film. Every image was of my neighbor's peach tree laden with ripe fruit, saturated by unreal colors. Talk about a dream mask.

Maybe I shouldn't be so attached to objects either. But everyone keeps dying, leaving stuff behind, objects I can't usually get rid of. And I enjoy the company of the dead. They are so quiet. They know things I don't know. The dead leave clues, and life is a puzzle of trying to read and understand these mysterious hints before the game is over. Even if these clues are not coming from the dead. Even if I'm making the whole thing up.

My mom's house resembles a Nick Cave Soundsuit, Tyree Guyton's *The Heidelberg Project*, the pink installations of Portia Munson, Nelson Molina's Trash Museum, or the Song Dong piece *Waste Not*, which makes order from his mother's collections. So many of the artists and curators I admire are those who know how to re-present the things humans have owned. My mom has a drawerful of nail polishes beside a toy turtle beside a pink pillow beside an expired jar of my dad's cancer drugs beside a golden statuette of the Virgin. I make it make sense. I plot these points and create a chalk line around the ghost, all that's missing. What do I mean by "ghost"? A dead person, certainly. But is a bruise a ghost? Is the bruise your boyfriend gave you a ghost? In what ways is a postcard a ghost? How much dust is made by the dead? Is haunting the same thing as memory? Does reading make you more haunted by more ghosts? Are books dead? Are books ghosts? How many holes?

I work at Pratt Institute, a complex and glorious school. It is not without its skeletons. It dates back to 1887. Students create breathtakingly new work here, despite or even because of the skeletons. There's ivy and hidden places. There are actual secret tunnels underneath a number of the buildings. Alone in a gallery or a quiet classroom, time travel feels possible and likely. The library has books of maps as large as the desks they rest on, charting the streets of New York City from years long lost. The floors in the book stacks are made out of glass squares crafted by Tiffany in 1888. They show a bit of wear and scuffing. If someone is browsing over one's head on the floor above, their footsteps are hazy and ghostlike shadows through the glass. Pratt's power plant is a glittering Victorian jewel box. There's a clowder of semi-feral cats fed and sheltered by faculty, staff, and students.

Like most academic institutions, we are often organizing conferences to bring visiting scholars and thinkers to campus. One day I have a thought to organize a conference for ghosts, but really, ghosts are very hard to organize. Plus, the dead never really speak to me. I organize an Old Lady reading series instead with Rachel Levitsky. We don't formally call it "The Old Lady Reading

Series." A handful of people warn us this term is offensive, though when I say "Old Lady," I mean wisest person.

Our first season we invite Paula Fox and Judy Grahn. During Grahn's visit I feel greedy. A small sip of this woman creates only more thirst. An hour-long talk is severely insufficient to move through Grahn's same-sex elopement in 1958; her dishonorable discharge from the military; cat scratch fever and coma and waking up to poetry; eating disorders; women's mythology; the Gay Women's Liberation group; the Women's Press collective; *Metaformia*, a journal about menstruation; Metaformic Theory, Grahn's tracing of culture to early menstrual rituals; books and books of poetry and essays. It might take an hour to simply read Grahn's epic nine-part work, *A Woman Is Talking to Death*. It might take an hour to discuss these two lines:

> *a woman who talks to death*
> *is a dirty traitor*

A dirty traitor, or someone who trades in dirt. Yes, I think. Yes, that might be me.

Paula Fox had been lost from the public eye multiple times in her life. Her parents left her at a foundling hospital in 1923 and her novels, some of the twentieth century's finest, were mostly lost until a copy of *Desperate Characters* was plucked off a dusty shelf at a writers' colony by the novelist Jonathan Franzen, who then helped bring her work back into the light. I found the real person Paula Fox living in Brooklyn on an ordinary street.

After a morning class, I made my way over to the auditorium where I'd introduce Fox. She'd warned us that reading might be a challenge. She said she would bring her magnifying glass. I checked my voice mails. Fox's husband had left a message saying there was no way Fox could do the reading. He asked, did I realize she was ninety-one years old? I entered the auditorium. Would she be there?

Paula Fox wore a chic brown pantsuit. She took to the stage with her magnifying glass. She brought down the house. She spent the next hour running up and down the auditorium stairs, greeting students and answering questions. She was courageous, triumphant, and gracious. Fox died at ninety-three, on March 1, 2017.

We hoped to next bring Paule Marshall to campus. Her brilliant book *Brown Girl, Brownstones* considers the body of a girl against the architecture of a neighborhood. The book begins, "In the somnolent July afternoon the unbroken line of brown stone houses down the long Brooklyn street resembled an army massed at attention." Then teenager Selina comes strolling through the park, the very opposite of these armies. Her free movements poke holes in fearful ideas of safety, property, and capitalism. The book is set in Pratt's neighborhood. To walk these streets, having read Marshall's book, invites understanding, embodiment. Having taught her book for over a decade, I could not wait for Marshall to visit.

In the summer of 2019, Levitsky texted me from another time zone. "So sad to read that Paule Marshall has passed. Love from the cathedral in Reims. Here's a fallen and magnificent Eve with serpent." Levitsky attached an image of an alert Eve carved in marble, holding a snarling creature in her hands. I read Marshall's obituary in *The New York Times*. It was late at night. My thinking was misty. A small part of me hoped, schemed, wondered: Would Marshall still be able to come to Pratt to visit us?

In this room where I'm working right now, an ant collects the bodies of her departed brethren, creatures I squished earlier, accidently I try to tell myself, though I know better. What will she do with the bodies of her dead? The ant is a hard worker. Me too, I tell the ant. A dirty traitor knows dirt well. Ants have undertakers, those members of the community charged with collecting the dead into middens to keep disease away from the colony; also, because ants use chemical pheromones to communicate, a dead and decomposing ant might release chemical pheromones without sentient intention. Imagine the confusion. Imagine what mixed message a decaying, dead ant might broadcast, or, for that matter, a dead aunt.

In this room where I am working now (a different now, a different room from the previous paragraph) my family is sheltering in place to stop the spread of a virus. Our new intimacy with death does not feel calm and wise. It is often marked with fear. Last week a woman in a parking lot could not stop screaming at me. She was so stressed out. People were hoarding groceries. People were fearful. She was trying to care for an elderly mother in a wheelchair. I tried to help but could not find a way past her stress. We were too close. Our hearts beat too fast, a tempo of panic. One friend lost her father and mother to the virus within a few days of each other. Death often does not behave the way I want it to. A woman in my town, mother to three, ended her life this week. And death, sometimes, takes children. Death leaves the living raw and ruined. I grabbed at the empty air for weeks and even months after my father died, trying to catch a trace of him in the skein of my fingers. Nothing there. Mary Oliver writes that she thinks our world is "the prettiest world—so long as you don't mind / a little dying." But we do mind. It hurts. James Baldwin writes that white Americans do not believe in death. He writes, "Perhaps the whole root of our trouble, the human trouble, is that we will sacrifice all the beauty of our lives, will imprison ourselves in totems, taboos, crosses, blood sacrifices, steeples, mosques, races, armies, flags, nations, in order to deny the fact of death, which is the only fact we have. It seems to me that one ought to rejoice in the fact of death."

I wrote a short story with two titles, "Three Days" and "Cortes the Killer." In the story a horse drowns because he slips into a lake of frozen ice. I wrote that story because my sister-in-law Nancy told me our cousin's horse died exactly that way and I was struck by the solid fact of humans' inability to stop death, despite our best efforts. My cousin could do nothing to save his horse when it had fallen through the frozen pond. He watched the horse die. Later, I heard from a reader who was angry at me for killing the horse in my story. She thought the animal's death was gratuitous. She even rewrote my story and made the horse live. The horse was rescued in her version. As if fiction could be the place where death does not exist.

This book is not fiction. It is an experiment written over many years, and while someone might read it in a day, in a week, it was years in the making. Patterns occurred, themes returned, as with anything that one observes over a long enough period. Surely this is part of the reason death hurts us. We want to stay and look longer, to conduct our experiments, to see the patterns repeat and confirm what we might have suspected all along: In the distance, this makes sense and even more than sense, in the distance this makes beauty.

I have no authority to write about the dead as I have not been dead, at least not that I remember. My work is absolute appropriation, total conjecture. For this forgery, perhaps I'll face some sort of zombie tribunal, a scolding and retribution. The dead will demand an apology. The dead will revoke my tenure. "How," the dead will ask, "did you think you could speak for us?" Dirty traitor, indeed. I'll point out that they don't do much talking. And I am not speaking for the dead. I am only trying to read alphabets and signs they left behind. Maybe I'm a bad reader. Maybe I'm ignorant. Faced with their steely silence I'll plead senselessness. It's true, my love of language, words, books, humans, my love of being alive has driven me almost mad, seeing things that don't exist, constructing an endless library, an infinity archive, a forest, where in beginning we end; in the end we begin.

Table of Contents

Dread of Death is seated between *Craven Need for Approval* and *Malignant Narcissism. Out-of-sorts artist who works with sound and light, used to be quite the gamin, but peri-menopause ruined her sleep pattern* sits across from *Novelist and Playwright with a colossal amount of rage in his soul that only emerges when he drinks too much—like, every night at 8.*

Amy Sillman made a series of pen-and-ink seating-arrangement charts that map tables full of human neuroses. Inspired by Sillman, I'm thinking of the table of contents as a table, though one where the seating chart is blurry. The chairs keep moving, like unbound pages that shuffle freely and mingle. Collisions happen. Chapters become drunk. Some are arm in arm, some fight. Ideas overlap on the path of obsession. Still, one theme emerges around a centerpiece of lush if slightly rotted flowers: How We Are Haunted.

At one moment in time, this one, my table of contents looks like this:

Devour

I grew up in a house built in 1765. Old for America. My family has lived in the same house for more than fifty years, which has given me time to consider the other humans who haunted these rooms: daughters of 1803, brothers of 1920, teenagers of 1792.

I wasn't alive when my family moved in, but I like to imagine that first day, when the rooms were bare, empty, quiet. When the house was like this,

packed with emptiness.

It's not like that anymore.

In the 1960s, my father and mother came to the house after tough times: bad first marriages, custody battles, lost loved ones. They wanted a new start. My mom was pregnant. When they moved in, she spoke frankly to the ghosts even though she doesn't really believe in ghosts. Except for when she does. "You're welcome to stay but please, never show yourselves." Perhaps my mother's sense of hospitality or curiosity prevented her from asking the ghosts to simply leave. So far, a deal is a deal. None of us have ever seen a ghost in our old house.

Students from the elementary school used to visit our house to learn about colonial dwellings. Once, my mom set the date with the schoolteachers, then forgot. My parents went traveling and left us home with an auntie who was surprised when a busload of elementary school children arrived expecting a tour. She showed them the brick oven built into our enormous chimney. She showed them our outhouse and chicken coop. Then, not wanting accuracy to stand in the way of effective storytelling, she showed the children the back, secret staircase built as a fire escape. "This, children, is where they hid from the Redcoats." A statement that, while perhaps untrue, speaks to the fearful history of my small town, the site of both a Revolutionary War battle and, earlier—during Kieft's War—a massacre of five to seven hundred Wappinger people over the course of one night in 1644. For many years I had imagined that, because my town is small, it might somehow have escaped violence and fear, as if in being little it might hide from what is huge and horrible; a story I created.

Our outhouse is a double-seater. When I consider the number of people who may have lived in this house before me, I multiply the number by two, like the toilet seats. I have no idea how many people this house and land have held. A lot. Our narrow dining room and all the Decembers that have happened inside it are like glass slides held up to the light, singularly or layered. The others who sat here before me, warm from wine. What part of this dust is theirs?

The house has beams cut from American chestnut, a species that, more or less, no longer exists. These beams tempt me to think of the house as a living tree. Before furnaces, families hung blankets from the beams in winter to close off rooms and trap the fireplace's heat in a smaller space. The family would gather in these blanket rooms.

The historical society wants to include my parents' house in their registers but my mom likes her freedom. She says they can have it when she moves out. I don't think she's ever going to move out of that house.

My mother is a beauty, a serious practical joker, an opera fan, a painter, a lover of literature, flowers, carnivals, dessert, travel, children, and people. She is kind, funny, and intelligent. She is a sharp dresser. When I plug a description of her house into the National Study Group on Chronic Organization's Clutter Scale, it ranks between a Level III and a Level IV. There are five levels. The blindness of categories is a tool to flatten the story.

Olympia Dukakis delivers the best line in Norman Jewison's 1987 film *Moonstruck*. To her cheating husband she says, "Cosmo, I just want you to know, no matter what you do, you're going to die, like everybody else."

If my mom keeps all her stuff, maybe she'll keep on living? Seems worth a shot. She doesn't buy new things. The stuff in her house is old. A copy of *Treasure Island* inscribed to my father— *To Walter Jr. from Dewell and Phelps Christmas 1940*, my mother's

well-played-with Ziegfeld Girls paper dolls from 1941—Patricia
Dane, Louise LaPlanche, Anya Taranda, and even the inventor
Hedy Lamarr, their undergarments printed with stars that seem
distant, as if we are seeing their light across the universe and
they've already burnt out. I find a xylophone made to look like a
green caterpillar; a miniature stuffed pink hot-air balloon whose
basket hides a music box; an empty tin of lotus tea, a souvenir
from my wedding; a tin of pickup sticks; and a cookie box printed
to resemble needlepoint—"Saturday's child is full of grace"—
stuffed with crayons. I was born on a Saturday. There's beauty in
her house and lots to look at. Thrift store clothes and art books.
There's little of financial value but much that's rich in color and
meaning. If I started reading the books in my parents' house right
now, I'd die still reading.

   In between my visits some things disappear, others emerge. I
suspect things in the house are reproducing. The child of a Dutch

windmill salt shaker and the old brown velvet couch might be the elegant secretary with an angled tabletop that one day appeared in the kitchen. My mom doesn't buy things, but things I've never seen before, sometimes, suddenly appear.

I tell her, "You can't hold on to every beautiful thing." But watching her sort through a pile of old magazines is like watching an Arctic hunter carving up a seal. There's no part of the beast without a purpose; nothing goes to waste under my mother's attentions. She finds value in things others might discard. An article about South American frescoes that was written in 1992 holds just as much value to her today as it did when first published— perhaps even more now that a periodical from 1992 might be hard to find. I admire her thriftiness, even if I sometimes worry that what she's done is built herself a very colorful tomb.

Every now and then, important things do get lost in the ramble of her home. We had my dad cremated. My mom put his ashes in an old cookie tin, then she put the tin into his well-loved briefcase. Then she put the whole thing under the bed they had shared for thirty-odd years.

After some time, my mom started to date other people. Maybe it became strange to have the ashes of her dead husband underneath her bed when she had a boyfriend. She moved my dad into another room.

A few years later one of my daughters asked, "Where's your dad?"

"He smoked cigarettes so he died."

"But what happened to his body?"

"We burned him."

I've been honest with my daughters from the start. I tell them what I can about sex, death, birth, all of it. It seems easier to slip these truths in from the beginning when everything is equally surprising/unsurprising. Carrots, sandwiches, cancer, hand jobs, menstruation, tulips, decay.

My daughter wanted to see what my dad's ashes looked like. I asked my mom, "Where's Dad?" We looked. My dad was lost. She knew he was in the house. She just couldn't, at that moment, say where.

There's a peace that comes over me in this house. Something similar to floating in a warm ocean. Maybe it's a desire to drown. It is impossible not to find beauty there, interesting ideas everywhere I look, the detritus of humans who make art. The house also winnows out from my life anyone who is uptight. The house reminds me that order is temporary and that it is better to learn to feel at home in spaces that lack order, rooms that don't make a human sense. The peace I find in this house is that of being lost with no desire to ever be found. It is surrender and the realization that I am also part of the house and my mom's collections.

I left New York City soon after my landlords replaced the wooden front doors—doors that had stood since the turn of the last century—with plastic ones. Now, only a decade later, those new doors have already peeled and paled. They are self-destructing. The lies capitalism tells in order to sell more things. I was out of my apartment barely a week when, passing back by, I found our seven-foot-long pink cast-iron tub. It had been left at the curb as rubbish. It had cleaned bodies since the 1940s. It was one of the best things in the apartment. Nieces and nephews would come visit just to bathe in our pink tub. I tried to take it with me but couldn't even lift one corner of that old tub, made, as it had been, to last forever. I wonder where that tub is now.

As a family of eight, camping was how we spent our vacations.

It was cheap enough. Our tent was a heavy green canvas number, so difficult to erect that it often took half the family to set it up.

I remember one victorious camping trip. My mom and her sister, both married to alcoholics, were fed up, so they packed me and my cousin Christine into a station wagon and we left. We didn't arrive at our campsite until after dark. The moms went to battle with that tent. In the past they'd always relied on the men. That night turned out to be no different. After cursing so loudly, for so long, they stirred our campground neighbors to sympathy. Two brothers arrived with a hammer and had the tent set up shortly thereafter.

Recently I found that old green tent in my basement. It hadn't been set up in over twenty years, but none of us have the stomach to junk it. How long and well it held us all together. It leaked in the rain. My mother would wake and construct beach towel dikes to divert the flood. Such tenderness in that tent, a place I remember as being kind, sturdy, exhausted. I set the tent up with my daughters, thinking it would make a summer fort. And it did, for a day. But now the tent's been up for weeks and I'm the only one playing in it. The daily thunderstorms that rip through here knock it down, soak its insides every afternoon. So I set it up again, in order to dry it out before I put it away. Or I set it up again because each time I step inside, the musty, earthy odor zooms me into the past, a terrifically fast time machine. I mentioned the scent to my sister Amy over the phone. It's such a deeply lodged sense memory that even six hours away, she could smell that old tent too.

I'm happy to make meaning out of any old thing I find. Here's the past in my backyard. The past is hard to keep standing up. The past is also hard to take down. The tent weighs more than I do. I note that the past has completely killed the summer grass that had been growing beneath it. I hoist the bagged-up old tent onto my shoulder. I carry it across my back. It's easy to imagine the tent is my father's dead body. It's the right shape, the right weight. He loved this tent. I lug, I hug, and sometimes I even ask myself, Why am I carrying around this heavy dead thing that kills the grass?

After my dad was gone I took books from his library, thinking I could build a small replica of him inside of me by reading what he had read. My father had been so smart. He had been full of book learning. Having him with me was like having a walking work of reference before the internet. I could ask him anything and chances were good that he knew something—not necessarily on every topic, but near every topic. If my interests were Irish holy wells, he might tell me something about Appalachian springs. A tangent that might become a new path, like browsing the stacks in a library and not finding the book you're looking for but finding the book you weren't looking for.

One of the books I took from my dad was Joseph Twaddell Shipley's *The Dictionary of Word Origins*. I'm not sure what this book meant to my father or even how often he referred to it in life, but after he was gone I asked the dictionary the things I could no longer ask him. *Word Origins* became a place for talking with the dead, a tool of divination. It's never far from my hand. One of the best parts about Shipley's dictionary is that, in an effort to be efficient, he points out the relationships between words. He builds beautiful and astonishing connections. On a day when I miss my dad I might look up the word "die," searching for a hint or a way to better understand sorrow, and Shipley, because his dictionary is capacious, responds with:

die, *See* sequin

The hole death made isn't filled but it flashes with glitter. Romantic trouble? I ask and Shipley, sounding much like my dad, writes:

boy, *See* alas

When my body was battered by doctors, Shipley told me:

gynecology, *See* banshee

His work is poetry. It illuminates and broadens my understanding, as verse does. It makes me feel a part of all. It makes gentle sense, spreading joy and curiosity. It suggests that wisdom is not hierarchical—there's no ladder going up—but cyclical, relational. Sometimes I have no question but open Shipley to any old page, throwing the bones. **phantom**, *See* focus. **fashion**, *See* defeat. **rape (turnip)**, *See* alcohol. Sometimes I don't even follow up with Shipley's reference word, enjoying and imagining the electric distance between phantom and focus. Other times, I keep reading and I'm further rewarded.

devour, *See* sarcophagus

sarcophagus
The ancient Greeks buried bodies in coffins (or pits) made of a kind of limestone, which supposedly consumed them. They called this coffin a sarcophagus (from Gr. *sarx, sarc—*, flesh + *phagein*, to eat).

The full definition goes on to include references to geophagy, omnibus, carnal, coronation, carnival, sarcasm, morsel, and mausoleum, among others. Shipley's act of reference, X, *See* y, teaches me that everything is connected, everyone is related. X, *See* y. Y, *See* o. O, *See* 3. 3, *See* tree. In Shipley we are linked. We are part of a whole.

Merlin Sheldrake, the author of *Entangled Life: How Fungi Make Our Worlds, Change Our Minds & Shape Our Futures*, writes, "The authors of a seminal paper on the symbiotic view of life take a clear stance on this point. 'There have never been individuals,' they declare. 'We are all lichens.'" And lichens, Sheldrake tells us, "flicker between 'wholes' and 'collections of parts' . . . Lichens are stabilized networks of relationships; they never stop lichenizing; they are verbs as well as nouns."

What book do you use as oracle? What book don't you use that way? What book is not a work of reference, pointing in the direction of every book our author has read, job her parents have worked, meal she's eaten, film she's seen, road she's walked, rock she's kicked, microbe she's never even imagined?

My dad had been sick for about a year with lung and colon cancer when he collapsed upstairs. I was at work, but my brother Charley took care of him. From the floor, my dad said, maybe if he had something to eat he'd regain his strength. Charley brought him a chocolate doughnut with rainbow sprinkles, the sort of confection my father loved. My dad ate half of the doughnut before admitting that something more serious was wrong with his body. Charley and my mom took him to the hospital.

We created a lot of stories when our dad was sick, things to believe in, like: Hospitals stop death, or, Maybe you just need something sweet to eat, then you'll feel better. Once, my dad sent me to the store for some Preparation H and we shared a moment of believing that the tumors in his colon might actually just be hemorrhoids, a fiction that felt temporarily courageous as hope. When my dad was still in our home, we felt we were still in charge of the narrative. We are good with fictions. Our house is made for fictions. They seem to crop up there like mushrooms. When my dad was admitted to the hospital, the story changed. Our beliefs, however fungal, were scrubbed clean. Other people got involved, people who side with nonfiction. One doctor, perhaps noticing my skill in self-delusion, told me, "He's going to die. You know he's going to die, right?" I asked her to leave. Denying death is foolish, I know, but there's still a part of me, a very immature part of me, that believes my dad would still be alive if I'd kept him better wrapped up in stories.

The morning after he died, I lay down in that place where he'd collapsed at home. It had been a week since he'd fallen there. From this position I had a good view underneath the cabinet. There among the dust bunnies, I found the other half of the chocolate doughnut. I swallowed the half doughnut quickly, before I could think. I suspected that if I didn't eat it right away I'd be stuck with this doughnut for the rest of my life, making a monument out of a half-eaten piece of cake. Yes, I shouldn't be so attached to objects. I went on to eat the hairs that remained in my dad's humble hairbrush, remembering some distorted childhood wisdom that said hair lasts seven years in the stomach. It was an experiment. I enjoy conducting experiments. I thought if I could keep him with me for seven years, maybe, by then, death would hurt me less. That turned out to be very true. Seven years later his death hurt far less. But that day with the doughnut, I was still unhinged by my dad's dying. He was seventy-one, not too young, but it seemed there was much more he should have seen in life. His death seemed an impossible thing—like someone vanishing into thin air right in front of my eyes. I was distraught by the loss of stories he hadn't yet told me.

Like Shipley's, the poet Heather McHugh's knowledge of etymologies runs deep. Sometimes her sentences overwhelm with doubled and tripled meanings, some of them maybe even unintended. Her lectures are built like New Orleans graveyards; coffins and meanings are stacked three or four high. McHugh once told me, "Language's orders are of means: grammar and syntax. Its disorders are of meaning." Like finding eros in the word "erosive." That's an important one for me, student of geology, the place where desire and rocks meet. McHugh went on to tell me, "Etymology is etiology." I had to look up the word "etiology." It's a term most often used in medicine, meaning the cause of a disease or abnormal condition. So, words as illness.

Soon after I ate the doughnut, I went searching through the house for more of my dad. What else could I eat? He'd lived in that house for more than thirty years. He was everywhere, except that he was gone. I found his Blackwing pencils in each room. Crosswords finished and unfinished. I started collecting everything, like a detective bagging up evidence I'd use to make a new narrative. In one desk drawer I found a handful of typed pages.

My dad wrote a novel in the eighties, called *The Land of Counterpane*. I asked if I could read the manuscript when I was in high school. The book is about a silent-movie star coming into the age of talkies. Much of his book went over my head at the time that I read it, but I liked having something to talk about with him. I wanted to know him well. That wasn't always easy. He had a lot of children and he was a quiet, modest man who didn't readily share the stories of his life unless you could get him alone.

My dad was never able to get *The Land of Counterpane* published, and after years of his and his agent's trying and failing to find a publisher, he stopped talking about his writing. Maybe he had even stopped writing. In the rush of ambition that I felt in my twenties, I rarely moved slowly enough to ask him about his own work. Though I was with him the day he died, I left at midday. I had a reading that night at the Bowery Ballroom. As I left I told my dad not to die. At dress rehearsal, a phone call told me that he was gone. For a strange half hour I sat in the theater imagining I would still perform that night, some high school sense of *the show must go on*. As if the show were important. But then a rush of blood filled my ears, loud as a flood. Whose blood? I couldn't hear anything but the rush. It can be horrible to be a self, an ego. I didn't want the flood—the blood of those who'd come before—to go away without me. I want to be part of that blood, that flood. Such a rush of sound, I couldn't hear the words the people in the theater were saying, so I left. I went to go find what remained of my family. I sometimes regret the ambition of my youth and wish I'd spent more time moving slowly. Or I wish for more than one life. I wish to try life more than one way.

The pages I found in that desk drawer a couple weeks after his death were not from *The Land of Counterpane*. These were something else, from a book I hadn't read before. I clung to those pages. I had so many unanswered questions for my father, some really basic ones, like What hospital were you born in? Where is the money you left for Mom? What happened when you were drafted? Who were your childhood friends? How did you make that pot roast with onion soup mix? Some questions were less basic. Where are you? What are you thinking? Do you miss us as much as we miss you? Even more than the books in his library, the pages in my hand were something I could work with. With these pages, I thought, I'll talk with the dead. And I knew, even at the start, that the answers to my questions might not be simply presented. They might not be clear. Clarity is a lot to ask from someone who can no longer breathe. But I could read my dad's writing. I could make interpretations and solve mysteries. I could build references. Even when the rocks are busted up into tiny bits or transformed by heat and erosion, geologists can still gather information. These pages felt like that, my dad had changed but he'd left behind clues, building materials. I didn't eat my father's book, I devoured it.

As I first read the pages, the ground felt uncertain in a way that excited me, like beginning an adventure. I didn't know what I was looking at. Was this fiction or nonfiction? The pages from his desk drawer start with an epigraph. There's no title, no dedication, no middle, no end, just a section of a book, a handful of pages, a start that I will reproduce here. But before I start with that start, a quick note on what I've done here. When I was breastfeeding my twins, one kid per boob, I'd rest a book between their heads and consider the tremendous symmetry of bodies. It frustrated me that unlike my boobs, my eyes had to work together. I could not read two separate streams of text at once. One eye on the left, one on the right. I wanted to read two books at the same time. What greed. What hunger for books. I couldn't do it. Maybe you can. Below, scattered throughout my book, are parts of my dad's unfinished book mixed with and marred by my thoughts, a work of reference. In one eye, a fragment from a methodically constructed

I Already the third epigraph in a book I said was not a collection of epigraphs. How many more times will you have to begin?

grow to be men What of when we grow to be women? I had an irritation with sexist language even at a young age. When I was ten, I wondered about the language used for God in church, *he, the father*. Why? I asked. Fathers were removed and, in my neighborhood, often alcoholics. I didn't want a removed god but rather one more like my mom, kind and present. My questions about language were a testament to the free-thinking that pervaded our home, a place where there were no wrong questions. My father, rather than agreeing with me, hoped to ease my suspicion that the world was stacked against my gender. He explained that the inclusion of women was understood in the word "man." But it never was to me. It only felt like a narrow-minded exclusion, something like the night I was given lodgings for work at the University Club in New York and found that parts of that club are off-limits to women. I didn't sleep well that night. What were the men doing in these off-limits chambers? Why would we call God a he? As we look for ways to loosen the narrowness of pronouns and other words that suffocate, I love pounding on language, insisting on less cruelty, wedging hard clay until it is supple, stretchable, and large enough to hold us all.

within a space so small we should have founded a kingdom Saint-Exupéry shares my attraction to miniatures—his prince is *petit*, after all—though it seems Saint-Exupéry felt left out of the small as he became an adult. I would ask Saint-Exupéry, What is a book if not a miniaturization and a magnification of life? Except that he and his plane disappeared while on a reconnaissance mission collecting intelligence on German troop movements. Saint-Exupéry has been dead since 1944 and so I will have to ask his books instead.

that we have lost How does this epigraph illustrate the unfinished book my father wrote? In all his writing he centers the loss of childhood, a loss that he felt keenly. *The Land of Counterpane* is titled after Robert Louis Stevenson's poem that tells the story of a sick child making an imaginary world of his bedspread, or counterpane. My dad's brother, my uncle Chuckie, was sick his whole short life. They always knew Chuckie would die young, and yet my father, three years older than his brother, was charged by his parents with protecting Chuckie, a horrible assignment, as he was destined to fail. My father could not stop death. And he didn't. His brother died at age eight. Though evicted from innocence too soon, my father held on to the literature of childhood. He did not believe "other laws" that say it is time to put these books away. He had six kids. He never really stopped reading C. S. Lewis, George MacDonald, Laura Ingalls Wilder, J.R.R. Tolkien, E. B. White, Richard Bach, Saint-Exupéry. This epigraph contains the story my father was always telling: In books we can find our ways back to the worlds we thought were lost, the world of childhood, the world of the dead.

narrative written by Walter Hunt. In the other eye, evidence collected by a daughter/detective trying to interrogate her dead dad. If I were a good detective and thorough scientist there would be marginalia from all six of his children. While we are close, we remember the past differently, each one of us having our own relationship with our dad, our own way of understanding his life.

Here is the start of the pages I found in my dad's desk, beginning with, yes, another epigraph.

I remember the games of my childhood—the dark and golden park we peopled with gods, the limitless kingdom we made of this square mile, never thoroughly explored, never thoroughly charted. We created a secret civilization where footfalls had a meaning and things a savor known in no other world.

And when we grow to be men and live under other laws what remains of that park filled with the shadows of childhood, magical, freezing, burning? What do we learn when we return to it and stroll with a sort of despair along the outside of its little wall of gray stone, marveling that within a space so small we should have founded a kingdom that had seemed to us infinite—what do we learn except that in this infinity we shall never again set foot, and that it is into the game and not the park that we have lost the power to enter?

—*WIND, SAND AND STARS* BY ANTOINE DE SAINT EXUPERY

journal I found my father's Boy Scout diary from 1941, written when he was twelve. The last entry was made on February 14. "Hooray! Got lots." Chuckie died a few weeks later, marking an end to my father's childhood. The rest of the journal is empty.

My father is writing a novel disguised as a journal. However, much of his novel is true to his life, tempting me to ask, Is it all true? Then, as someone who writes fiction, I know of course it is, regardless of whether it is called fiction or nonfiction. And anyway, it has no title or title page. No assertion of fiction or nonfiction. How many times will we strike up the same commotion when once-popular memoirs are revealed to be fabrications? People are enraged to learn that the border between fiction and nonfiction is slippery. I am delighted as it confirms a truth I've always known: Fiction Wins! (She writes in a book of nonfiction.)

work *Reader's Digest*'s Pleasantville campus was made beautiful by the magazine's founders, Lila and DeWitt Wallace. They were generous to their employees. There were beautiful gardens and art, health insurance, turkeys delivered on Thanksgiving, family days at amusement parks, spouses invited on business trips. Tellingly perhaps, *Reader's Digest* was not physically located in Pleasantville, New York, but in nearby Chappaqua. The Wallaces created a fiction by using a remote mailbox in the actual Pleasantville, the town where my mother grew up. The Wallaces were Republicans during the Cold War and maintained some dubious ties to the government. I think a number of my father's colleagues were in the CIA. Despite being conservative and stridently anti-communist, the Wallaces ran their company like socialists, and my father, a lifelong Democrat, repaid them with his loyalty. He was often perplexed by my habit of leaving a job after only a year or two. He wondered why I had no fidelity to any company. I wondered how he didn't understand that most companies treated workers like cogs, not humans. He'd soon learn. The Wallaces died in the early eighties and though they had been capitalists who made quite a bit of money, after their deaths many employees felt that *Reader's Digest* went from being a venture dedicated to reading—DeWitt spent most of the first year he was in business at the New York Public Library simply reading—to a venture dedicated to making money. A series of presidents and CEOs in the eighties and nineties focused on profits and cost-cutting restructures that included closing down many of the international offices. The top staff became bloated, some of them escaping on million-dollar golden parachutes, though not before gutting the benefits the Wallaces had built for their employees. In 1998 the Wallaces' art collection was sold off. One of the CEOs was quoted in *The New York Times* saying, "It was fabulous living with those paintings. It will also be fabulous living with the money." My dad was writing this book during the years of that fleecing.

dream When I picture my father dreaming, I see the tiny bed he and my mother shared for more than thirty years. In sleep, he often looked like a child, as most of us do. Innocent.

Chapter 1

It is not my custom to keep a **journal** (I have always found it boring), but I wish to record now the astonishing interview I had last Wednesday. Actually, I have had two astonishing and disturbing interviews in the past week, and it is the second which has prompted me to put down the details before time bevels the edges of my memory, for it is the second interview which has now made me realize that the first had a significance that initially I denied.

I had arrived at **work** about half an hour early that morning, that is, about eight a.m. Because of our suburban location, we have always opened at 8:30, the idea being that this allows us to go home earlier and enjoy the fruits of suburban living without the one-hour-plus commute to New York City. I had no pressing business; I was just awake early. The kids had already left for school, and I hadn't anything much to do around home at that time of the morning, so I came to work. It was a nice ride in. I had the top down and the radio up.

What had awakened me early was a bad **dream**. Oh, I know. I hate listening to other people's dreams, too, but this one later

Ted, John In the eighties my father's boss and friend Ed was replaced by Ken, a man my dad had a more complicated relationship with. My father was often drunk at work. His friends protected him, his job, and my family for years until my dad got sober. The names here are a fiction, though barely. The dream seems quite real.

New York Times A crossword puzzler and a book lover, he was devoted to *The New York Times*. I still find yellowing reviews cut from the paper tucked into his books. I now write book reviews for the *Times*. He didn't live to see many of the seeds he'd planted flourish. None of my books had been published, and barely a handful of my short stories had appeared in obscure publications, when he died.

seemed to have something to do with the interview. I'll make it brief. The dream didn't start out badly. It was a flying dream, which I have had all of my life, and which I normally enjoy immensely. I was flying about blissfully when I looked down below and there on the ground was my boss. Not my old boss, **Ted**, but my new boss, **John**. He was shouting at me, "Get down here. Are you drunk?" He kept shouting it, and the more he shouted, the bigger he grew. It was as if he were inhaling, and with each breath, inflating himself like a balloon. I could see that he was trying to grab me and bring me down, and as he grew, his clutching hands got closer and closer. I tried to fly a little higher, but I couldn't. Instead, I woke up, the dream disappeared, and I probably wouldn't have remembered it at all except for later events.

Carol, the receptionist, who relieves the night guard at eight, was at her desk when I came in. I said hi to her, picked up my **New York Times**, and went on down the hall to my office. No one much else was in.

I opened the Times to the daily book review, always the first order of my day. The book being reviewed was a biography of the Wright brothers, Orville and Wilbur, and it was the book I was looking for to be reviewed. That was because today was the official publication date of the book, and normally, if they could, the Times printed its reviews to coincide with this date. Unfortunately, the Times did one of its dust-off reviews of the book, in which it acknowledged certain good qualities in the writing, etc., but more or less suppressed a yawn, as if to say, "The Times knows all about the Wright brothers, and so do its readers, and what, after all, does this book, competently put together though it may be, add to the Times' great store of wisdom?" I hated that kind of review, and I hated this one in particular because I believed that

Talbot's Monthly Why did he change the names of his colleagues and company? He must have hoped this book would be published one day. He was reporting on a time when work in America was changing drastically: the return of robber barons, the birth of the CEOs, the death of the middle class, and a rise of have/have-not capitalism. Maybe my dad changed the names because being free from familiar words allowed him license to imagine the unknown parts of people. He enjoyed mysteries. Who doesn't? So why the word "Talbot's"? The only Talbot's I can think of is the women's clothing shop, an outpost of which my dad passed twice a day on his way to and from work. I like to picture him writing books in his head, driving in his Oldsmobile Starfire on his commute. Commutes can be such fertile spaces. I often write on the train to work. I often think about the word "commute" too. (Shipley: **commute**, *See* immunity.) Especially when I ride the train that passes by my grandma Norma's grave. I use my commute to commune with the dead. There's an exchange in com*mute*, something *mut*able, a com*mune*, com*mun*ion, which is precisely how I feel when I write.

("All the news that fits, we print.") This inversion of *The New York Times*' motto was also used by *The Yale Record*, where my father was once editor in chief.

a good biography of the Wrights had never been written until this one appeared. I had read it already. Indeed, the magazine I worked for, **Talbot's Monthly**, one of the few big, general interest magazines left in America, was using the biography in its May issue due on the stands in a few days. (This, too, was planned to coincide with the publication date of the hard-cover book.) Like many other periodicals, Talbot's ran one or two books every issue, in a shortened form. The Reader's Digest called it "a condensed book" (like soup), others called it an abridgement, or an excerpt; the Times itself, in its Sunday magazine called it an "adaptation." In house, at Talbot's, our shortened books were called "briefs," and I was the head "briefer." Actually, my title was book editor, and along with six other editors, I was responsible for finding the twelve to twenty-four books that Talbot's used every year and making them short. (**"All the news that fits, we print."**)

So, in a sense, I had a vested interest in the Wright brothers book, and I was disappointed in the Times review. I had always had a sneaking suspicion that Wilbur was the real genius of the two, and this new biography confirmed it. The trouble was that Wilbur had died in 1912 of typhoid fever when he was only in his mid-forties. A few years later, Orville sold out his interest in the American Wright Company, and after that was a consultant, which I have always thought to be a euphemism for not doing much of anything. He lived on until 1948, when he was in his late seventies. When it came time for a biography, Orville picked a friend of his, an Ohio newspaperman named Fred C. Kelly, and the result was a sort of jokey, fuzzy, boy's story, as if two old cronies were sitting around the stove spinning yarns about their youthful days. And since then, silence. Oh, there were the journals and notebooks (mostly Wilbur's), but that wasn't a story, and it seemed to

spiritual My dad wanted to believe in God, but what God would kill his eight-year-old brother, Chuckie? Still, my dad tried belief. When he was sick, I told him I was going to perform psychic surgery on his tumors, a process I had absolutely no experience with or faith in. I put my hands above his back and we closed our eyes and really tried to shrink his tumors with our thoughts and hearts. I don't know what he believed just then, but he let me try. He wanted to stay alive. And not believing never stopped either one of us from trying.

fifty-one If all goes well, I will be fifty-one years old in 2022, the year *The Unwritten Book* is to be published.

widower He was not a widower. In addition to two sons, he also had four daughters, of whom I am the youngest. It stings a bit to be written out of the narrative, to be unwritten in this fiction that is very close to nonfiction. This seems further evidence that my dad was a bit befuddled by daughters. Or else he is writing his own childhood, where he was one of two boys.

Stephen Vincent Benét Though he won the Pulitzer Prize for his epic poem *John Brown's Body*, and the USPS honored him with a stamp in 1998, I'd never heard of Benét before my dad's book. (Per Shipley's **X**, *See* Y, I'll write here: **Stephen Vincent Benét**, *See* Spirits, for more on Benét. You don't really need to flip ahead to the section titled "Spirits" just now, but I mark it here to suggest that all things are related'in this book as if I've written a work of reference, as if I am tracking the relationships between objects, between sections, between parts of a whole. As if we are all lichen. *See* Devour.) Benét's "Good Picker" is a story about showing early promise, then not becoming famous. It is a story about staying small. Benét's obsolescence pains me, like any remainder table at a bookstore. Did my father, who left the Midwest and made it to Yale, feel that he too had shown early promise and then faded?

Benet Like my dad, Benét went to Yale. His ghost is said to still haunt the offices of Yale University Press.

St. Paul St. Paul, or Saul of Tarsus, along with being the patron saint of writers, is a hero of the sudden turning, transformation, the ability to change. St. Paul is my dad's hometown.

we listened for the mail plane, too In the early days of the 2020 coronavirus quarantine, I spent time sitting outside listening to the new quiet of the world. There were no planes flying overhead. There were nearly no trucks or trains or barges and so, when something did pass, I really heard it. I had time and space to consider. Where was this vehicle heading? Who was driving? Quarantine is perhaps the closest I'll ever get to knowing the silence of the 1930s and my father's childhood.

me that the first flight was the greatest story of my century. There had been other significant advances, of course, like better bombs, but flying wasn't an advance to me, unless one categorized it as a form of transportation. It was a lot more than that, it was an adventure into the unknown and the unseen. I wasn't alone in thinking that. One has only to read Antoine de St. Exupery, or the Lindberghs, or talk to the early pilots (if any are left) to know that flying often brings one in touch with the **spiritual**.

I suppose I'm just old-fashioned, or out-of-date. Here it is, 1981 and I am **fifty-one** years old, a **widower** already, settling into discomfort with my own era. My two boys, seventeen and nineteen, think of airplanes simply as a way of getting somewhere. Flying, to them, is an expression of time. It's faster. I think of a short story by **Stephen Vincent Benet**. (Speaking of being old-fashioned, I suppose no one reads Benet anymore. Certainly, no one writes as he did.) It's called "Good Picker," and he begins, "I wonder what sound they listen for now at night, in the small towns sunk in the wheat of the mid-continent—the young and ambitious, the ones who mean to get away? The drone of the mail plane, I suppose . . . In our day, it was the long, shaking whistle of the Limited."

Benet was born thirty years before I was, but we still listened for the Limited when I was young. In my day it was the North Coast Limited which left the Union Depot in my hometown, **St. Paul**, Minnesota, and began the long grinding grade up from the Mississippi toward Minneapolis where it turned west for the Pacific Ocean. And **we listened for the mail plane, too**, the passage of some lone eagle in the night. We had the best of both worlds before they vanished. In those days, when I was young, my parents would drive me down to Holman Field, St. Paul's airport,

not even thirty Holman was thirty-two when he died, which means my dad was working from memory here. He was two years old when Holman died.

mother My grandmother lived to be ninety-seven. She never once flew on an airplane.

I flew out to see my mother He took my sister Amy to St. Paul on this trip. The three of them went to the Minnesota State Fair, where my grandma won the largest prize in a fairway contest, a huge gray bear she gave to my sister.

The Spirit of St. Louis *See* Spirits. Just kidding! The *Spirit of St. Louis* was designed by Donald Hall, a Pratt alumnus.

Lindbergh memorabilia Did these memorabilia trace the history of Lindbergh's white supremacy and anti-Semitism? What were the clues in these memorabilia?

on the west side of the Mississippi. Holman had been an early pilot. One day at an airshow, he was doing loops, flipping over at the top, and descending so that he flew along the ground upside down, then zooming up to repeat the maneuver. He had just passed the stands upside down about three feet off the ground when something went wrong and he crashed. He was a young man, **not even thirty**.

Airports were ramshackle affairs in those days, a few low buildings, an air sock, an X-shaped strip and a hangar. We stood by a chain-link fence and watched the planes take off for an hour or two and then went home. My **mother** always said we'd never get her in one of those things, and we never have. (She always added, "unless I can keep one foot on the ground.") Later on, when planes got bigger, Holman Field couldn't be used by passengers. The high banks on the far side of the Mississippi made it too dangerous to take off. Airline traffic moved over to Wold-Chamberlain Field which lay out in the cornfields near Minneapolis and allowed for endless expansion. That irritated St. Paul's city fathers, but St. Paul was a railroad town anyway, not much given to flying. Not long ago, **I flew out to see my mother** who still lives in St. Paul. Naturally, we landed at Wold-Chamberlain, which is how I thought of it. But I discovered that somewhere along the way it had been named after Charles Lindbergh, also a Minnesota boy, and in the main concourse, a full-scale, silvery model of **The Spirit of St. Louis** hung atilt (as if circling to come in) over several display cases of **Lindbergh memorabilia**. When I was leaving to return to New York, I had to walk out one of those long radial arms that seem to get you half-way to your destination, and came upon a bar for thirsty travelers. It had no true entrance, but was open along the front in the way they do things

"Wold-Chamberlain Cocktail Lounge." My dad was wrestling with sobriety at this point in his life. Part of that struggle involves living in the present. Alcohol, as a fermented beverage, bottles up the past, allows us to return to former times where we might dwell with our dead. The temptation to stay in the past can be overwhelming. *See* Spirits. I'm a bit like a broken record now, but the spirits, both booze and the dead, have a lot to do with my family.

But it And that was it for the pages I found in the drawer. The End. The text dropped off here, right after "But it." Only no punctuation, just a cliff in the story. But it what? A Mad Libs blank I had to fill in, or a crossword clue. *See* The Blanks. But it meant x, y, and z. But it is certain, everything will be all right, daughter. But it blah blah blah. But it what, Dad? But it what?

There's a moment in Ali Smith's story "Erosive" when two friends are on the phone. One, on board a train, says, "Listen, I'm going into a—" And the other friend is left to wonder, "Monastery? Coma? Sulk? Whichever. Her voice is gone."

Word processing and computing were technologies my father learned later in his life. They seemed a marvel to a man who had spent a career editing reams of work on pulpy yellow paper and a manual Royal typewriter. But the pages I found were not typed on a typewriter. They'd been made by a computer. Faced with the above, "But it," I fired up his computer and went looking for more. And there was more! Still not an entire novel at all. But I found six files, three chapters. FLY-EX, FLYING, FLY2, FLY2A, FLY3, and EXUPERY.DOC. The files repeat themselves and overlap some. There are versions and revisions. He saved each draft. The years I spent working paste-up at *Seven Days* and *The Village Voice* served me well. From these digital bits, I reassembled the start of my dad's book. So, picking up from where the hard copy dropped us off, we enter the digital version of my father's unwritten book.

in airports. At either side of this gaping, hangar-like opening was a giant photograph, each of a man in uniform and puttees standing beside a SPAD, or a Sopwith, or a Jenny, one of those planes, and connecting the photographs across the top, on the lintel of the elongated entranceway, was a legend reading: "**Wold-Chamberlain Cocktail Lounge.**" But at least I could remember listening at night to the Limited, and the mail plane, too. And in my mind, as I heard those lonely sounds, I could picture the mist rising over a favored realm that was both my past and my future. I was one of those Benet speaks of "who mean to get away." I didn't think about staying, or worry about returning, so the phrase, popularized by Thomas Wolfe, "you can't go home again," had no meaning. Later on, the saying came true, but not, I think, for the reason Wolfe intended. I can't go back because it isn't there anymore.

You can see these were nothing more than morning thoughts, confused and random. I suppose I should delete "you can see." These are private notes, not something for Talbot's ten million readers. **But it**

get them moving The airplanes he writes of so lovingly were the start of speed culture and a pace of life that would go on to destroy most things my father held dear. Holman's nickname was Speed.

Stet the whole thing! An early reader of this book suggested I condense my father's materials, thinking these chapters boring. That might be true, but I am a detective collecting clues around a disappearance. I can't even bring myself to fix some of the typos in my dad's work because I might destroy a crucial bit of evidence and really, his life has already been condensed. So, stet the whole thing! And apologies if this is boring you. I promise, things are about to get juicy for our narrator, Sam.

But it has become hard for me to write anything these days without taking those faceless millions into consideration. Keep it short. Get the reader hooked in the first sentence, the first paragraph. Drop in some conversation right away. Cut out all the extraneous garbage, the Stephen Vincent Benet, the Wold-Chamberlain; don't let characters stand around with egg on their faces, **get them moving**, acting. I forget I am keeping this journal, or starting it anyway, only for myself. I don't have to make it short, I don't have to "brief" it. What a luxury! Stet "you can see." **Stet the whole thing!**

Having finished reading the book review, impatient with my irritation at the Times, I got up to go get a cup of coffee from the dispenser down stairs. But just as I stood, Carol, the receptionist, appeared in my doorway. "Mr. Cate," she said, "there's a man at the desk who wants to see you. I tried to ring Marjorie, but she isn't in yet." Marjorie is my secretary. "I told him we aren't open yet. I didn't say you were in. I just said I'd check to see."

"What's he want?" I asked. "Did he say?"

"No, but he asked for you by name. He gave me his card."

She handed me a business card. It read "I. Crane," and centered under that, "Consultant." No company name, no address, no telephone number. "Is this a joke?" I asked.

"I didn't look at it," Carol said.

"His name is I. Crane, according to this," I said. "Ichabod? Is there a headless horseman in the parking lot?"

She laughed, but nervously. Like many receptionists, she basically wanted only to do her job: greet visitors, steer them in the right direction, deflect the crazies and the nuisances who occasionally showed up and keep them from getting through to the editors. Carol held editors in awe, almost worshipfully. That was

seen us up close There was a tremendous amount of bad behavior among these editors. Marjorie is the one character here who gets to keep her real name. She was an essential part of my father's work; I don't think he could imagine this character having any other name. My father treated Marjorie with great respect and Marjorie *did* worship my dad. Who knows what other sort of bosses she'd had in life, perhaps some men less kind and respectful. So, according to my mom, he could do nothing wrong in Marjorie's eyes, a stance my mother thought was uninformed. She knew my dad. She knew just how many faults he did have. My mom tells the story of how, one night, the three of them drove home from a party. My dad, completely wasted, insisted on driving. My mom says he was sailing across all three lanes of the FDR Drive. And every time she asked him to pull over and let her drive, Marjorie piped in from the backseat, "He's fine, Diane."

Sam Cate My name + my sister Cathryn's name, though she spells it Kate. Finally, his daughters, or at least two of us, make an appearance.

plastic lid It's hard not to lament the trash of the 1980s and to think where we might be now if we'd heeded early warnings about pollution, climate change, and the destruction of our planet. What if we'd made actual changes back in the eighties? Instead, I begin to tally the staggering number of plastic coffee cup lids expended since then, lids that still flood our planet with fresh trash every morning.

nice, because mostly the secretaries, Marjorie included, didn't. They had **seen us up close.**

I looked at my watch. Eight-fifteen. We weren't even open yet, officially. I shrugged my shoulders at Carol. "You want to bring him down?" She hesitated, and I could see she was still nervous, so I added, "Oh, well, I'll come get him. Just let me get some coffee." She headed back to the reception area, and I nipped around the corner, down to the basement, where the coffee machine was, then back upstairs by another staircase that brought me directly to the open area at the front of our building. Seeing me, Carol pointed to the reception room, a lounge off of the main entrance. I walked into the room, smiling, and held out my hand to the only occupant.

"Mr. Crane? I'm **Sam Cate.**"

The man stood up. I always pictured the original Ichabod Crane as tall, thin, loose-jointed, but this one was about my height (medium-short), older than I, brown-haired, wearing a gray business suit. He had a ruddy complexion, and wore eyeglasses with thick, brown rims. When talking to a person, I usually look at his mouth forming the words, but I noticed Mr. Crane had dark blue eyes, bristly brows and crow's feet that extended almost across his temples. The skin over his forehead and around his cheekbones was taut, as if he were standing at the tiller in a high wind.

We shook hands. I indicated my coffee cup. It had a **plastic lid** on it and I carried it, thumb on top, index finger below. "You want some coffee?"

"No. No, thank you," he said. His voice was soft. "I've had some."

"I drink coffee all morning," I informed him, which was true enough, but slightly inane to be saying. I was in that initial stage

Not a Falcon—a Mustang Not a bird of the sky, but a beast of the land.

convertibles My dad had a convertible when I was very young. Before the time of car seats, all three of his youngest kids would ride together standing up on the passenger seat, no roof. Eventually, this car was replaced by an Oldsmobile Starfire with a back seat. I've never before considered the connection between flying and driving with the top down. And now, I wonder about the fathers who drive convertibles and what it means to fly if you are a parent. I guess I think parents shouldn't fly. Parents should parent from here on Earth, right? Or at least, if parents are going to fly, teach your children to fly too.

mid-April My father would die on April 30.

The Cardinals We had already decided my dead dad was a cardinal before I read this. He wasn't really a follower of any sports and didn't root for the Cardinals above any other team. I imagine he chose the Cardinals here because the team is Midwestern like him and because they are magnificent, if common, birds.

of awkwardness with a person when inanities often bubbled out of my mouth. I led the way for him, out of the reception room and into the hall toward my office. He trailed slightly behind me, and I had to talk to him across my shoulder.

"Normally," I said, "I wouldn't be here. We don't open until eight-thirty." Too late, I realized how rude this might sound. I plunged on. "I was up early today, so I came in."

"Yes," he said quietly. "I didn't mean to bother you at your office. But I saw that you had already left."

"Oh," I said, disquieted. "You were at my house?"

"I saw your car. You drive that red Falcon, the old one."

"Yes," I said, bothered by his answer, or lack of one. "It's a 1968. Not a Falcon—a Mustang. They're hard to find these days. Especially the convertibles."

"Do you like driving with the top down?" he asked. It seemed a rather stupid question, but since I didn't take him to be a stupid man, I supplied a reason for the question. It was only mid-April, not that warm yet in these parts. "I suppose I'm rushing the season a bit," I said. "But, you know, it's really fresh these early spring mornings. The air is so fresh, I mean. It smells different. I like it better now than in mid-summer. The top down, I mean." We had reached my office, and I stood back from the door to let him enter first. "What the heck," I said, because for all I knew he was one of those religious nuts that Talbot's drew more than its fair share of, who would object to strong language, "the baseball season is well underway."

"Yes," he said, taking the seat I pointed out to him. "Are you a Mets fan? Or the Yankees?"

"The Cardinals," I replied. He looked at me suspiciously, and I could see him wondering if I was pulling his leg.

Do you like birds? As far as I know, my dad knew very little about birds. One summer after college I moved home so I could pay off some of my student loans. I set up a bird feeder in the yard. My then mostly retired dad feverishly took on the job of keeping squirrels off the feeder. I appreciated his work. I still wage a daily battle against the squirrels who steal from my bird feeders though lately I've made peace with a squirrel who has moved into the barn where I write, believing that we might peacefully coexist.

keeping an open and curious mind My editor, Jenna Johnson, does indeed possess an open and curious mind; however, I'm very aware as I write this that I may indeed be one of "the nuts" my father speaks of. I am certainly among "the secretive." I've been writing this book for five years and haven't told anyone about it. Not Jenna, not PJ, not even my husband. I work in secret because secrets are my power plant. Secrets give me energy to keep working on a book. Once the secret is out of the bag, the energy dissipates into thin air. If you are trying to write a book, don't tell anyone about it.

accidents or disasters Sometimes my father was responsible for editing the "Drama in Real Life" section at the *Digest*. It was a favorite of mine. Shipwrecks, plane crashes, lost in the Arctic. I couldn't get enough.

"Do you like birds?" he asked.

"Not especially," I said. "Tell me"—I had moved behind my desk and was folding up the New York Times, which I had left open—"is your first name Ichabod?"

"No," he said with a smile. "I see you were looking at the book review, the one about the Wright brothers."

I noted Mr. Crane's lack of an answer again. He was beginning to irritate me. It is, unfortunately, an editor's job to see every nut who asks to see him, to read every nutty manuscript that comes in—or part of it, anyway—on the off-chance that something useful for the magazine will come out of it. An editor must condition himself to say "yes"—the editorial "oui." And by and large, this necessity—of keeping an open and curious mind—was one of the joys of an editorial job, that and the anticipation of discovering an exciting, fresh story. But from years of experience, I knew that the surprises came rarely. More often came the nuts—the walking insane, the fanatics, the ideologues, the paranoiacs, and the secretive, those who had a great story (they said), but wouldn't tell it for fear that I (that is, Talbot's) would steal it, distort it, tell it to the world without crediting them. I was getting the first tell-tale antennae quiverings of secretiveness from Mr. Crane.

"That's what I want to talk about," he went on.

"The Wright brothers?" I asked. "Well, we've just done the book ourselves, you know."

"Not the Wright brothers, specifically," he expanded. "More generally, flying. Flying, in general."

I experienced a sense of disappointment. Flying, treated as a general subject, is something that encyclopedias do. General magazines don't. They—we—write about specific events, like Lindbergh's transatlantic solo, or accidents or disasters, even minor

Do you have dreams about flying? My father asked me once if I had flying dreams. I was tempted to lie and tell him yes, but I didn't. I told the truth. My sister Amy does have flying dreams. Maybe that's why he took her to Minnesota! His mom also had flying dreams. Maybe they had a conference of the people with flying dreams while they were at the fair. Maybe they rode the large Ferris wheel and thought about flight. That would have made my father very happy.

crises. (Talbots, particularly, was addicted to articles about small plane flying in which the pilot suffers a heart attack and the only other person aboard, a non-flyer, has brought the plane in.) I began to try to explain this to Mr. Crane, but he interrupted me.

"**Do you have dreams about flying?**" he asked.

"You mean dreams when I'm asleep?"

He nodded. "Yes."

"Yes, I do. I suppose most people do."

"Less than you think," he said. "Very few, in fact. I once told someone that I dreamed at night about flying and he—it was a man I knew casually—said yes, he did, too. He'd had a dream just the other night when the engines had conked out and he was the only one able to land the plane."

"Ta-pocketa-pocketa," I said.

"Yes," he said, picking up the allusion, "a Walter Mitty type situation. I tried to explain to my friend that I didn't mean that kind of . . ."

"Not in a plane," I interjected.

"Exactly," Mr. Crane said.

"I had one of those last night," I said. "Not too pleasant, though. Someone was trying to pull me down by my feet."

"That happens sometimes. Other anxieties get mixed into the dream."

"I suppose so," I said. I was thinking, and I dropped back a reference or two. "That's what you meant, wasn't it? Flying without a plane? Without anything, no wings or motors, just yourself aloft and flying around?"

"Yes," he said.

I looked at him for a moment. "You're not here about a story, are you?" I asked.

"No." He pondered this. "Is that what you thought? That I wanted to sell you a story? I suppose that makes sense, doesn't it? I'm sorry. I haven't come here to sell a story—an article, do you call it?"

"Yes, or in my case, a book. Like the Wright brothers. Why are you here, then?"

"I wanted to ask if you had flying dreams."

"I see," I said, "you're one of those people who drops into offices unheralded, and asks by name for someone just to see if they have flying dreams. Does someone pay you to do this, or is it a hobby?"

"Yes," he replied, "you might say it's a hobby." He fell silent for several seconds, looking down at his feet. He had his shoes turned up, the soles almost together, like a nervous schoolboy in the principal's office for an infraction of rules. "It's always difficult in the beginning," he went on at last, still staring down. "I've never found a way to make it easy. I'm not the glib type, but I don't think glibness would help, anyway. Let me put it this way. We are worried about your safety."

I noted the "we." Perhaps it was the editorial we. Ha, ha. I had once agreed to see a man who said he had a hot new angle on the Jekyll and Hyde story, a *new* Jekyll and Hyde story. He talked about "we" also. It turned out he thought he *was* Dr. Jekyll and Mr. Hyde.

"Oh?" I said.

Again, he was silent, as if he found it difficult to formulate his thoughts. "Do you remember a story recently, it was in the newspapers, about a man who climbed the Washington monument, I mean like a mountain climber, and when the police got called in, they had to get a helicopter to take him off?"

twin towers In 1977 George Willig, also known as "The Human Fly," a toymaker and mountain climber from Queens, scaled up the outside of 2 World Trade Center, two and a half years after Philippe Petit crossed the span between the twin towers on his tightrope. My dad met Philippe Petit after editing an account of his famous feat of daring. I also met Philippe Petit, about thirty years after my dad. My friend Sophia, an artist who builds processions that often involve puppets four times human size, invited me to watch Petit rehearse. I was able to witness his daily exercises. This during the pandemic, when my eyes were starved for any sort of theater. To watch Petit work was miraculous. After he finished I approached him shyly, though I needn't have been shy. He is very affable. I told him that my father had met him years earlier and that my father, while not a wire walker, often dreamed he could fly. I said, "My father wondered if you also have flying dreams." Petit looked up. "You know," he said, "it is funny. I never dream that I am walking on the wire, but I often have dreams that I can fly." It wasn't until much later that night that it dawned on me how much Philippe Petit resembles the wiry and strong body of Saint-Exupéry's hero.

the man dreamed he had flown People are reluctant to admit that strange things happen all the time. Even those same people who have eyeballs and lungs. Even people who have seen the crystal formations of snowflakes. *See* Ghost Story.

"Yes," I said. I did remember the story vaguely. I hadn't paid much attention to it because it was beginning to be an old story. A man had climbed up a pier on the Brooklyn Bridge; a man climbed, or tried to climb, the outside of one of the **twin towers** (the World Trade Center in lower Manhattan); others were parachuting into unlikely places; it had become the thing to do, despite the threat of arrest and a fine.

I was growing impatient with Mr. Crane. I had work to do. The day had begun. Marjorie had come in. She had looked through her door into my office, inspected Mr. Crane and smiled at me behind his back before going out of sight to her desk. We were connected by a buzzer. If I buzzed three times, she knew to cook up an interruption, a summons to another editor's office, something urgent.

If I let Mr. Crane proceed at his own pace, he would be with me all morning. "What you're going to tell me," I said, "is that this man on the Washington monument didn't climb it, he flew up there, right?"

"No," he said. "I was going to tell you that **the man dreamed he had flown** to the top of the monument."

"Okay," I said. "But how come when the police came, he wasn't dreaming anymore, but was up on top and they had to get a helicopter to bring him down?"

"Well," he said, "that's the riddle, isn't it?"

"Only if you believe he flew up there by himself in a dream and then woke up and found himself actually on the monument."

"That's exactly what I believe."

I slid my hand along the underside of my desk toward the buzzer.

"Please don't call for someone," Mr. Crane said. "I'll be going in a moment. I'm only here to tell you that we are worried for your

feel that someone is staring at you I had the great pleasure of interviewing the British biologist Rupert Sheldrake. Sheldrake's work is a marvel. He investigates this very phenomenon: Why do we know when we are being stared at? And why do so many people insist on placing this investigation outside the realm of science? *See* Queer Theorem.

anonymous Alcoholics Anonymous saved my father's life. He got sober when I was a teenager. While he sponsored many people on their journey to sobriety, he thought he made a poor sponsor, awkward with the language people use to encourage and convince. He couldn't do it. He'd say things like, "Just don't drink." He really did want people to stop drinking, he really wanted to help, but he couldn't find the right words. My mom told me that sometimes he'd ask her what he should tell people.

safety. We have named this sort of thing a break-through, an emer-
gence, if you will, from the dream, or something that is very like a
dream, into reality. It is like a bell that is ringing in a dream which
turns out to be ringing in reality also. You will notice that I use the
word we. We are a society, quite small as yet, that concerns itself
with such matters. We meet regularly on Friday nights to discuss
this dangerous situation and other matters that concern us. The
purpose of my visit is to make you aware of this, to tell you about
our society and invite you to attend a meeting, where I assure you
that you will be completely anonymous and where you will learn
a little more about our concerns and how they apply to your . . .
your predicament. You see, we sometimes have intimations that
a break-through is occurring, or is about to occur. By intimations
I mean that we feel a presence, just as, for instance, you may **feel
that someone is staring at you** in a room. We feel, as it were, that
you are staring at us. We can identify you, but no contact has yet
been made. That concerns us, worries us. Our society, I mean.
There have been accidents in the past, which, we feel, might have
been avoided. And there has been publicity, on occasion, that has
been baffling and also should be avoided, if possible. Like our
friend in Washington."

He reached into an inside jacket pocket. "Let me just leave this
card. It has our address on it, and a reminder that it is on Fridays
we meet. That's all. As I said, at the beginning it is very difficult.
We are most often dismissed as crackpots, so I will say no more.
But I urge you, for your own sake, to attend a meeting. It's **anonymous**, and I promise you, worthwhile."

He stood up and handed me the card. "I can find my own
way out," he said. I navigate very well. I am sorry to have had to

420 Watts My brother Andy lived on Watts Street for years, though the street is a short one and there is no number 420. I imagine the 420 is a tip of the hat to my other brother, Charley, who would have enjoyed telling our dad secrets about marijuana culture. My dad really listened to his children, and as he got older, we became his link to the world, his way of learning. We became the only people he was actually interested in besides our mother. He once told me he didn't really have friends, a statement that, I imagine, would have come as a big surprise to the many people who were his friends.

Crane The human bird plus the bird bird in one man's name.

Icarus Icarus implicates the father. Daedalus constructed the wax wings that would cause the death of his son. My grandfather, also named Walter, was not a flexible man. When my mother once told him how much she loved the movie *Elvira Madigan*, he told her it was disgusting because it portrayed adultery. Later in life, after retiring from the railroad, my grandfather became a painter. He died while painting a still life of flowers. My grandmother marked the painting with a note to preserve it forever. My mom, years later, thought she could improve on this painting and added some deep reds, putting her signature below his. Despite giving him life, my grandparents did a lot to mess up and repress my dad with sorrow, guilt, and propriety. I'm not trying to blame them. I'm sure they did their best with the grief they carried. My mom and her deep reds, a free spirit, tried to help free my dad from the guilt his parents gave him. One of the many reasons I wish he hadn't died young is that I believe, in retirement and older age, he would have finally had the time and the self-confidence to make the art he'd dreamed of making.

interrupt your work, and I apologize for the unsettling nature of this interview. We hope to see you soon."

I took him at his word, and did not follow him out. I had not even removed the plastic lid from my coffee cup. I did so now, but the coffee was cold. "Oh, shoot," I said to myself, and then realizing that Mr. Crane was gone, I re-phrased it. "Oh, shit," I said, and felt better.

I looked at the two cards he had left behind. I. Crane, Consultant. And the second:

SOI 420 WATTS MANHATTAN
FRIDAY 8 P.M.

SOI? Clearly that didn't stand for South, as in South Watts Street. More likely it was the name of the society that I. Crane had mentioned. Of course. Society of something-or-other. Suddenly I had a notion that I knew what Mr. **Crane's** first name was. It seemed just nutty enough. SOI. Society of **Icarus**.

The Blanks

When I found the pages of my dad's unfinished book, I first thought I might try to finish it, fill in the blanks. The more I read his book, though, the less of an idea I had about what belonged in those blanks. I could write anything, but that didn't mean it would be right or satisfying. Was there a secret society whose anonymous members can fly without wings? And if so, how to meet them and join their ranks?

In *Hauntings*, an installation by the filmmaker Guy Maddin, a number of lost films from the silent era are reimagined. Maddin channeled and re-created storied films by F. W. Murnau, Fritz Lang, Hollis Frampton, Victor Sjöström, Jean Vigo, Kenji Mizoguchi, and Josef von Sternberg, works that were known to have existed or had been planned but were either destroyed or never produced by the original filmmaker. When I sat down to take up where my dad left off after chapter 3, it felt wrong. I didn't know what happened next.

My friend Jenn's father went to West Point. At his funeral, there was a soldier who graduated the same year as Mr. LaBelle.

Their class had been decimated by the war in Vietnam. The man stood up at the funeral and explained that when he and Mr. La-Belle were students, they conducted roll call at the school. One cadet would call out the others' last names. These calls were met with the response, "Present." At the funeral, the classmate paused in his explanation and asked, into the silence, "LaBelle?" No answer. "LaBelle?" Nothing. Then, one last time, "Gary LaBelle?" He waited and a beautiful, blank silence held the room.

In third grade one of my daughters wrote a biography of the rock climber Alex Honnold for school. Honnold is known for climbing Yosemite's El Capitan using no ropes, a free solo, up two thousand and nine hundred feet, half a mile straight up, or sometimes worse than straight up, obtuse angles, with no ancillary support. The filmmakers Elizabeth Chai Vasarhelyi and Jimmy Chin followed, with ropes, and recorded Honnold's ascent. I've watched the film *Free Solo* many times now and, spoiler alert, Honnold completes and survives the climb. The film is still harrowing. What would have happened to the footage if Honnold had fallen, if they'd recorded his body bouncing off the rocks far below? Would there be no film? Would the filmmakers cut off the ending and leave us hanging, thousands of feet above the valley floor? What *do* flying and dying have to do with each other?

My dad writes that early aviators are always associated with the spiritual. Some idea that they are flying closer to heaven. In this present moment of environmental catastrophe, it is clear that ideas of a heaven removed or above Earth have allowed humans to poison our planet. Who cares about this Earth when we will fly off up to a removed god? But heaven is here on Earth, in the forest, in the soil, in the sea. This is where we will go when we are dead. Every aviator has returned to Earth, whether by choice or not. The connection with flying and dying has nothing to do with staying in the sky forever, but rather with our desire to crash back into our beloved Earth. To never leave this holy place.

In *The White Diamond* Werner Herzog films his crew filming the space behind Kaieteur Falls in Guyana, a place the Patamona people hold sacred. The footage exists, and some sacrilege has been trespassed, even though Herzog never shows us what lies behind the sacred waterfall. If we know the mystery's been filmed does that mystery still exist?

A few summers back, my daughters, husband, and I listened to the audiobook of S. E. Hinton's *The Outsiders*. Three-quarters of the way through, something shifted in my oldest child. She was ten. She's sensitive and observant. She sometimes tells us things that are going to happen before they happen. Her comprehension of narrative arc was in tune and as we listened, she sensed death nearby. If we kept listening to the book, Johnny and Dally would die. We would somehow be responsible for their deaths if we kept listening to the story unfold. So, my daughter stopped us. She wouldn't let us continue the book. She turned it off before the beautiful, messed up boys were dead. If she was in control, there would be no dying. Stop the film before we hit the rocks below. Stop here, while it looks like we are only flying.

Ghost Books

The Invisible Library is an archive of books that exists only within other books. One of its cofounders, Ed Park, writes:

> In Raymond Chandler's posthumously published note-books, we find 36 unused titles, from "The Man With the Shredded Ear" to "The Black-Eyed Blonde," as well as reference to Aaron Klopstein, author of such books as "Cat Hairs in the Custard" and "Twenty Inches of Monkey."

The list of books that don't exist, like the Invisible Library itself, is without border or end. In his essay "La biblioteca total," Borges writes:

> Everything would be in its blind volumes. Everything: the detailed history of the future, Aeschylus' *The Egyptians*, the exact number of times that the waters of the Ganges have reflected the flight of a falcon, the secret and true nature of

Rome, the encyclopedia Novalis would have constructed,
my dreams and half-dreams at dawn on August 14, 1934.

Have you read *The Vixen, the Patriot, and the Fanatic* by Anya
Partridge; *The Father* by Benno von Archimboldi; *Miriam: The
Disappearance of a New England Girl* by Karl E. Hammer; the
Necronomicon by Abdul Alhazred; Thelonius Ellison's *The Second
Failure*, published by Endangered Species Press; or Kilgore Trout's
oeuvre?

Juan Rulfo's *Pedro Páramo*, like *The Rings of Saturn*, is a story
of a journey under the Dog Star of August. Susan Sontag, in her
introduction to *Pedro Páramo*, writes, "It is rare for a writer to
publish his first books when he is already in his mid-forties, even
rarer for first books to immediately be acknowledged as master-
pieces. And rarer still for such a writer never to publish another
book. A novel called *La Cordillera* was announced as forthcoming
by Rulfo's publisher for many years, starting in the late 1960s—
and announced by the author as destroyed, a few years before his
death in 1986."

The broken volumes from Italo Calvino's *If on a winter's night
a traveler* might be considered ghost books of the second degree.
Their immateriality is only partial, like *The Canterbury Tales*, like
Sappho undone by worms and time, like my father's book: somewhat unwritten.

What about books that can only be read once? Where to
shelve them? Alaska McFadden made me such a book years ago,
a vampire story. At the end of the book, it asked the reader to
stab it with a provided wooden stake. Curiosity beat out preserva-
tion. I raised the stake and stabbed the book. A pile of ashes was

deposited in my lap, released from a secret chamber. I had killed the book and remain its only and ever complete reader.

I told McFadden about the joy and sorrow I felt having read her book to its end. A few years later, she and Jessica Elsaesser of A Wrecked Tangle Press created an entire edition of books that could be read only once. They hid the texts inside the evacuated shells of a number of chicken eggs. They presented me with one of these eggs, a book that must be destroyed in order to read it. I wasn't going to make the same mistake twice. The egg remains. The book unread but intact.

What about books so potent or voluminous they cannot be read in one lifetime? Raymond Queneau's *Cent mille milliard de poèmes* is a thin volume—no thicker than the Saver booklets once made for holding S&H Green Stamps (speaking of ghosts!). Queneau's text is the poetic response to the mathematical function 10^{14}. Ten sonnets of fourteen lines. Each line is printed on its own strip of paper, allowing for an interchangeability of lines; every permutation makes a new poem. By Queneau's calculations, a person reading at a rate of one sonnet per minute, eight hours a day, two hundred days a year (roughly the hours of a full-time job), would take more than a million centuries to finish reading every possible poem inside this thin, thin book. A text that has our own mortality stitched into its pages. You cannot live long enough to read this book. Perhaps I'm wrong to classify *Cent mille milliards de poèmes* as a ghost book. It's not the book that will be a ghost, it's you.

As kids, we draped our washcloths over an old iron radiator after bath time. Eventually all of our washcloths were covered with rust stains. When we saw these stains, my brother Charley, my sister Amy, and I would cry out, "Franka-ki-ee's blood!

Franka-ki-ee's blood!" I don't know who Franka-ki-ee was. We made him up to hold all the frightening unknown things, the essence of mystery. And I often felt him just behind me, in hot pursuit as they say, when I ran screaming at night through the backyard. The scream, the run, the darkness. I always managed to escape Franka-ki-ee's grasp.

I wrote my college essay about bath time, an unorthodox topic, I now realize. I didn't get into my first choice, Brown University. I went to a state school instead. Years later, when I was super-pregnant with twins, Brown University asked me to come teach their students about my novel *The Invention of Everything Else*. That felt good, like an admission that they'd been wrong about the importance of bath time and the mysteries of Franka-ki-ee.

A few weeks after my visit to Providence I received an email from Brian Evenson, the magnificent writer who had organized my visit. The note from Brian contained a postscript. He wrote:

P.S. (And I wanted to ask you about Wanda LaFontaine, the author you mention on page 27. I'm assuming she's made up? I haven't in any case been able to find her easily in the usual places. But, at the same time, I knew I'd heard her name somewhere before, and then realized after wracking my brains and paging through together too many books, that Lucius Shepard had mentioned her in *The Jaguar Hunter*. Is your Wanda LaFontaine happy coincidence, deliberate allusion to Lucius's or is she actually real?)

Wanda was a fabrication. I've never written a book that doesn't contain mention of at least one book that doesn't exist. At first that was unintentional, though now it's something considered.

Evenson's fantastic memory plus strange coincidence had detected this ghost author.

I checked on my Wanda. Here she is on page 27:

> *On the Aft Deck* by Wanda LaFontaine is a ladies' novel. It had been left behind at the hotel and stuffed into Louisa's purse before she realized how silly it was.

I'd never heard of *The Jaguar Hunter* or Lucius Shepard. I assumed Evenson was returning my volley, that he'd fabricated both author and text. A few days later my twins were born and I forgot all about Wanda.

Time passed. Children grew. Four and a half years after my reading at Brown, I finished writing a new novel, *Mr. Splitfoot*. Inside its pages I placed another book that doesn't fully exist. *The Book of Ether*, a religious text, consisting of lines recycled from the Book of Mormon, the Bible, Carl Sagan's *Cosmos*, some scattered lyrics from Cher and Queen, and the U.S. Constitution:

> *1 We are approaching the greatest of mysteries.*
> *We float like a mote of dust in the morning sky.*
> *We know that this is impossible.*
>
> *2 We the people.*
> *We believe all the words which thou hast spoken.*
> *We cannot understand the words.*
> *We fled all that day into the wilderness, even until it was dark.*
> *We commanded the rocks and the mountains to fall upon us to*
>   *hide us.*
> *We will, we will rock you.*

3 *We cross this great water in darkness.*
We lost a great number of our choice men.
We will change them into cedars.
We see there was no chance they should live forever.
We will change them into cedars.

4 *We have spoken, which is the end.*
We should call the name.
We should call the name. We know that this is impossible.

Wanda LaFontaine returned to me. I reread Evenson's long-ago email, and one internet search later, I found Lucius Shepard, a real person, not a fiction at all. The internet instantly provided me with his Wanda passage:

> The publishers would keep the title; they would change it to *The Keening* or *The Huffing and Puffing*, package it with a garish cover, and stick it next to *Love's Tormenting Itch* by Wanda LaFontaine on the grocery store racks. But none of that mattered as long as the words were good, and they were.

Lucius Shepard was not only real, it was clear that *his* Wanda and *my* Wanda were the same author, a cruel stereotype of a woman I never even gave a fair chance, a woman doused in cheap perfume to disguise the scent of her own decay.

This excerpt was from Shepard's short story "How the Wind Spoke at Madaket." Strangely, Madaket is a pinprick village at the faraway end of the postage-stamp island two hours out to sea where two of my sisters have lived year-round for twenty-odd years.

Who was Lucius Shepard? I told many friends this story. I must have said his name a hundred times or more. My children, hiding under dinner tables, listening through vents, overheard the man's name. I told the story so often, I began to doubt Shepard's reality again and found myself checking the internet to confirm that Shepard was in fact a real person, with a photo and even a real Facebook account. On February 27, 2014, I sent a fast message off to Shepard, explaining that from separate lives we had stumbled upon the same ghost author. I waited for his reply. On March 18, I was at a drive-through coffee shop outside Jackson, Mississippi, when I received an email from Ed Park. Lucius Shepard, seventy years old, had been found dead in his Oregon home.

I'm embarrassed to say it now, but in that moment, I thought, My God, I've killed the man by noticing that he dealt in ghosts and their books. In that Mississippi drive-through, another branch of the Invisible Library opened its doors. All the books Shepard would not write, on a special shelf beside the never-completed works of Wanda LaFontaine.

A few weeks after Shepard's death I was sitting outside in the cool air. Through a window I heard my daughters taking on roles, whispering in their own patois, a shadowy game. They repeated an incantation, something they'd overheard and adopted. "Loooo-cius. Loooocius," as shapeless as Franka-ki-ee, giving the dead man voice, magical and alive and dead and, in their mouths, alive again, alive.

Spirits

There's a ditch at the end of our driveway that consistently swallowed vehicles heading home after parties at our house. My siblings and I would help drunk adults push wobbly cars out of that ditch and back up onto the road. Seeing them off on their drunken way home. We never considered the hazards. Everyone we knew drank. Everyone drove. And the ditch, streetside, late at night, was an exciting place to be: disheveled clothes, jealous brawls, dirty songs at 2:00 a.m.

My siblings and I studied adult behaviors. My father would strum "We'll Build a Bungalow" on a banjo he had carried home from the Korean War. Moments later a searing passion would consume him. He'd ask my sister and me, "Do you understand what a great artist your brother Andy is?" Yes, we'd nod. We did understand, but my dad wasn't really talking to us. He was just noticing things. We were unseen, free to observe uncles stumbling down staircases, visiting editors sleeping on the living room floor. Or my dad. Just step over him. It wasn't unusual to have a house filled with passionate adults from all over the world, lovers of books, music, and dancing. Like getting drunk, it was fun until it wasn't. Watching adults act wild meant we had total freedom. There were a lot of us. We could help ourselves to anything— whipped cream, the barn roof, tonic water. We could dance with the adults; enough of them were jolly rather than drunk, though still, my mom says I'd often ask, "Can I please go to bed now?"

In the cranky sunlight of morning, we felt fine even if the adults, especially my father, sat frozen, trying not to move his head, his eyes, petting the family bunny like it was the only friend he had in the world.

There were non-parties too, and my father continued to drink. He nestled cans of Schlitz between his thighs on car rides. He drank gin from a bottle he'd hidden in our woodpile or in the pantry under the stairs, underneath the kitchen sink. From the living room, watching TV, we'd hear the pantry door open. We'd hear the quiet of him trying to not make a sound, gulping Gilbey's. Then a feeling of sinking under and down.

My oldest daughter and I drive past a sign, "Spirit Shoppe." "For a minute," she says, "I thought we could buy a ghost there." A sudden dawn. Yes, we could. Ghosts are exactly what we're buying at the spirit shop. Booze is haunted. We drink what's fermented and distilled. We drink the past, the dead, and even past the point of dead, something so fermented it lives again in those of us who swallow these spirits.

My siblings and I remain uncommonly close even as adults. We are still a gang of Hunts. One friend of mine, who does not get along with his family, explained our closeness. "You had a common enemy to fight against." Maybe, but none of us ever thought my dad was the enemy. A more gentle man than he would be hard to imagine. Perhaps booze was the enemy. At the time, thick with shame, the enemy looked like other people, because my father's drinking wasn't always contained. He'd pick me up at birthday parties drunk or he'd put on a good show if a friend spent the night. His drinking ran straight into the cruelty of middle school, mean girls, and the public nature of small-town life. At those times, the enemy was clear. The enemy was anyone not in our family, anyone who couldn't see that my dad was swimming in the spirits because he was looking for sunken treasure, or at least looking for something buoyant enough to hold on to, a word or sentence, in the sea of his dead. Other people—the cruelty of their judgment—were what left me feeling dirty, a classification I still carry, though now with more pride. Now I know how much I like the dirt.

My siblings and I are close because we saved one another. My sister Amy protected me like the prow of a ship, breaking the waves before they hit me full force. One morning my dad, Amy, and I left at dawn to drive the Starfire to Vermont. It was so early Amy and I wore our pajamas, so early my dad hadn't yet had a drink. At the end of our driveway he said, "Oops. I forgot something." Then a horrible wait in the car for his return and our assessment of him. The children of alcoholics really are detectives, alert to the slightest changes in scent, demeanor, and language. A survival tactic that has become a secret superpower I now use to notice birds, flowers, and tiny fluctuations in the natural world.

What our dad had forgotten that morning was to chug half a handle of gin. Off we went to Vermont with a new precarity to the drive. Just south of New Haven the highway grew crowded. At that time the Sikorsky Memorial Bridge over the Housatonic had an open steel-grid deck with two lanes of traffic in both directions.

The metal road surface was like driving on black ice eighty-five feet above the river below, difficult to navigate even for a sober person. The bridge is named for Igor Sikorsky, an aviation pioneer. Aviation was the last thing I wanted to consider as we started across that slippery bridge with a very drunk dad at the wheel. Yet it was all I could think of—the guardrail, the edge of the bridge. It was very close, and I found it easy to imagine swerving over it and out into the air, a moment of flying in our Oldsmobile before sinking swiftly into the river below. Never have flying and dying felt as close. Amy and I held our breath. Did he want to fly off the bridge? He swerved across both lanes. I willed myself to think, This is normal, this is normal. It's a slippery bridge. Everyone probably uses two lanes to get across. Everyone gets this close to the edge.

Amy was thirteen and in the front seat. I was nine, tucked in back. On the far side of the bridge—we made it across—as soon as we could draw breath again, Amy said, "Dad, I have to pee." He pulled over at the Orange, Connecticut, rest stop. In a move extremely clever and loving, Amy said, "Come with me, Mandy." That's my nickname. I climbed out and once she had me on the sidewalk, out of the car, she turned back and told him, "We are not getting in the car with you. You're drunk."

At first, he tried kindness. "Come on, girls. It'll be okay. Just get back in the car."

"No," Amy said and held me there, standing beside her.

Then he got louder, less kind. Amy, steel-faced, only a girl, repeated what she was certain of, "No." Her bravery was breathtaking, such strength in her small body. My sister saved my life. It wasn't the only time. Our dad left us there, two little girls, at a gas station on a highway in our pajamas. We watched him swerve away from us, uncertain where he was going and how he would get there.

Amy explained everything to the man working at the gas station. He took us into the garage where he was a fixing a car. He invited us to sit on a dark bench and gave us something to eat. Our PJs were the only bit of brightness in that greasy garage. And the man's kindness. In a few hours one of my father's friends came and picked us up, a ride that had been arranged by my mom. My dad's friend was also an alcoholic, but luckily for us he hadn't yet started drinking that day. When we got home my dad was there in one piece, petting our poor bunny.

On my cousin's sixteenth birthday, my uncle loaded too many of us into an open dory with a weak engine and a pitiful dinghy towed behind. We headed out to one of the unpopulated islands off the coast of the town in Maine where my uncle sometimes lived. The men of my childhood loved adventure and living near the edge. The boat was brimming with food, drink, sweatshirts, a motley crew of people young and old. We cooked lunch over an open fire on a deserted island. It was a perfect day. We collected crabs and explored the island while our parents got wasted. I felt like I was living in one of my favorite picture books, Liesel Moak Skorpen's *We Were Tired of Living in a House*, illustrated by Doris Burn.

That evening, during our attempt to journey back to the mainland, it became clear that we were in trouble. My dad and his friend Roy rocked that dinghy until it capsized with them in it. They did it on purpose. Their wool sweaters were soaked. The ocean in Maine, even in September, is frigid. Such drama. They swore like the sailors we wished they'd been. We had no light on the boat and the sun set. At one point on the journey home my uncle tangled the engine on a lobster pot line and cut it free, an offense for which some in that area still extracted payment with a bullet. He was not sufficiently sober to navigate. We drifted on the open, very cold ocean in the dark of night in an overloaded boat. We didn't know which direction meant land, which meant the opposite. The stars were infinite. The men were always liquid. The moms—choking on anger at idiot men—were our saviors, our solidity and happiness. My aunt and mother drew our attention to the Northern Lights, to something larger. The mothers were powered by love and it lifted us. Though this love also meant our mom was trapped in a dangerous marriage. She had no money, no job, and few marketable skills. She'd been raising children for years. She once asked a therapist for help. She was scared we would all die. She wanted to leave my dad. The therapist, a man, told her, "How can you leave him? You have no way to support your children."

That night in the boat, people kept singing and fighting. People kept drinking. No one we knew died that night. But all those men are dead now. All the women are still alive. What was inside the men of my childhood that drew them so quickly to death?

My cousin's been sober for well over twenty years. We celebrated her oldest daughter's sweet sixteen with a family camping trip, a late September dip in the ocean, s'mores and singing. We went without alcohol the whole trip, as many people there were in recovery. No booze is hard for a lot of us. It's hard for me. I thought about a glass of red wine all night. I sometimes need the burn of alcohol to cut through the noise in my blood. That night, sober, I measured the distance between my cousin's sixteenth birthday and her daughter's. I watched my siblings and cousins, those of us who'd been in the boat so many years ago, as we sat around this campfire. We made eye contact across the flames, recognizing a permanent mark in one another, an opening where ribbons of green rip across the black sky and the dark sea below.

In high school I became best friends with girls from families living with substance abuse. These girls became my friends before I even knew the truth about their families. Somehow, we recognized this stain in one another. We found comfort and non-judgment in other families marked by addiction.

What did the spirits do? Where did they take us? One brother jokes about digging a moat around his home. He and his wife are slowly building a cabin in a ravine a mile away from any road. Two of my siblings live so far north, the snow melts in May. Two of my siblings live on an island two hours out to sea where the ocean is wild, and sometimes I worry one big storm might wash my sister's tiny, basement-less house away. When bad weather strikes their island, the boats stop running. No one can leave. No food can arrive, a surrender to the weather and the water, a proximity to danger and beauty. Amy was pregnant on the island and went into labor after the boats had stopped running for the night. She called me and I asked her what she was going to do. "Hold it," she said, and she did. The following morning, she boarded the boat for the mainland, where my niece was born. When we talk about the drinking, Amy says, "That's why we live on the edge out here." The edge is familiar. The edge feels right. We have found places where the depths are close, within view, and there, we've tried to build calm lives for our own children.

When I was a kid, adults were above me in a complex world. I didn't enter my parents' bedroom if I knew my dad was there. I was afraid of the adult mysteries I might witness: sex, hangovers, death, sadness. There was space between child and adult. Now, my daughters wake me at night. They join me in bed. They tell me things and I listen. I cry in front of them. I know the lyrics to their favorite songs. When we visit my mom, no one drinks Schlitz on the drive down. Still, my parenting skills are in no way superior to my parents'. I'm messing my kids up in my own way. My daughters live closer to an adult world than I did. That creates its own sort of damage and neuroses. We talk about cancer, climate destruction, school shootings. We talk about alcoholism and all the people we love who have died from substance abuse. There's still a very deep sea below. Indeed, it often seems deeper than ever.

In the *Dictionary of Word Origins*, Shipley's take on the word "spirit" is a faceted doozy.

spirit, *See* trophy

trophy.

A *trophy* was originally a monument erected where an enemy was turned back. Gr. *trepein*, to turn, whence *trope*, turning . . . A *trope*, figure of speech, is a turning of a word from its literal sense . . . Those interested in aviation will note that one range of the *atmosphere* (Gr. *atmos*, vapor) is the *troposphere*, where there are convective (turning) disturbances . . . *Sphere* is via Fr. From Gr. *sphaira*, ball, Gr. *speira*,winding, give us Eng. *spiral*; but the church *spire* is a later sense (from the shape of AS. *spir*, long blade of grass, related to *spar* and *spear*, for which *see affluent*. To *aspire*, however, was first to breathe upon (much the same as *inspire, inspiration, q.v.*) then to breathe toward, to seek, to reach, from L. *ad*, to + *spirare*, *spirat*—to breathe—whence also the *spirit*, L. *spiritus*, originally the breath of life or animating principle in each of us. The various meanings of *spirit* follow from this, as the evil *spirit* that directs a person, the *spirits* summoned by a *spiritualist*. Hence also the use as a basic principle or essence of anything: as the four *spirits* of the medieval alchemists. They were quicksilver (mercury), orpiment (yellow arsenic), sal ammoniac and brimstone (sulphur). Hence, too, *spirits* of turpentine, and animal *spirits* more exuberant with alcoholic *spirits*.

I found a box of old letters at my mom's. Some from my grandma, some from my great-grandma, along with a number of editions of my uncle Chuckie's Funnies Book, a craft paper compilation filled with clever drawings. Ten cents a copy. The craft paper decomposed in my hands. Tiny bits of paper were airborne. The scent of old things, small bits of the drawings inside my lungs. The breath of life is also the breath of death.

When I stepped away from the box, I was dizzy, as if I'd been zooming through time, seasick, drunk on those other kinds of spirits.

When I travel for work I am less lonely in hotel rooms if I have a glass of red wine with me, as if in drinking, I keep my kin close. I use the past and alcohol in similar ways. They are comforts, reminders of our cohesion. I must moderate my consumption of both, so as not to grow senseless to the present.

In late March 2020, a book arrived, one I'd ordered before the pandemic, Stephen Vincent Benét's *The Last Circle*. I wanted to read "Good Picker," the Benét story my father quoted in his manuscript. According to a number of bookplates and markings inside the book, this copy had had a long journey before arriving at my house. It had been deaccessioned from the University of Manchester's library before landing on the shelves of Blackwell's in Oxford, before an outfit called Any Book, Ltd, UK, sold it to me.

In "The Universal Story" Ali Smith writes about the previous lives of our books, in this case, a paperback edition of *The Great Gatsby*.

The novel had first been bought for 30p (6/-) in 1974 in a Devon bookshop by Rosemary Child who was twenty-two and who had felt the urge to read the book before she saw the film. She married her fiancé Roger two years later. They mixed their books and gave their doubles to a Cornwall hospital. This one had been picked off the hospital library trolley in Ward 14 one long hot July afternoon in 1977 by Sharon Patten, a fourteen-year-old girl with a broken hip who was stuck in bed in traction and bored because Wimbledon was over. Her father had seemed pleased at visiting hour when he saw it on her locker and though she'd given up reading it halfway through she kept it there by the water jug for her whole stay and smuggled it home with her when she was discharged. Three years later, when she didn't care anymore what her father thought of what she did, she gave it to her schoolfriend David Connor who was going to university to do English, telling him it was the most boring book in the world. David read it. It was perfect. It was just like life is. Everything is beautiful, everything is hopeless.

I like thinking of used books as contagions, things that spread through the world. I cracked open the Benét on a day I couldn't stop coughing. I was waiting for the results of my Covid-19 test. It would take more than two weeks for me to get the results. By the time I did, I was feeling better. At the start of the pandemic, we knew so little. Terror and panic were everywhere. Would I die? Had I infected others? Would they die because of me? Could my children survive? While I was, like many, feeling grateful for the pause the pandemic provided, it came with a bristling fear.

Rather than turning straight to "Good Picker," the piece I'd
waited months to read, I was stopped by the first sentence of the
book's introduction, written by Rosemary Benét, Stephen's widow.
"As I re-read these stories and poems, there seems to be in them
a premonition of death." I closed *The Last Circle*. What a creepy
title. How can there be a last circle? Sometimes collecting clues
is spooky. They can be so adamant in their message, Thou shalt
surely die. I know. I know. But at that moment, my daughter had
a trick she wanted to show me, dangling from the branches of
a tree.

There is no last circle. I stand in my mom's barn looking for
her rake while I am also stacking firewood there in 1985. Sometimes I feel years before I existed, 1967, 1938, 1802, as shouted
declarations. I'm guilty of trying to drown the present moment—
one filled with greed, celebrity culture, questionable technologies,
and a virus smarter than humans—in the past, to move through
life conscious of the dead and the moments they lived in. I am
comforted by the smallness of my life and by ancient things. What
if we were less drawn to the new? The new will not stop us from
dying.

There is a lake near where I grew up, Lost Lake. It isn't lost to
me, but it is hidden in the woods and hard to find. No roads lead
to the lake. My siblings and I grew up swimming here. It was never
clear who owned the land, and we trespassed there so often, we
thought we owned the lake, or, really, rather that the lake owned
us. The morning of my wedding, we all swam there together, a
ritual to prepare me for the day and life to come. I didn't shower
or wash my hair after our swim. I wanted to get married with
the lake in me and on me. Years later my husband and I baptized
our daughters in Lost Lake. It wasn't always a lake. Once it was a

farm, and when the light is right, you can see down into the lake, underneath the water. You can see the stone walls that divided the farm fields. Walls built by humans are under ten feet of water. I imagine the woman who lived on this land and think of her there underwater, seeing fish in the same sky where once she saw birds. The past, present, and future are all there in the water, and I swim in all three. Time, I mean to say, is not a river. It's a lake.

Perhaps this is a self-help book I'm writing, a wellness manual that urges us to live closer to our dead. If we imagine our planet as populated by our dearly departed—and, people, it is—if we lift up our eyes unto the hills, down into the ditches, and see our mothers' and fathers' bones, we would take better care of the land. People used to know this. People have amnesia or they've become numb to the Earth's kindness that allows us to become her dirt again, a kindness that, at this point, I quite frankly can't believe the Earth still offers humans. That is true mother love, unconditional and unfathomable. Everywhere we walk or swim is a cemetery. Everywhere is sacred.

When my children were still very young, we met my in-laws in South Carolina. The ocean was lovely and we spent much time swimming. One day in the waves something struck me in the head. At first it appeared to be some floating garbage, a box sealed in a plastic bag. I felt disgust, until I saw words through the plastic. I carried the box out of the ocean and eventually, with my family near, found the courage to open it. Like a small, seaworthy craft, the box was carrying some of the cremated remains of a man gorgeously named Klemens C. Walters, who hailed from the astonishing town of Mars Hill, PA. Inside we found a lovingly lettered card, "Here Lie the Ashes of a Good Man." It was so tender and touching. We contacted Klemens's family, wanting to know their wishes. Should we send the package back out to sea? Back to them? They asked us to instead free Klemens's remains from the sturdy box/boat. We said some words of peace and released Klemens into the water. Death had struck me in the head while swimming in the ocean. Of course it had. The ocean is full of dead things.

At my dad's funeral I realized that his name, Walter, is only one small sliver of an easily eroded "l" away from the word "water."

The ocean near where my sisters live has riptides and huge waves. There are great white sharks not far off the coast. Still, we visit every year. One of our favorite things to do as a family is put our bodies in that deadly ocean. I don't sleep well on their island. We drink too much when we are together and later I'll lie in bed worrying about my daughters. Like me, they love this wild ocean. The shore here gives us a gradual approach to the depths, a way to sip from the place beyond the edge without drowning in it. No swerving over the rail. This salt of what we once were and will be again. Before and after. We float in our familiars, swimming in the deep, the dark, the spirited sea.

There Is Only One Direction

The girls' shriek is tidal, solid as a wall of water. These girls love love. They love hope. They love Harry. He plumbs the depths. He lifts the mic to damp lips, sharpens his steel eyes. He sings a message of hope out onto the sea of screaming fans. Do they notice that tonight he seems slightly off? Tired. His eyes wander and shift. Harry Styles has a cold or a hangover or a broken heart. The Jumbotron tightens its focus. Styles prepares for another moment of intensity: Sudden silence and a deep stare. The tossed, greased hair. It's late August all over the world. How many nights in a row can Harry sing his words of hope?

The boy band One Direction has sold out Gillette Stadium. Seventy thousand people in the New England Patriots' home arena. A generous tally would have a hundred males in attendance. Most of these men are fathers staring into their devices, ignoring their daughters' antics. This is a land of girls, for girls. There are very few boys at One Direction shows except for *the* boys, Harry, Zayn, Liam, Niall, and Louis, strutting onstage in tight jeans.

Simon Cowell assembled these five teenagers, UK talent-show

losers, into a boy band known to fans as 1D. They soon became a massive weather system, chasing summer nights around the globe. One world tour ends in the United States as the next starts up in Australia, and every night that the boys perform, no matter the continent, a temporary volcanic island of girls appears. I love it here. I love girls, my girls in particular, but I also love the sea of hormonal girls who fill the ranks of 1D's fans, Directioners. Here girls are permitted to be unembarrassed by the extreme manifestations of their passions. These girls are honestly mad for love or whatever chemistry it is that the band ignites in the girls' bodies. The documentary film *Crazy About One Direction* records one fan admitting she had braces put on her teeth not because she needed them but because Niall had braces. Another girl says that if the boys asked her to chop off her arm, she would. A third confesses she'd kill a cat, no, a goat, in order to meet the boys.

Tonight, the mass of girls before me in the arena, swarming like insects, also raises a question of economy. How many waitressing shifts, humid summer jobs, and hours babysitting does it take to lift these five boys up into the stratosphere of fame and wealth? How else might these girls' energies be spent? How best to understand their mania and avoid dismissing it as a fault of their youth or gender?

It's this last question that interests me most, because I too am here, willingly, happily, and I am not a girl. I am a mom whose daughters introduced me to the band, though I swiftly became a rabid 1D fan even when my daughters were not around. One Direction makes me feel light and lifted and full of gladness. Even as I write this, it is all I can do not to watch the video for "Steal My Girl" on a loop.

Friends who claim to know better urge me to listen to

something more age-appropriate. They wonder why I, a mother, writer, and college professor, still pick at the scab of teenage drama. They wonder how I became addicted to music produced in marketing laboratories. They ask, "Is One Direction actually that good? Will I like them?"

"No. You won't." The reason I love 1D isn't because they are so good; it's because they are good for me, as if they are a code sequenced for my DNA, made to produce emotions I want to feel, thoughts I want to think.

During the rise of Britney Spears, Simon Doonan wrote an article for *The New York Observer* lamenting the passing of a time when people worshipped elegance: Elizabeth Taylor in a muu-muu with a martini. What, Doonan wondered, had eroded adult worship and why was the new goal forever twenty-one? I grew up in a world that was so adult, so *Who's Afraid of Virginia Woolf?*, that I grew old when I was still young. In my rush to control the chaos of my childhood, I too soon departed the place where this music belongs, girl land. Then, after three small daughters, I was no longer young but my house was suddenly filled with music that made me feel like I was.

The winter my oldest daughter was two, my twins were born and I moved to a new town—not the best conditions for maintaining a stable mind. I told my friend Lisa that wolves and bears and coyotes were circling my house. I told her the animals wanted to eat my babies. She thought I was speaking metaphorically until she understood I was not.

When my twins were three weeks old, I gave a reading and told an auditorium full of people that, because everyone had been so kind and welcoming in this new town, I now knew they were vampires who wanted to suck the blood of my newborns.

I imagined that, through enough worry and fear, I could control our lives and keep us safe. Listening to One Direction became
an antidote to my worry, because it doesn't ignore the fear but
engages with it. There's a darkness in this light music that stirs
thoughts of life, death, gender, literature, and the multiple concerns of aging. The boys sing and it triggers a chemical response
of joy in my body so intense, it sets my mind zooming through
history; it unclogs stopped-up neural pathways last touched in
the 1980s. That sounds disgusting. I suppose it is. But it is the
truth of aging. The boys shout, "I don't care what people say when
we're together." And I think, Okay, okay, me neither, and raise my
hands in the air because it is true, at this point in my life, I just
don't care. This liberty, not caring what others think of me, is not
something I knew as a girl, or not in public, at least. Losing this
fear and settling into my body, with all its humiliations, is a wonderful benefit of aging.

The boys and their fans are a reminder that the intellect does
not solely belong to suffering and seriousness. Wisdom populates
girly things just as fully. One Direction reminds me that love, joy,
giddiness, even hysteria are crucibles of intelligence. There are
few questions more important than, How do we love? What are
the conditions for joy? What are we here to share? How do humans grow? How best to use this short time we've been given?

I'm the last appointment of the day. The room is mostly dark.
The ultrasound techs are sleepy and want to go home. "Feet in
stirrups. You want to insert the wand or should I?" one asks.
I'm unfamiliar with proper protocol for wand insertion. I'm naked but for a pink sweater and ankle socks. "You?" I'm showing

symptoms of ovarian cancer, a disease—the terrifying internet has told me—that has no symptoms until it's too late. Insert the wand any way you want.

The tech goes from being tired to being a poor actor. She adjusts the wand hoping for a nicer view. She asks the other tech to join her. They both look into the screen. Neither is tired anymore. They take a sudden interest in me. "Where do you live upstate?" I translate her question to mean, *There's a bad-looking thing here on your ovary.* She continues, "How many kids do you have?" This translation's even easier. *Who's going to take care of them when you're dead?*

The hallways of the Foxboro, Massachusetts, Comfort Inn are a raucous girls' dormitory. In our room, I cue up an MP3 player. My sister Amy pours two glasses of wine. The ritual is familiar, since 1D goes on tour every summer and we've yet to miss a year. My oldest daughter and my niece get to work creating handmade T-shirts for the show. My daughter cuts a fringe on her shirt before attacking it with a rainbow of Sharpies. Directioners make their own concert T-shirts, a gesture of DIY anti-capitalism that provides some relief from the marketing morass of most arena shows. My daughter is young enough to need help spelling favorite lyrics on her shirt. She doesn't need help spelling Harry's name. She's scrawled it on notebooks, sneakers, sidewalks. She writes "I heart Harry" on her forearm, then passes me the marker for my own fake permanent tattoo, an arrow heart with her name inside.

The boys sing, "From the moment I met you, everything changed." I think of my daughters. The boys sing, "Your hand fits

in mine like it's made just for me." Yes. "Baby, I loved you first."
As a zygote. "Even if you scream and shout, I'll be here for you."
Right. "You're all I think about, baby." I haven't slept in years.
"You're everything I see." Mostly. "Nothing can come between
you and I." I really hope not.

"Girls," I say. "Before tonight gets started, I have some sad
news." Amy and the girls wince. Not tonight. We bought our tickets a year ago. We've planned for weeks. "Louis and I broke up,"
I tell them. "But it's cool. I'm dating Zayn now." My niece laughs,
embarrassed and half-delighted by an aunt so devoted to a boy
band twenty years her junior.

"No way," my sister says. "Zayn's mine. I gave you Louis." We
trade the boys like baseball cards. If we were forty-year-old men
talking this way about twenty-year-old girls, I would hate us.

"Well, sorry," I tell my sister. "I want Zayn. Also."

"Okay. Okay." My niece takes account of what we've got. She'll
be the judge. She sizes both of us up, taking note of my Union
Jack hair kerchief. She makes her decision public. "You get Zayn,"
she tells me.

"Can I have Louis too?"

"What? Why?" My sister mocks outrage. "Why does she get
them?"

"Mom." My niece talks her down. "Mom. She knows all the
words."

There's a photograph of my cousin and me pressing our pregnant
stomachs together. With twice as many babies inside mine—a
twin pregnancy—my belly is an obese Pac-Man set to swallow

her tidy tan dot. I love showing people this photo because their inability to look away from the image confirms what I already know: My twin belly was a freakish sideshow attraction. It was the Mount Everest of Womanhood, a mountaintop I traveled to and returned from somewhat intact.

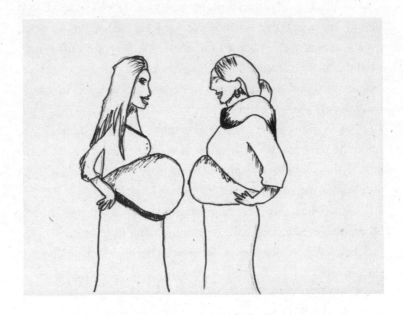

Toward the end of that pregnancy, I had three items of clothing that still fit. Each garment was soiled with food spills, a result of having a belly so large that my food had a long, treacherous journey from my plate to my mouth. I'd been invited to a benefit. Marc Jacobs was being honored. Beautiful, intelligent people in gorgeous outfits would be in attendance. I went anyway. Ten minutes after arriving, I had to pee. I pushed into the ladies' room just as the farthest stall door was kicked open from inside. A long leg in a black boot stepped out. I put my hands in front of my belly and waited to see what demon lay within. The stall occupant swayed on her way out, still zipping up her fly. She was tall as a man and slender. I waited and watched until, with fly secured, she looked up to see what monstrosity was blocking her way. I didn't disappoint. I stood before her enormous, food-dribbled. She broke into a huge grin, displaying gray teeth. She nodded at my belly, blessed my babies with her happiness, her surety, her tough guts. We exchanged places, and by the time we had, I realized I was looking at Patti Smith, poet, rocker, mother of all things cool, mother of Jesse, mother of Jackson.

I ask my husband what he thinks of 1D.

"They make serviceable pop songs."

"Come on."

"I don't know," he confesses. "It's kind of like I have Stockholm syndrome." He doesn't even realize that "Stockholm Syndrome" is the title of a 1D song. "Know what I mean?" he asks.

In my house, there is 1D duct tape, sunglasses, T-shirts, calendars, wrapping paper. I know what he means.

I hear Billy Joel, Blondie, Tom Petty. I hear Queen and "Summer Nights" when I listen to 1D. That makes sense, since a lot of their songs are co-written by men my age. In fact, one of their biggest hits, "Rock Me," was written by Sam Hollander, my friend from middle school. The argument that 1D's music is unoriginal is consistently hurled at me by haters; my counterargument is that the boys are not sampling sounds unaware. In "Stand Up," One Direction sings, "I'm a thief, I'm a thief." Their song "Better

Than Words," my favorite, is made up of lyrical quotes taken from
the Bee Gees, Beyoncé, Lionel Richie, Boston, Cascada, Usher, the
Beach Boys, Britney Spears, Adele, Mariah Carey, Drake, Elvis,
Shakira, Gnarls Barkley, Daft Punk, and Maroon 5. A catholic,
generous, inclusive, cyclical, generational approach to the Western pop canon. Or else, perhaps, it is an attempt to break down the
ego with the admission that nothing we make is ever really new;
or perhaps they are just thieves. The boys' borrowed words are
linked by an original chorus. "Words ain't good enough. There's
no way I can explain your love." The One Direction wiki says that
"Liam Payne came up with the idea to use titles of other songs as
lyrics in the verses. Every line in each verse (except the bridge)
is the title of a popular song." "Better Than Words" attempts to
describe emotions so nuanced that all the pop music that's come
before fails to communicate the depth. To further underscore this
bottomless complexity of love, to offer proof of how words consistently fail us, the song is punctuated by two deep pauses, post-
modern silences that, beyond the obvious allusion to the grave,
have, in past live concert settings, provided opportune moments
for one of the boys to hip thrust or grab his crotch. Dance moves
for which all the girls go wild.

I am supposed to call the doctor for the test results. "Hold on,"
her nurse says. "Let me look at your chart." There's silence on the
line as she reads about me. "Okay. I've got it here in front of me."
     "And?"
     "I'll say a prayer for you," she tells me.
     Not only are words not good enough, they can be the unwill-
ing bearers of terror.

* * *

One common T-shirt design among fans is when a posse of girl-friends subverts the traditional team-jersey format. They print MALIK or PAYNE or TOMLINSON in capitals across their shoulder blades. They print a huge "1D" up front. A perfect girl team would be made up of five friends, each girl representing the separate object of her 1D crush. (Crush indeed. I fear that the boys, left unprotected in this arena, would be devoured, ripped apart by their loving fans.) These punked jerseys interest me because though we're gathered inside a football-field shrine to testosterone, the screams tonight don't come from battle, defeat, or competition. These jerseys and the girls wearing them subvert hateful American ideas of one side wins, one side loses. I see two girls in handmade tees both scrawled with the same message: "Future Mrs. Niall Horan." The girls are walking arm in arm, disregarding any constraints of logic, monogamy, or cardinal numbers. Everyone wins in this fantasy. The girls make peace, they make love. The screams tonight come from pure Hydra-headed joy and the act of creation, building dreams that won't last forever but are certainly strong enough to hold for a night. Who is the real object of their crush? Their friends. Themselves. Life.

One group of girls is different from the others. They're not wearing T-shirts but rather paper masks, photographs of the band members with cutout eyes. They don't want to marry 1D. They want to be 1D. Yes, I think. Me too. Give me some tight black jeans and a microphone. Give me a penis. I really do know all the words. I love to karaoke. Plus, Harry's off tonight. He needs a break. His moments of punctuation are fuzzy. His eyes seem un-clear, unable to meet the camera. I can do the steely stare-down. I'll be an understudy. The stage lights lift and an overwhelming roar greets the opening chords of a new song. I forget my body. I think of a line from Mary Robison's novel *Why Did I Ever*: "Something else that makes me angry is that I got too old to prostitute myself. I wasn't going to anyway but it was there, it was my Z plan."

I'll be Zayn. That's my Z plan.

In a music-theory course in college, a young man, a fellow music lover, was trying to court me. He asked, "What are your favorite bands?" It was the nineties. Grunge and riot grrrls urged listeners to demonstrate how their lives were more messed up than the next person's. Tragedies connoted gravitas. I knew the answer this young suitor expected/hoped I'd provide: Pavement, Television, and Bikini Kill. I kind of liked those bands, but they were indie bands, cool-kid bands. Cool kids so often are cruel kids, even in college.

"Bon Jovi," I told the boy. "Poison. Skid Row." That was the truth. I liked those bands. I liked how hair metal rockers played with gender. My friend Linda and I often dressed up as Bret Michaels, Axl Rose, or Sebastian Bach for fun. I also liked many, many other bands, but I could already feel how my classmate wanted me to join his narrow-minded thinking. He wanted to declare one team as winner.

"You can't," he told me. "You can't like those bands."

A few years ago, I saw the Who live in London for the band's fiftieth anniversary. The tickets had been given to me for free, otherwise I wouldn't have gone, though I enjoyed the evening and knew every song they played. I spent the night measuring the similarities between One Direction and the Who. I know all Who fans, old and male, will shudder at my exercise. All 1D fans, young and female, will ask, "Who?" I forced confluences on these two all-male, mostly white, mostly British bands. Roger Daltrey and Pete Townshend, the last two remaining Who members, performed surrounded by ghosts and old angers. It was haunting. I imagined forty-five years hence, 1D taking the stage in their seventies. Who will be there and who won't? The accounting on my end is a bit brutal.

The doctor calls it a "solid mass." She says we have to wait for further test results. This drop of new information is a gallon of gasoline on my fear fire. I picture something like the creature from the Black Lagoon eating my ovary, something dark green and slimy. I don't imagine the "solid mass" could be just as pink as the rest of my parts. I make things up for a living. The danger in my job is that I can't stop making things up.

   With my family asleep, the loneliness of death looms. Death feels separate, a place away from here. I don't want to go anywhere. I pass my laptop on my way to the bathroom and think, I should delete my new novel, Mr. Splitfoot, a recently completed book that took me five years to write. I haven't yet sent it to my agent or editor. I could delete it now and it would never exist. Next to this solid mass, literature, and the years of work I put into it, feels like ego, feels like separating myself from others, as if I have a special or different story to tell. I don't. All I want is to stay alive. That is better than words, living. Deleting the book would be the clearest example of what words mean against death. Deleting the book would mean there is no separateness or ego. I pause a moment at my laptop. I don't do it, though. I don't hit delete. If I'm going to die, my girls are going to need some money.

   "I love Harry for his voice," my oldest tells me. "And his hair." Me too.

*   *   *

The day they remove my right ovary, Zayn fails to show up at the world premiere of the new 1D record. It seems right in terms of my reproductive health. The boys make excuses, say it's a stomach bug. It isn't a stomach bug, but I make excuses also. I want to stay alive.

I think about the boys' moms a lot. Some of their moms are younger than I am. One of them also has twins. Zayn bought his mom a house, her first house ever. Louis's mom bought a life-size cardboard cutout of her son so she could "just go in and say good night." Fame came to them at such a young age. To the 1D moms, it must seem like their children were born, then sixteen, seventeen, eighteen years later their children left home for an afternoon *X-Factor* audition, and still haven't returned.

The mass is benign. This is good news, great news, the best possible news I could ever receive, though a small part of me is furious at how well my imagination makes untrue things true, my facility with worry and fiction. After my surgery, early menopause sets in. Hot flashes, night sweats. Fine. It's not like I want any more babies. But after a few weeks, these flashes make me sad. I wonder where my ovary is. Not that I need it, but it's been with me a long time, from the start. I don't want to arrive at my end prematurely just because I was careless and let some important parts slip away.

*   *   *

Then, four months after the surgery, menopause also departs. My
other ovary kicks into high gear. My period returns, replete with a
crazy surge of hormones and pimples. I enter puberty again in my
forties. This seems like a great sign, a definite step away from the
end. I'm singing. I'm dancing. Maybe I even put on some 1D. I'm
over the moon. The universe takes notice. You are not a teenager,
it says. And that afternoon, Zayn, my boyfriend, mid-tour, quits
the band, quits One Direction.

One of the most entrenched and elaborate fantasies among 1D
fans is that Harry Styles and Louis Tomlinson are lovers. To search
the term "Larry Stylinson"—their ship (relationship) name—is
to fall into a wormhole: hundreds of Tumblrs, Twitters, YouTube
videos, and Facebook accounts collect evidence of this love affair.
Larry Stylinson has an online presence as vast as any Kennedy
conspiracy theory, exegeses that unpack Louis's and Harry's many
tattoos, the alignments and secret meanings of these markings.
There are diatribes against Modest!, the management company
that, rumor says, no longer allows Harry and Louis to stand beside
each other in public in order to quash rumors of homosexuality.
There are warring factions among fans: the Larry Shippers (those
who want the boys to be together) versus the Shakespearean-
sounding Calderics (those fans who fly under the banner of
Louis's girlfriend, Eleanor Calder). There are reams of Larry Stylinson fan fiction. Some are innocent—kisses and snuggles in para-
graphs so prolonged, a reader's expectations for climax are never
fulfilled. Other pieces are more traditionally debauched. "Pretty
Boy," an anonymous work, comes with this summary: "Harry's
been forced into a high-class prostitution ring . . . Louis is the

crown prince of England and gets into a lot of mischief and thinks
it's normal to pay prostitutes."

The truth of these fantasies is that every fan makes her own
One Direction. There's an expansiveness in the number five, a creativity. This capaciousness is clear when 1D is juxtaposed against
a more narrowly defined singularity, say Justin Bieber or Drake. In
the video for 1D's song "Kiss You," the boys re-create Elvis's "Jail-
house Rock," but the director doubles, triples, quadruples their
bodies. He metastasizes Liams for everyone, Nialls enough to go
around. The boys are clay in their fans' hands, and when Harry
stares out from the Jumbotron, he's looking right at *you*.

The fantasies these girls create are so elaborate, it can be a
betrayal when the boys are revealed to be five mortal men who
like to sing, who might even be in love with someone else besides you.

The first time I saw Patti Smith in concert, I recognized in her
elements of Borges's definition of the aleph: that which contains
everything in the universe seen from every point of view simultaneously. She scowled, tough and bitten. She smiled like a beautiful girl who knows love. She spat onstage, a solid body dispersing
itself over the audience.

When my twins were born, I didn't care about literature anymore. I had three children under age three. The only book I managed to read that first year was Smith's *Just Kids*. This account of
her life with Robert Mapplethorpe returned me to the glorious
years I spent in love with a man who couldn't quite love me back.
It returned me to my wild youth. I wedged the book between my

daughters' heads as they tandem breastfed. At night, I had a man-
tra. "Patti Smith is a mom. Patti Smith is a mom."

Lucy Sante's article "The Mother Courage of Rock," in *The
New York Review of Books*, tracks Patti Smith from the first time
Sante heard Smith's name in 1971 through her life as a playwright,
poet, painter, lover, rocker, but then Sante herself arrives at a wonderful, deeply stirring wordless moment in the piece. She writes,
"In 1980, [Smith] did the unthinkable: at or near the height of her
powers she married Fred 'Sonic' Smith, late of the MC5, and retired from recording and performance to move to a Detroit suburb
and become a housewife and mother."

The page drops into white space. What is it Sante means to
leave unsaid? The shift from a public artist to a private parent? Or
is it something more sinister? Something so awful that we can't
say about mothers because there's no one who doesn't have some
semblance of one?

I already know what people think about moms: cookie reci-
pes, Halloween costumes, hysteria, laundry, yogurt, kitschy comforts of home, chicken breasts, regular old breasts, frivolousness,
pop music, minivans. No one has ever looked at my kids and said,
"You made three deaths. You must really understand life." I'd like
to see that Mother's Day card. The truth of this love I feel for my
daughters is that it's so penetrating, it's made a mush of my mind.
Perhaps that is clear in the way I (don't) organize a coherent argument, but my mind, in its mushy maternal state, has an ability to
ooze over boundaries, squish into thoughts a more logically solid
mind might never even dare to consider.

So, I'm waiting for Patti Smith's real Mother Courage, her
book filled with words about those wordless years of maternity

and her own kids, the baby she gave up for adoption at nineteen and the two she kept and raised. I trust Patti Smith will bury all notions of motherhood that measure only its unbearable lightness without mentioning the flip side of that coin.

It comes down to the simple truth of the band's name. In five years, five boys have become five men. And one direction is, of course, the only choice they, we, get.

I don't tell my girls that Zayn left the band. It feels too much like a death. My daughters aren't yet on social media but still, I know it's only a matter of time, a few days, before someone breaks their hearts with the news.

The internet explodes with an amazing clip. The theoretical physicist and cosmologist Stephen Hawking answers viewer questions for a live audience in Sydney, Australia. The male emcee poses a question submitted by the presumably female Samantha Su. "What do you think is the cosmological effect of Zayn leaving One Direction and consequently breaking the hearts of millions of girls across the world?" The emcee then adds his own commentary, behaving as if he, an older white man, has no responsibility whatsoever to try to understand an enormous population—girls— who, of course, are clearly so confoundingly incomprehensible he has wholly discounted their contributions to our planet. "I haven't a clue what that's about," he says. His attitude puts me in mind of bell hooks's book *Communion*, where she writes, "Patriarchy has always seen love as women's work, degraded and devalued labor."

But Stephen Hawking, generous and even more intelligent than I had already thought, answers. "Finally a question about something important," he says. "My advice to any heartbroken young girl is to pay close attention to the study of theoretical physics, because one day there may well be proof of multiple universes. It would not be beyond the realms of possibility that somewhere outside of our own universe lies a different universe. And in that universe, Zayn is still in One Direction."

Back in the arena, the sun has set. It's still warm and we've been dancing for hours. Liam, above an ocean of screaming girls, says, "Thank you," his West Midlands accent clear. "Thank you for supporting this boy band for the past four years." He laughs and looks at his four mates. "This boy band with chest hairs."

The Horseshoe Casino in Hammond, Indiana, recently hosted New Edition, the boy band of my own youth, and Ronnie DeVoe, the New Edition member whose gorgeous teenage smile and dance moves made my eleven-year-old heart beat wildly, now has a Twitter feed. "Even in the studio," he writes, "I'm reppin—> devoerealestate."

So, there's a time limit on boys. Harry, Zayn, Liam, Niall, and Louis gaze down at me at the grocery store, cardboard images hawking Ritz Crackers, Pepsi, and their own line of perfume while they can. In the aisles of Target, their images scream the truth of beauty. The photos gracing the five partitioned covers of a 1D Trapper Keeper were taken a while ago, when the boys were still boys, when they had a lot fewer tattoos. Perhaps the stick of the needle makes it easier to shill for huge corporations. There's even a wiki dedicated to the boys' tattoos. On this site, their body parts are parceled out, labeled, and deconstructed. The fans parse these markings as if encountering a system of iconography, a new alphabet or constellation that becomes inspiration for the girls' own tattoos. Copycats and stolen lyrics inked with the hope of pinning one singular moment in restless time to the wall. Stay young forever. Good luck with that. By the time you read this, One Direction merchandise will have long been replaced by the latest pop sensation.

I could never bring myself to get a tattoo after seeing a young woman in a Raleigh, North Carolina, bus station. Her forearm was covered by the word "Survivor." She attached to her grief and all I could think was how one day, in some morgue, her tattoo would no longer be true.

Recently, I had an etymological breakthrough standing nude before the mirror while waiting for the shower to heat up. Through the now-deflated skin of my abdomen, the term "old bag" shook with new resonance. How commodious. How wonderful. I, like an old bag, have held things—babies, lovers, friends. These droops and sags seem a clear sign of a life well lived, an unselfish, un-conservative use of the gifts my parents gave me. My stomach's a contour map of twin skin and cesarean scars, a different sort of tattoo.

Back at the concert, my daughter leans against me, exhausted but still swaying to the songs, enjoying perfect health while we stand in the irresistible pull of coming night, of late August. There's a time limit on girls too. Here we are, feeling light, feeling dark, feeling everything for a few hours, no matter the danger. Her name is on my wrist in permanent marker, the Girl Almighty, track 5, album 4, set to fade and age, but not tonight.

journal Is Sam Cate aware his "journal" is a novel? Is Sam Cate aware he is a character? Or does he know that he is really my dad, Walter Hunt?

"the next day" As far as I can tell, he didn't write "the next day" anywhere. At least not in any version of his book that I have. Are there other versions? Did he delete work or are there drafts that I simply haven't found yet?

April **26th** is four days before my dad died. It's the day he ate the half doughnut. *See* Devour. Every year we live right through the day we'll die, never marking it or knowing.

leaf pile He lost his eyeglasses in this leaf pile. *See* Re-Vision.

Chapter 2

I guess I should date these entries, because I can see that the above notation is confusing. I started this **journal** on April 25, 1981, which was a Saturday. It was also yesterday. When I wrote **"the next day,"** I meant that it is now Sunday, the **26th**, and I am continuing the entry. But what I have written so far concerns events that occurred on Wednesday, April 22, four days ago. And actually, I have a driblet more to say about that day, but it got late last night as I was making the entry, and I ran out of steam.

The boys have gone off with their friends. I got them started after breakfast cleaning up some of the winter debris in the yard, but their enthusiasm didn't last long. We have one good rake and one with a number of tines missing, and they began to scuffle over who should have the good one. I see from the windows in the den that they have left several large piles of leaves for me to get to the **leaf pile**. The garden cart, half-full, is abandoned in the orchard, where, no doubt, it will pick up a few more millimeters of rust before being returned to the sanctuary of the garage. In the end, I must blame myself for their lackadaisical performance.

Sam Jr. Why did he make me a boy? Though my parents named me Samantha, they've always called me Mandy because they did not want me to have a boy's name. Now, almost everyone I know calls me Sam. But I am not a Jr. My dad just liked the name Samantha. My mom liked it less. She wanted us all to have Irish names. She's Irish. He's not. If my mom had gotten her way, I would have been Deidre or Meghan. When I was twenty I moved to Dublin and oftentimes wished that I had a more Irish-sounding name. To be one nationality, rather than an American mutt, seemed a clear and solidly defined identity. The path of likes and dislikes had already been decided by others, and I look Irish. When I was young and more confused about who I am, I even admired the ease of identity available to a man I knew who had "I.R.A." tattooed on his knuckles. The slippery slope to hatred, the ease of the coward's path. Loving the other is the hard job. Now, I am grateful to be someone whose identity is unfixed and continues to change, to be a person with many names.

the raking This portrait of a landscaper is an acutely observed rendering of my mom. She maintains joy. She views the world with wonder. She constructs practical jokes. Once she taped a life-size portrait of a naked woman to her brother's front door on Halloween and had a friend call and feign outrage, threatening to alert the police. Once she stole another uncle's prizewinning pumpkin and his car. Recently, at age eighty-four, she lost her front tooth on an ice cream cone. She'd been using a Louisville Slugger bat as a cane, so started pretending she'd lost her tooth in a bar brawl with an anti-vaxxer. For fun. My father sometimes caught her joy but not often, though I recall one night when my sisters and I were awaiting the arrival of some boyfriends we weren't sure we liked. My dad greeted them by dancing the hopak while folding the laundry.

crossword puzzle He'd tell my mom, "Just do it lightly."

not the right one, anyway The patriarchy of crosswords!

I have never liked yard work. I got them started, but I deserted them. It is not that warm today. I got chilled and came inside. I saw **Sam Jr.** look up as I headed in and it was Amy's look, exactly hers. That is but another way in which I miss her and cannot seem to mend the loss. I miss her enthusiasm to be outdoors on these early spring days. It was never the tasks to be done, **the raking**, the clean-up, that mattered to her. She wanted to be outside, moving, coaxing the boys, laughing at their antics, encouraging them to breathe the new air. She was a lousy raker, anyway. A little pile here, one there, then, oh, look, the daffodils are up, and scrabble, scrabble with a trowel around the edges of the flower bed, then off her knees to cart a fallen branch to the pile, and then, oh, anything that caught her attention. I saw her bouncing up and down one day on the spongy earth out back, where the water drains from the hill, testing the earth, finding it elastic as the ground began to thaw. She kept it up for several minutes, just bouncing.

I came inside feeling chilled and lay some logs in the fireplace. I got the Times Sunday magazine and turned to the **crossword puzzle**. That too was an ache. We used to do them together, and I was the noble and forebearing husband who held back his eagerness to fill in the squares until I was sure Amy wasn't going to come up with the answer herself. Which she never did, **not the right one, anyway.** Her answers, the letters she put in, were always zany, and had to be erased to make the down-words work, but I remember her little smile of joy when she got the point, or the theme, of the puzzle. Like "novel by Herr Lewis," which turned out to be "Arrowschmidt," and she would give a little laugh and smile. Now I do the puzzle quickly, to get it over with, and sometimes I stop half-way through because I realize I'm

when I die My grandma and I sat with my father as he lay dying. She read us a story from her Christian reader, one with an easy moral. When she finished, she said, "I know you believe, Walter." Her eyes were twinkly. He smiled and said, "I believe in you, Norma." Later, after he was dead, my grandma said there'd been a deathbed conversion, that he admitted he believed. Maybe she needed that. He'd been her son-in-law a long time. Or else she just wasn't going to let the truth stand in the way of a tidy story. In regard to his recovery and AA, he often told my mom that he was moving toward a leap of faith, but wasn't there yet.

bizarre stories One story my dad pushed for and was able to get published was about Zé Arigó, a Brazilian faith healer who became famous after he claimed to have removed a cancerous tumor from the lung of a senator, using psychic surgery. My dad worked on this story years before he himself was diagnosed with lung cancer. Arigó was jailed for practicing medicine without a license but was later pardoned by the president of Brazil.

Dr. Rhine J. B. Rhine, a botanist and ESP researcher at Duke, wrote a paper exposing the medium Mina Crandon's séance tricks. Arthur Conan Doyle wrote, "J. B. Rhine is an Ass."

Hinchcliffe The pilot's name is spelled Hinchliffe. Misspelling as ghost.

bored. Maybe the puzzles aren't as clever as they used to be, I say, knowing that's not it at all.

And you know what I wish? I wish there was a Heaven where Amy and I will meet again **when I die**. But I don't believe there is. And then I find myself wondering, but suppose there really is a Heaven. If I don't believe in it, do I get to go there anyway?

After Mr. Crane left I went into Marjorie's office. She asked me who my visitor was, and I replied, "Some nut," and though I felt like saying more, I did not because I could not form my thoughts. I bought another cup of coffee from the machine and on my way back stopped by a friend's office. He started off on a story of his own, and when he had finished, I didn't feel like talking to him, either. So I went back and got to work. Soon, I had forgotten about Mr. Crane. In the course of a month, I would see two or three people with stories equally as bizarre.

Actually, I like **bizarre stories**. Of course, there are bizarre stories and then there are *bizarre* stories. At Talbot's a story can't be too bizarre or it won't get past the research department, even if it's true. We have done stories about UFOs, but only to the point that we report on various sightings, both positive and negative, and always conclude with the government findings that inevitably declare the whole thing to be hogwash. We have published ESP stories, but usually of the **Dr. Rhine** type—carefully controlled laboratory experiments which often don't prove much one way or the other. I did once get the Hinchcliffe story past research, but it was dicey all the way. **Hinchcliffe** was an early pilot who set out to duplicate Lindbergh's feat, except that he was going the other way,

Hart's I've used the last name Hart as alias for Hunt before, so I wonder, was this fictional dinner happening at our house?

east to west. He disappeared and pieces of wreckage were picked up off the Azores, nowhere near his last reported position. Then Hinchcliffe, or his ghost, began appearing to people, notably his wife, to explain what had happened to him, and to warn that disaster was awaiting the imminent flight of the R-101. The R-101 was a huge dirigible which took off from England and crashed in flames a few hours later in France, and then, my god, there were ghosts all over the place! I suppose I got away with it because it had all happened long ago, in the late 1920s and early 1930s, and because Arthur Conan Doyle involved himself in the case, and people tend to think that Doyle was as coldly logical as his fictional hero, Sherlock Holmes, besides being a doctor himself, when the truth is that Doyle was as nutty as they come in psychic matters, and awfully gullible.

Lately, Talbots has shied away from the bizarre altogether. The field has become tainted by those garish supermarket check-out tabloids which every week trumpet some new psychic or UFO or monstrous birth oddity, and let me say, if I may, that these publications do not have stringent research policies, if indeed they have them at all. Recently as I went through the check-out I saw the headline: COUPLE WILL KEEP TWO-HEADED BABY. Where, I wondered. In the freezer?

And yet I hold no inviolate brief for rigid fact-checkers. There are more things in heaven and earth than are dreamt of in their philosophy.

Wednesday ticked away in mundane tasks. Before going home to get the boys' dinner, I had a quick drink with Mavis, and she reminded me, for the third time, that I was to pick her up at seven on Saturday to go to the Hart's for dinner. She told me I was

I know why Why? Sex? Loneliness? Or because he likes someone to be mean to him because he thinks he deserves cruelty? Because when it hurts it feels like home?

This guy's in the White House My mom remembers this White House guy. She's lost his name but remembers that something scandalous happened with him. She thinks he might have shot someone with an unregistered gun.

getting fat. I wonder why I continue to see her. But, of course, **I know why**.

Thursday passed uneventfully, and it came Friday, payday, end of week, and I felt a sense of relief as I went in to work. Ever since Ted was fired and John took over as editor-in-chief, the joy has gone out of coming into the office, but I don't want to go into all that now. I arrived feeling a bit sodden as it was raining and I had left my umbrella behind Marjorie's door. I didn't have a hat either, and I went to the men's room to dry off my hair with a paper towel. As luck would have it, John was there, too, standing at the urinal.

"Oh, Sam." he said over his shoulder while I stood before the sink, "I've been trying to reach you. I want to talk to you." I looked at my watch guiltily. But I wasn't late. It was just eighty-thirty. That was one of the things about John. Just because he might be in early—and it happened randomly—everyone else was supposed to be there, too. Later, I came to see that John wasn't purposely trying to make me—or anyone else—feel guilty or inadequate. It was that he himself felt guilty and inadequate, and his low self-esteem spilled out into all of his dealings with others. Guilty, I don't know about. Inadequate, yes. John was not up the job.

"I've got someone coming up from Washington this morning," John continued. "He'll be here any minute. I'd like you to sit in. There might be a book in it. I'll have Judy give you a ring when he shows up. You're not busy, are you?"

"I'm free," I said. "What's it about?"

"**This guy's in the White House**. I don't know him, but I've been told he's very sharp. He wants to talk about some government program."

He asked especially glad I'm leaving my dad's typos intact. Maybe you already noticed. STET the whole thing!

black Caddy Some people at *Reader's Digest* had very sympathetic relationships with the CIA. My father didn't much like the government or the military, though, as a man who'd been drafted into a war himself, he was sympathetic to young men who found work and a steady income rising up through the military's ranks. It was the higher-ups he couldn't stomach. Their self-seriousness was so often accompanied by an egoism that wanted to control other people. When my dad was a student, the CIA came to Yale to recruit. There was a meeting after dinner. My dad did not attend. He was a poet, an artist with a tender heart that had already been broken by death. A handful of his classmates signed up with the CIA, including John "Jack" Downey, who would later get shot down behind Chinese lines and be held prisoner for twenty years because the CIA would not admit that he belonged to them.

Already I was yawning. But John was very big on "government programs," particularly now that a Republican was president.

"**He asked especially glad** that you be there."

"Oh?" I said. I knew from nobody in Washington, D. C. "What's his name?"

"Law. Colonel Vincent Law."

"Never heard of him. Is he in the army?"

"Marines, I think, detached for White House duty."

"Don't know him," I said.

"Maybe he was running his finger down the masthead. He asked about the 'Book Editor.' I told him your name and he said that would be fine."

I put my comb back in my breast pocket. "See you," I said.

John was zipping up his fly. "I'll give you call," he said.

I wanted to warn John that if the women editors found out he talked business in the men's can, they would demand admittance to it. But John was the type who wouldn't realize that I was joking.

I diddled around in my office for a while, glanced at the Times, told Marjorie I had a conference later on with John and would be gone I didn't know how long. My office was at the front of the building and a window looked out on the circular drive that brought visitors to the entrance. About nine o'clock I watched as a **black Caddy** limo drew up and stopped just outside the window. Two men sat in back, one of them in military uniform. He got out and I saw lieutenant's bars on his shoulders as he raced around to the other rear door and opened it. The man he was attending wore civilian clothes, or at least the trouser legs were, which I could see below his trench coat. It was still raining. The officer popped a black umbrella, obscuring the man's face, and the two of them hurried in tandem toward the front entrance. An olive

drab Chevrolet had pulled in behind the Cadillac, chauffeured by a Marine sergeant. He waited until the limousine pulled out for the visitor's parking lot, then moved up to the entrance. A woman sat by herself in the back. She didn't get the open-door treatment. The rear door released slightly, then swung slowly outward as the woman pushed on it with her rump. She exited backward, bent over. She had nice legs. As she pulled erect, I saw she had a briefcase in each hand. She was wearing a yellow slicker, a stylish interpretation of fishermen's gear, and a yellow rainhat over her blonde hair. I couldn't really see her face, but I got the impression she was pretty and in her mid twenties. One of our company guards came to meet her—he was in a slicker as well—and as he drew up she made a half-comic movement of sagging under her load. He relieved her of the briefcases and she turned toward him—and me—with a gorgeous, warm, heart-breaking smile, and a few words, a thank-you no doubt, before they drifted out of my suddenly lascivious gaze.

I went to my door and into the hallway. Looking down the hall, I could see the reception desk and the large foyer. I walked nonchalantly in that direction as if on an errand. The two men had given their names to Carol, the receptionist, and she was on the phone. The man in civvies looked about, saw me, looked away, turned toward the door. I reached the foyer just as the young woman came in. She was ahead of the guard, momentarily alone. Briefcaseless. The man in the trench coat stiffened as he saw her and broke for the door, almost in a trot. It would have been a trot if the distance had been longer. The woman's face showed alarm, she started to say something, but the man stiff-armed her aside and hit the doorway full tilt where he ran smack into the guard coming through the door sideways to make the briefcases fit more

girl Sam Cate has referred to this character as a woman, above. I like that my father noticed that the bad guys are the sexists who think of twenty-five-year-old women as girls.

Korean War My dad told us little about his time in Korea. I associate it with a Rolleiflex camera he brought home from the war, and with his banjo. He did tell me that on the ship he took there, a huge thing loaded with men, he hid out on a stairwell used mainly for vomiting. Many soldiers were seasick crossing the Pacific. My dad read *Tristram Shandy* in the stairwell, avoiding KP, undisturbed there but for the smell of puke.

easily. The jolt was strong enough to loosen the guard's hold on
one of the cases, and it fell to the floor with a thump. Trench coat
stooped, retrieved it with one, swift movement and then wrested
the other briefcase from the guard's hand.

"Thank you," he said. Brusquely, he turned and marched back
to the front desk, not looking at the **girl** or speaking to her. She
stood to one side where he had knocked her, her face flushed with
distress and embarrassment. She glanced in my direction, but I
had already resumed my semi-purposeful walk and donned the
blank mask of one who in his preoccupation has seen nothing
unusual. I nipped into the stairwell, descended to the basement,
passed the coffee machine, then went back and dropped a quar-
ter in. Just on my way to get a cup of coffee, sir. Then I hurried
along the basement corridor and up the stairs near my office. I
empathized with the woman's situation, but I accepted what had
happened with the equanimity of one who, having been drafted
during the **Korean War**, had effortlessly adopted the enlisted
man's unshakeable prejudice that all military officers were ass-
holes. For, of course, I took the man to be our guest from Washington, Colonel Vincent Law.

As for his paranoid distrust of the guard, I could accept that,
too. John acted the same way with his numerous articles about
"government programs," especially the ones dealing with military
projects, a subject dear to his heart. The articles were never mentioned, never listed on work-sheets, had to be typed up in secret,
edited only by trusted lieutenants, and kept off the table of contents until the last minute. Needless to say, the articles contained
such highly secret matter that it had all appeared in The Washington Post twelve months previously. I mean, the colonel probably
kept a change of underwear in his briefcases—you know, the pair

Valentine's Day As my dad's Boy Scout diary of 1941 says, "Hooray! Got lots."

(God forbid) John (Ken) died in 2006.

I would rather the Russians had some piffling secret of ours than stiff-arm a lady for it My hero.

decorated by his predecessor, plus one I only entered Lila Wallace's office once and I was very young. I think she had a Monet water lily painting inside. Once my father went to the Wallaces' house and brought us home a book of matches with the name of the house, High Winds, printed on the box. I was obsessed with this matchbook. I couldn't believe a private house had its own matches. I'd never seen wealth that excessive before.

with a pattern of red kiss-marks that his wife gave him on St. **Valentine's Day**. It wouldn't do to have them fall into the hands of the KGB.

The odd thing is, if John were ever to read these words (**God forbid**), he would take them seriously, and would honestly and sincerely argue with me that, of course, it was easy to overdo the secrecy business, but just the same, it was wise to be on the safe side. And I would respond to his genuine concern, his earnestness, his need to be understood, and agree. But then back home, in bed ready for sleep, I would realize that deep down I didn't agree, that **I would rather the Russians had some piffling secret of ours than stiff-arm a lady for it**. (Mavis has almost, but not quite, got me out of the habit of saying "lady.")

Fifteen minutes passed and I tried to read the paper without much success. At last Judy rang me, asking me to come along to John's. I waved to Marjorie, said, "I'm off," and walked to the other end of the building. John had a big corner office, **decorated by his predecessor, plus one**, in French antiques and several valuable paintings from the Impressionist period, acquired in one of the hiatuses between recurring "economy drives." I've been at Talbot's for twenty-five years and lived through seven economy drives so far. They seem to last about six months.

John's door was shut, but Judy waved me in, so I knocked and entered. John was standing in back of his big mahogany desk. "Hi, Sam," he said, "come on in." John is tall, over six feet, with light brown hair that tends to curl. He's not handsome, but he doesn't scare babies either. One doesn't really look at his face; one watches his hands. At the moment they were engaged with a letter opener, which they had picked up and didn't seem to know why. The hands were shaking, so one judged that John was

nervous Turns out he had Parkinson's.

Colonel Law, **Lieutenant Noble** An echo of Ian Fleming's absurd character names.

football quarterback In my grandma's papers, I found two programs from St. Paul Academy's football games—the military high school my father attended. The programs list "Probable Starters." My dad does not make the cut, but my grandma held on to the programs. My father was no athlete. He also was no military man, but that didn't keep his parents from enrolling him in military school. The lack of imagination, the anemic starring roles America offers boys: sports hero, war hero, working stiff, or millionaire.

nervous. He came forward. He seemed to be suffering from his hip dysfunction this morning, a periodic affliction, so that his bottom half appeared to be in more of a hurry than his top half.

"This is Sam Cate," he said, "our book editor." The two men were standing to one side near an arrangement of chairs and a sofa. I faced them, and John made the introductions. The man in civvies was, as I had guessed, **Colonel Law**. The other was **Lieutenant Noble**, an "aide." I heard but did not hang onto his first name. John held out a hand, in which he still clasped the letter opener, indicating that we should sit down. He sat on the sofa with me and we faced the other two in chairs with a coffee table between us. I had brought a yellow pad and a pencil with me. I put them down on the table.

Colonel Law cocked a finger at me. He was smiling. "Sam," he said, "no notes. Please."

I nodded.

I guessed Law to be about forty years old, perhaps a little younger. He had a boyish face so that it was hard to judge. He was not a big man, about average height, but beneath his gray business suit, he gave the impression of being strongly made. His wrists were large, and his chest filled his shirt snugly. The image that came to mind was of a scrappy **football quarterback**, too small for college play, but a star in high school, speedy, smart, elusive.

"John, may I?" he asked.

John waved his letter opener expansively, meaning the floor is yours, but dropped the opener and had to lean over to retrieve it. It had slid under the sofa and he got down on his hands and knees to find it. We all watched silently. He sat again, put the implement

T.S. My husband's the first man in his family not to join the military. His father urged him to apply to the Coast Guard Academy, even wrote the essay for him. My husband did not get in. He went to a state school, tripped on LSD, and immediately changed his major from business to English. He's a writer now also and loves his work. His dad is very proud of him even though he pursued a career his father hadn't considered. When I first met my father-in-law, I didn't understand much of the military language he speaks. I'd often have no idea what was being said, but I like codes, even those I can't understand. I've worked in corporate America and academia, where, as in the military, people also speak created languages. It's fascinating. Why do we try not to communicate with outsiders? To show a greater allegiance or state our membership in a club? Like the BFF necklaces given to some girls in middle school. I was never given a half heart. Indeed, the girl I thought was my BFF, Kim, got a necklace with another girl, Julie. After that I was done with BFFs. Maybe created languages are one of the ways adults replicate the games of childhood? Making elaborate codes and puzzles. Stating, "You belong to me, and you don't."

innate distrust My dad got drafted to fight in the Korean War immediately after college graduation. His mother tried to keep him out of the war, saying she already had one dead son, but that wasn't reason enough. My dad fudged his typing skills when he arrived and was sent to an office in Seoul to keep records. He never referred to his military service as an honor, or even called it "service," a term that will irritate me until public school teachers' jobs are also called service, and early boarding and airport lounges are provided for our teachers as well. My dad never wanted to talk about the war much at all except to say that Korea was no World War II, meaning that in World War II, the humanitarian necessity of fighting was evident, while the Korean War seemed to him to be American strong-arm meddling, those higher-ups practicing their powers of world manipulation.

in his other hand, looked at Law, then placed it on the table and
sat back.

"Let me be blunt," Law began, "this stuff is T.S."

The only meaning I knew for T.S. was "tough shit." My confusion must have shown.

"Top secret," Law explained. "My sink [that I got; CINC for
commander in chief] is the President, so when I say this has CINC's
approval you know it comes straight from the horse's mouth."

Already my mind was drifting. If this came from the horse's
mouth, how did one characterize pronouncements from under-
lings? Right!

This would not do. I had to pay attention and stop being
silly.

"You know, John," the colonel said, in a less official tone,
"we're beginning to get things sorted out down there. CINC believes in delegating responsibility. Before this everything had to
clear the O.O. and nothing got done."

"Oh, oh?" I questioned.

"Oval office," he said. "We've set of up a proper COC and if it
can be handled by someone before it reaches CINC, it never goes
to O.O. at all. We can get CINCSIG later. That's SOP now."

I surrendered. It was like trying to keep up with foreign sub-
titles before the frame changed. I guessed that COC was chain of
command. SIG was probably signature. SOP was army talk for
standard operating procedure. But by the time I puzzled this out,
Colonel Law had pushed on to new matters and I had lost all
sense of what was being said.

I had an almost **innate distrust** for military abbreviations. I
sensed that they often wrapped the meaning with an aura of truth
and significance which they did not possess. My introduction to

this argot had occurred in Korea where I had been assigned to a behind-the-lines personnel office. One of the major tasks of the office was the issuance of special orders, those mimeographed sheets which accompanied and made official every single move by an individual or a unit. It was a common joke that one could hardly go to the latrine without the authorization of special orders. One of the orders I liked best was issued when, as in real life, someone went some place without special orders. Then orders had to be issued after the fact. The introductory form used went thusly: Exig of the svc having precl prev iss of ords. That stood for, Exigencies of the service having precluded previous issuance of orders, and then the post facto authorization was given. But the words didn't really mean that. What they meant was that someone had goofed, forgotten, had not issued orders in time, and the person involved, officer or enlisted man, had gone off without them, just as if he were a civilian. To cover up the goof, to make matters official after they had already taken place, exigencies were called upon. Now the word exigencies connotes an atmosphere of urgency, events in crisis, so demanding that common everyday matters like issuing orders must be put aside. But the situation was precisely the opposite of this. The top-sergeant was sleeping off a hang-over, we peons were lazing at our desks, the adjutant was worrying about his latest performance appraisal, and the commanding officer was up at the officers' club arranging for a shipment of booze from Japan.

I had come by this insight at a fairly young age, and I assumed most men had, too. What it meant to me was this. When Colonel Law said they had established a chain of command, I assumed there was no chain at all, and that power had been gathered into a small knot of people below the President, men who knew how

two of my colleagues This woman would become that man's third wife. I know all of his wives and each one is, or was, a truly magnificent human. My mom says in the seventies, everybody was sleeping with everybody. But not my dad. He was an innocent in many ways. My mom recently described her former self as a flibbertigibbet, a word I've only ever heard in the Rodgers and Hammerstein song "How Do You Solve a Problem Like Maria?" The frenzied coupling of the seventies relied on the fact that women's career ambitions for any life outside of being a wife were squashed by patriarchy. The only chance for change came in finding a new man. How depressing and dangerous. My mother describes her first experience with college in the 1950s as "a ring by spring or your money back." She got a ring, and a first husband who abused her and nearly killed them both.

backfire My father is confusing innocence for ignorance.

power really worked, the guiding principle being, The less anyone else knows, the better. I also believed that the much praised
ability to delegate responsibility frequently meant only that the
executive in question did not know what was going on, or if he
did, understood mostly that it had been described to him as an
"initiative." These were the words that began to form in my mind
around the figure of Colonel Law: For him, everything was top
secret, everything had a top priority, everything was exigent and
must be initiated immediately.

I have noticed in the past that no prescience attaches to my
notions of how things really work. I'm interested is the mechan-
ics; the result stays veiled. I also have a misplaced sense of innocence. I tend, initially, never to think badly of individuals working
things out according to the formulae at hand, goofy as those may
be. Thus, though I had not taken a shine to Colonel Law so far,
I didn't think there was anything particularly sinister in the way
he was going about things, so long as he hadn't misled himself,
and so long as all the players he was playing with understood
the rules, too. But my presumption of innocence sometimes over-
rode good sense. A couple of years ago when I ran into—well, I
won't put their names down—two of my colleagues, one male,
one female, having a drink in a local pub after work, I thought,
"how friendly." A year later, when the man's wife sued for divorce
on grounds of adultery, I was astonished, but it turned out that
most of the others in the office had known for months. I think
of that coupling of innocence with a curiosity about how things
really work as a peculiarly mid-western trait. The Wright brothers had it. So did Lindbergh. But it's often a combination that can
backfire.

I had noticed another thing. Just as some people, like me,

southern accent My dad's own narrow-minded system of stereotyping here. Suspicious Southerners. Maybe that is why I fell in love with a Southerner and oftentimes feel disappointed that my husband, as a young man, actively worked to eradicate his accent.

We can't expect much help from the press. Clearly pre–Fox News.

Russkis My parents would guess which of my dad's colleagues secretly worked for the government. Strange to not know. My mother remembers our phone getting tapped when my dad was editing a story about Kennedy's assassination. She'd conduct long conversations about absolutely nothing with her sister and mom, some bureaucrat listening in. The misguided, paranoid buffoonery of Noble and Law.

Jesus Is Phoebe Jesus-like? Or is Colonel Law disgusted by female biology? Both?

made presumptions of innocence, others made presumptions of guilt. They were suspicious of everyone and everything. A lot of these people seemed to come from the South—like John who was from Virginia, and like Colonel Law, who had a noticeable **southern accent**.

"The time has come to take the initiative," Colonel Law said. "We're doing that in several areas. We're getting the B-1 back on track. Thanks, John, for all your help on that." The B-1 was a new plane, a bomber of course, that had been dumped by the previous administration. Talbot's, in the last year, since John had taken over the job of editor-in-chief, had done two articles calling for the revival of the project.

"**We can't expect much help from the press**. The Washington Post and the Times are hopeless. The little we can do doesn't change the management. But we're making ourselves felt elsewhere. The defense situation is bad, but the new budget is a beginning. We'll need a few years. As to the **Russkis** and the Chicoms, there won't be any more sappy deals as in the past, and no more talk of detente. But now we get down to where the rubber meets the road. Where do I fit into all this? What's my job, and how can you help me? Basically, I'm taking on subversion in this hemisphere. We don't want our enemies sneaking in the backdoor, do we? The situation in Latin America is critical, getting worse. You can help there, John. You've helped already. But we're going to need a lot more." He paused a moment, then called over his shoulder, "Phoebe!"

"I think she's still in the ladies," Lieutenant Noble said.

"**Jesus**," Colonel Law remarked. But at that moment, the door opened, and the young woman entered. Colonel Law had turned

FWOW On my first read, I had no idea what "FWOW" meant. The internet, oddly enough, suggests "fatherly words of wisdom."

sweetie My dad did not use terms of endearment. Not even for his kids. This helps explain why. They really can be hateful words.

mammaries "Mammaries" is not a sexy word, but it does a lot of work, reminding us that we are mammals and that much of what defines us as mammals comes from female bodies. "Mammaries" also points out my father's nerdiness. He often played at being stupefied by pretty women. Boobs are funny. It's true. Boobs make me laugh all the time. "Mammaries" is not a word often used in literature. I can think of only one other usage. It comes in one of my favorite short stories, Ed Park's "An Oral History of Atlantis." Park writes of a magical sort of peep show called the Wandering Womb, "the initials like mammaries." WW. Ed and I have been friends since we met while working at *The Village Voice* during a period of layoffs. This was in the months right after my father died. Each day, those of us who remained at the *Voice* would sit in our cubicles, awaiting firing. *See* Ghost Books or Ed's novel *Personal Days*. *The Village Voice* is also initialed like mammaries, VV, albeit pokey ones. Those 1950s bras shaped like rocket ships come to mind. Besides being a brilliant writer, Ed Park is many things: a scholar of the ouroboros, an editor (as his name implies), a keeper of the Invisible Library, the publisher of *The New York Ghost*. While I'm loath to implicate others in my sloppy detective work, especially someone I admire as much as Ed, in the name of thoroughness, I'll record how, in 2002, Ed published "An Oral History of Atlantis," a story jam-packed with evidence, some of it only making sense to me now, twenty years later. Is he a time traveler? He may be. Have I drafted him into my loopy theories without his consent? Most certainly. For example, once, at lunch, Ed told me a bit about his parents' younger lives in Korea. I told him how my dad had been drafted, but avoided battle by typing in triplicate in Seoul. Spared by a Royal, or perhaps a Smith Corona Skyriter, a model made for Korean War correspondents. There was a silence at our lunch table. Ed nodded. I nodded, embarrassed by my compunction to draw lines of connection that probably don't exist. And now I will embarrass myself again. I don't know what the evidence means to Ed. I don't even know what the evidence means to me. But here's what I have: Like my father (and, yes, thousands of other people), Ed Park attended Yale and worked for *The Yale Record*. Ed's story "An Oral History of Atlantis" paints a picture of a Manhattan held in the sway of a virus, the Metaphor virus. The protagonist starts following a writer named Walter Walter, a doubling of my dad's name. There's even a pair of lost eyeglasses. *See* Re-Vision. There are spectral whales. Two of my sisters and I live in former whaling communities where the only whales now are ghosts. "An Oral History of Atlantis" pays attention to the absurd neighborhood acronyms of New York City. *See* chapter 3. In Ed's story, New York is being erased in a way I liken to the influx of wealth that forced my family out of the city a decade ago. Ed writes, "As each level went, I could see nothing of human life but thousands of sheets of paper, perhaps all of Walter Walter's hopeless writing whirling like birds as they blew away." I recall the papers that littered our city after 9/11, an event that transpired while Ed and I were both employed by *The Village Voice*. I also now imagine the pages of this book, the words of Walter Hunt, one day scattered to the wind, Skyriter, taking flight, finally and at last.

in his chair. "Oh, there you are," he said. "Can I have the **FWOW** papers, please? That's a **sweetie**." He pronounced the acronym as if it were baby-talk for "throw," so it was almost impossible, in speech, to pick out the individual letters.

The young woman went to one of the briefcases, knelt and worked at the combination lock. She had taken her raingear off and was dressed in a light blue women's suit, jacket and skirt, edged with white piping, of the style popularized by Coco Chanel. She had attended to her hair; it blossomed out at the sides in a roll like Farah Fawcett's. She pulled out a slim file, approached us, and placed it on the coffee table with a Bunny dip. I wondered if she had once worked in a Playboy Club. She had the looks and the figure, especially the **mammaries** that so fascinated Hugh Hefner. She was a stunner, although in the Olympics run in Hollywood, the ultimate American scale of beauty, I suppose she just missed.

"This is my assistant," Colonel Law said, "Miss Phoebe Poon. Say hello, Phoebe."

Empty Boxes

That's not the end of chapter 2, but I pause here so poor Phoebe Poon doesn't have to say anything if she doesn't want to. I suspect Phoebe's already been asked to do too much. Her last name, an abbreviation of "poontang," a word that possibly comes from the Limba word *puntuŋ*, vagina; or from the French *putain*, prostitute. It's never made sense that so many of the words for an organ of warmth, generosity, and strength should so often be uttered with cruel intention, and yet, poon has a tang. Trevor Noah says:

> "Don't be a pussy." Yes. Because it implies weakness . . . and yet, in my personal experience, I have found the pussy to be one of the strongest things I have ever come across in my life . . . vaginas can start revolutions and end wars. You realize, even on a physical level, the vagina is one of the strongest things that have ever existed . . . You just sit on a penis wrong and it breaks. "Don't be a penis," that should be the phrase. I wish I was a pussy.

So far, my dad has made Noble, Law, Crane, and Poon. I can already tell that Noble and Law aren't either of those things. Maybe Poon will also be more complicated than her reductive name and blond Farrah Fawcett hair. Maybe she has a surprise or two up her sleeve, or wherever she keeps her surprises.

The artist Narcissister has a piece called *Marilyn*. Wearing a mask and a blond wig, Narcissister does a reverse striptease, getting dressed in garments she pulls from her vagina.

What is my father's intention with Phoebe Poon? Might she have a set of wings tucked up inside her womb? Might she take flight in the book's final, unwritten scenes, swooping in like a giant heron powered by poontang, lifting Sam Cate up and away from danger, on the wings of love or something like that?

My mom says my dad's agent, Millie, suggested he should "sex up" his writing in order to sell it. He must have wanted to sell it, a man with six children, all of us with hopes to attend college someday. Maybe Phoebe Poon's name is a jab at Millie, a frustration with books that reduce women to one organ in order to move copies. Or maybe my dad actually thought a leggy blond, a walking, talking vagina (the Wandering Womb!), could help him get his book published, pay off the mortgage, pay for us to go to school. In which case, work it, Phoebe.

In Adrienne Truscott's brilliant show *Asking for It: A One-Lady Rape About Comedy Starring Her Pussy and Little Else!*, Truscott performs a stand-up routine while surrounded by the headshots of comedians who tell rape jokes. Truscott wears high heels, many huge push-up bras, a trashed blond wig, a tight jean jacket, and nothing else. She's nude from the waist down. Truscott consumes a good number of Coors Lights as she delivers scathing bits that target rape culture's wrongheaded thinking, where a woman's clothing is somehow responsible for a rapist's violence. Truscott smiles, giggles, flirts, chugs beer, while saying, "If you don't want to get raped, just don't do any of those things, right, so no makeup, no miniskirts, no booze, no sexy dancing, and you should be pretty much just fine. Like in India and Iran." Truscott projects footage onto her body of men telling their rape jokes. Their chins align with her pubic hair and, voila, goatees. Having come up in the world of burlesque, Truscott is campy, candid, and extremely comfortable having both a beautiful body and a brilliant brain. Even if her audience isn't.

The name Phoebe means "bright," so perhaps there is some sense of brains meeting body in this character. In Carolee Schneemann's *Interior Scroll* (1975), a naked Schneemann pulls a scroll from her vagina, reading as the scroll unfurls out of her body. The text is a letter written to the art critic Annette Michelson, who claimed she could not watch Schneemann's films because they contained "the personal clutter / the persistence of feelings / the hand-touch sensibility / the diaristic indulgence / the painterly mess / the dense gestalt / the primitive techniques" rather than the masculine "system the grid / the numerical rational."

Clutter, feelings, diaries, and painterly messes is, more or less, an accurate description of my home and my brain. Schneemann's work also thrills me because there's a real excitement imagining the texts (entire libraries) that might exist inside of me, in the now vacant space, this womb that all the people have already moved out of. A void of possibilities, just waiting to be filled with meaning. To exist with open space is to exist with potential.

After my grandma Norma died, I was cleaning out her condo, looking for something of her I could hold on to. I missed her and

still do. I found a box in her attic. On the side of the box she'd
written "Empty Boxes." I opened the box. There was nothing inside. It was empty. Things like that—the real, heavy presence of
emptiness, all that is missing—drive me out of my mind in the
finest way.

Haruki Murakami's story "UFO in Kushiro" is built around
the idea of an empty box. Komura's wife has left him after the
Kobe earthquake. A co-worker urges Komura to travel to Hok-
kaido. He says he will even pay for the trip if Komura will deliver
a small box to the man's sister there. Komura agrees. He travels.
He delivers the box to the sister. Later, after the sister has left with
the box, Komura asks the sister's friend Shimao:

> "What's the something inside that box I brought up here?"
>
> "Is that bothering you?"
>
> "It wasn't bothering me before. But now, I don't know,
> it's starting to."
>
> "Since when?"
>
> "Just now."
>
> "All of a sudden?"
>
> "Yeah, once I started thinking about it, all of a sudden."
>
> "I wonder why it's started to bother you now, all of a
> sudden."
>
> Komura stared at the ceiling for a minute. "I wonder."
>
> The two listened to the moaning of the wind. The wind
> came from someplace unknown to Komura, and it blew
> past, to another place unknown to him.
>
> "I'll tell you why," Shimao said in a low voice. "It's be-
> cause that box contains the something that was inside you.
> You didn't know that when you carried it here and gave

it to Keiko with your own hands. Now you'll never get it back . . . Just kidding," Shimao said.

Murakami addresses how humans are discomforted by mystery. How we deal, or don't, with the unknown inside.

What surprise does Phoebe Poon hold inside? What surprise does any unwritten book, or for that matter, any uterus, any body hold?

In *As I Lay Dying*, William Faulkner sketches two empty boxes right into the text, solid, breathtaking vacancies. Addie Bundren, the mother who delivers a narrative though she is dead, comes with two voids: her womb and her tomb. Not to mention the deaths she made in giving birth, the births she made by having a daughter, Dewey Dell, and the deaths she made in having a daughter. In Addie's voice Faulkner writes:

> Why are you Anse. I would think about his name until after a while I could see the word as a shape, a vessel, like cold molasses flowing out of the darkness into the vessel, until the jar stood full and motionless: a significant shape profoundly without life like an empty door frame; and then I would find that I had forgotten the name of the jar. I would think: The shape of my body where I used to be a virgin is in the shape of a   and I couldn't think Anse.

This vacant shape is a refrain of an earlier hole in the text. Faulkner drops a coffin-shaped pictogram right into the book. The empty boxes of womb and tomb share a link deeper than their rhyme.

I'm overthinking things, but was my father speaking to this

void, this mystery? Or was he trying to sell out with Phoebe? To sex things up?

A few days ago, swimming at a waterfall, I watched two young women methodically labor to capture a series of "nature" photos. They took turns posing in the falls, butts out, boobs forward. The curve in their backs was so deep, as if butts and boobs were detachable, stand-alone parts, as if we can separate the sex from the person. With toes turned in, the women performed some idea of hotness. In between shots, their bodies would relax and actually look beautiful, but as soon as the camera was raised, they fell back into their "sexy" poses and Instagram bodies. Working on their brands. The marketing of bodies disturbs me, especially when it comes with a whiff of dismemberment.

My parents would talk about writing one "bad" book, full of scandal, sex, and drugs, something that would sell. I don't think the book I found in my dad's desk is that book, but as it is unfinished, who knows what Phoebe was meant to hold? My dad's unwritten book could be anything: *New York Times* bestseller, Pulitzer Prize winner, denizen of the free box at the used bookstore. It could be compost.

My parents never wrote their book of scandal. How many ideas did they abandon because they were making breakfast, washing up, doing laundry, working? What projects don't exist because I exist instead? How many unfinished works have I abandoned? More than I can count.

Andrew Goldman's interview with Richard Ford, published in *The New York Times* in 2012, has always stayed with me.

GOLDMAN: You don't have any children. In fact, you once said, "I hate children."

FORD: No, no, no. I don't hate children. My wife and I just
    didn't think we would be good parents, and also by the
    time we got married in 1968, we were pretty nose-down
    toward what we wanted to do, and having a child was
    going to be an excuse to fail.

GOLDMAN: So you think a person has to choose to be ei-
    ther a great novelist or a parent?

FORD: I can only speak about myself, not for anybody else.
    I'm not smart enough to do that kind of multitasking. I
    would always be wishing I were doing the other thing
    and not doing either one well.

Because I write about my children, I often receive emails from
young women writers who want to know: Can I be a writer and
a mother? I never get that question from any potential fathers.
Maybe they are only asking other men, or maybe they don't ask
that question at all. But it's a good question. What do creating
people and creating art have to do with each other? I still wonder
if I can be both a mother and a writer. I am both, every day, but
can I be a good mother and a good writer? I rise early, 4:00 a.m.,
5:00 a.m., to find writing time before my daughters wake, before
I head off to my teaching job. Do children stop art? Should artists
have kids? Like Ford, I can only answer for me.

    And when I do, I keep Mary Shelley close. Unlike her con-
temporaries Emily Dickinson, Louisa May Alcott, and Jane Aus-
ten, Shelley had many pregnancies, miscarriages, multiple dead
children, and one child who survived his parents, Percy Florence.
Tomb and womb rhymed perhaps too well in Shelley's life. Her
own mother, the feminist scholar and writer Mary Wollstonecraft,
died eleven days after Shelley's birth of an infection caught from

the dirty fingers her male physician inserted into Wollstonecraft's body to remove the afterbirth, its own sort of scroll. Stories from young Shelley's life have her both learning to read and, later, courting Percy on top of her mother's grave. Her diary records these entries: "Go to the tomb and read," and "Go with Shelley to the churchyard."

Besides being a womb, Mary Wollstonecraft Godwin Shelley also wrote an eternal book that births itself afresh each time I read it, carrying and miscarrying the story of Shelley's creature (a *creat*ure is *creat*ed) into future iterations and meanings. Shelley would not have written the same *Frankenstein* if she hadn't been a mother, living as close as she did to life and death.

To treat women as only a womb or only a vagina, as my dad perhaps did in his book, is dismemberment. I hope all my parts can find a peaceful coexistence. That's why I stopped where Phoebe is all poon. I might be reading too much into her. I might be really showing the seams of my revisionist thinking, but I want to remember my dad as a feminist, or, at least, not a sexist. Once, coming out of a restaurant in the city, we stopped to light our cigarettes and he said to me, "Ladies don't smoke on the street." I gave him a nod, as if to say, "Okay. Noted, but I'm not trying to be a lady," and we walked on, both of us enjoying a smoke after our meal. It's the only time I remember him acting like the rules were different for males and females. He raised four powerful daughters and two kind sons. His own mother, a former farmgirl, could do anything, make anything, but she definitely had some wild ideas about the limits on girls. I remember her telling all of us, "If you live with a man before you are married, don't bother inviting me to the wedding!" She didn't make it to my wedding. But then again, neither did my dad. Or maybe they were there, my dad, my grandma, my uncle Chuckie, my grandpas, all the family I've missed, queued up in the receiving line, my invisible and intractable dead.

Phoebe's author is gone. There's a certain freedom there. No one left to control her and tell her what it is to be female. What it is to have an empty place inside. She can be done with the hustle of marketing. She can even be done with meaning. Say hello, Phoebe. Or don't. You don't have to. Unfurl your wings, uncurl your hair, and fly away from here. Or have a baby. Or don't. Or die, or live forever in the pages of a book that will always be unfurling, unscrolling, unread, undead.

Hormones

One daughter asks, "How'd you get milk to come out of your boobs?" I didn't know the answer. I didn't use this bit of Sebald to explain it either, even if I did think of it.

> There was a door in the wall. Through it, one entered a dark stairwell; and on every floor hidden passageways branched off, running behind walls in such a way that the servants, ceaselessly hurrying to and fro laden with coal scuttles, baskets of firewood, cleaning materials, bed linen and tea trays, never had to cross the paths of their betters. Often I tried to imagine what went on inside the heads of people who led their lives knowing that, behind the walls of the rooms they were in, the shadows of the servants were perpetually flitting past. I fancied they ought to have been afraid of those ghostly creatures who, for scant wages, dealt with the tedious tasks that had to be performed daily.

My mom's house has a secret staircase somewhat like the one Sebald describes in *The Emigrants*. It's a dark passage, cluttered and steep. It's not for servants but in case of fire, a real danger in 1765, in a house built around a tremendous chimney. There's a fireplace in almost every room. We no longer heat the house with wood, and the stairway is blocked by cases of beer, paper towels, rubber boots, snow pants, and skates. I haven't used it as a staircase in decades.

Hormones both care for me and sabotage me, or so it sometimes feels. They lurk behind walls, behind skin. I can be overwhelmed by these ghostly creatures and wonder, inside our bodies, who is the servant, the human or the hormone?

Maybe there is no separating the human from the hormone. I tell my daughter, "Our bodies are filled with secret elixirs. So secret, sometimes we don't even know what they do."

"What's an elixir?"

"Like a liquid." I'm not doing a great job explaining. Are hormones liquid? I have no idea.

"Like milk?"

"Milk is a liquid. It's not a hormone. But hormones are the things that tell the milk to come to a body. Plus, they do a bunch of other things."

"What?"

"They make us grow." She nods. Beyond milk, hormones play a part in many M-words: masturbation, murder, motherhood, menopause. I do a bad job explaining the world to my daughters because I get hung up on language and its patterns. Recently one of my daughters reminded me that when she was younger she asked why a friend of mine had died. He'd killed himself. He had depression. She says I told her that my friend died from crying. I don't remember having said that, but it sounds like something I would say, not wanting her to know, at her young age, that suicide or depression are possibilities. She said this confused her for years, thinking a person could die from crying too much.

I have also been confused by incomplete explanations. In fifth grade they broke us up into boys and girls. The girls watched a film about periods. My brother Charley said their movie had something to do with using soap and holding doors open for girls.

I was full of questions but embarrassed to ask. Mostly I wondered what it would feel like when my period arrived. I imagined a river of blood and was glad when a friend's mom told me no, not a river. The film was animated. A young woman showering against a brown background. To demonstrate how hormones were triggered by our brains, switching on womanhood, the film used small white polka dots, like sonar signals launched from the cartoon girl's head to her ovaries.

Around that time, I wore a necklace made of coral beads, the kind surfers wore. I hoped it gave me an identity of "hanging loose," or a connection to the ocean, or a projected wealth.

Then my period arrived and I knew it was my period because I felt those small white polka dots trickle down my body. "My period!" I was victorious. I checked my undies. No blood. But I saw those small white polka dots pool on the floor at my feet. The cord of my coral necklace had frayed and busted.

Thirty-six years later, my oldest daughter told me, "We have to watch the period movie next week." She said her movie was "like, an hour, and the boys' movie is two minutes."

Nothing had evolved. "Why don't the boys have to know about periods?" I asked.

"I don't know."

I asked the superintendent and the principal to show both films to all genders. I said boys need to be responsible for human biology too and that it's unfair to leave them out of this critical education. The superintendent and the principal both saw my point but the principal said no, that the boys weren't ready. A few months after the film, my daughter, also not ready, began menstruating.

Emily Wilson from Babe.net does a brilliant interview series called Man Libs. She poses a statement about women's bodies and leaves a blank for the man she's interviewing to fill in. The interviews are conducted as a sort of quiz. For example, "Getting her period usually means that she is not _____." Answers from men range widely. Ovulating. Fertile. Pregnant. One man, unsure, says, "I feel like I should know this." Wilson adds, "I feel like you should too."

If boys don't know how girls' bodies work, they will imagine things to fill in those blanks. They might think it is a big powerful secret. And while human biology is big and powerful, it shouldn't be secret. They might think witchcraft. They might think girls' bodies are gross and scary. They might be frightened by mysterious, powerful things they do not understand.

Sebald's death was hard for me, an aneurysm that led to a car crash, eight months after my dad's death, two months after 9/11. Sebald's daughter Anna survived the crash. His death was the start of the ghost books, the start of my imagining all the books dead authors would never write because they had died too young. It was the start of imagining a library of these nonexistent books.

My daughter adds one more M to the list of M-words. "Magic?"

Magic is a cop-out when it comes to explaining the hormonal wonder of this world. But when my daughter asks if hormones also make magic, I'm thinking about how the books Sebald didn't get to write might get written. I'm thinking boys will suddenly understand girls, not fear girls, not hurt girls. I'm thinking that hormones made my daughters. "Yeah. Magic. Right."

A Thousand Deaths

Ada Mills was one of nine sisters. She grew up in Jefferson, Iowa, in the late 1800s. Much of what I know of her life comes from a memoir my grandma Marcella wrote. Ada was Marcella's mother.

In front of Grandmother Mills lovely house was a huge Maple tree and while young the girls practically lived up in the tree—the great limbs making marvelous safe spots to read, write letters or hide from unwanted company—After all the girls were married and away in their own homes they started "The Maple Tree" a round robin letter—each one adding her letter—pictures etc when it arrived and when read thoroughly sending it on to the next in line—It used to arrive at our house a huge fat bundle and Mother would be in seventh heaven forgetting all the mundane jobs around the house until it had been read many times— then her old letter etc. removed and her new contribution packaged and sent on its way.

I have two photos of the Mills girls climbing their maple tree in ankle-length skirts. Ada, the oldest, was first to marry. She and Billie Dewell decamped to Logan, a small town near Magnolia, Iowa, where Billie had grown up. My grandmother writes:

They had a son Philip who died when he was about 18 mo. old—a grief my mother could never overcome—She felt she had starved him to death—She did not have enough milk to breast feed Philip—but the old ladies of Logan (well meaning but dumb) told this poor, innocent young mother she must not give him a bottle—it just wasn't done—and so fearful of her good name she followed their advice until Philip became so malnourished he apparently got a bug and died.

Mother's grief was so severe (I understand) that she

strained her vocal chords necessitating the drastic opera-
tion a few years later to remove growths from her vocal
chords causing her to be unable to speak above a whisper
and to wear a silver tube in her throat her entire remaining years . . . as children we were never allowed to ask
about it (actually as grownups either) until we began to
feel there was something about it all that was shameful.
My younger sister Barbara grew to High School age suffering a thousand deaths if someone innocently asked her
why her mother couldn't speak above a whisper. She had
no idea but felt it must be a disgrace.

Ada spoke little after Philip's death, but still, her daughter describes her as "a superb storyteller." I have a book of Ada's poems and many of her letters. For all her storytelling, she never
mentions Philip. How did my grandma come to understand this
version of her brother's short life? Did Ada tell her children she'd
starved their brother? Did Ada actually starve Philip or did she
imagine that narrative as a way to blame herself for her child's
death? Philip's death certificate lists the cause as cholera infantum, an illness of diarrhea and vomiting. *The Boston Surgical and
Medical Journal* of 1851 writes:

Among the *causes* of cholera infantum, in my humble
opinion there is none more conducive to its devastations
than *over-feeding*. The anxious mother seeing her child la-
boring under other predisposing causes, and perhaps weak
and feeble, imagines the "dear little thing" needs more
nourishment, and consequently she is never satisfied unless when loading the already weak stomach of her darling

with some nice preparation to "give it strength," not realizing that she is to see her kind and unwearied endeavors,
and anxious solicitude, rewarded only by a fearful and often fatal disease! She does not realize that she is killing her
child with kindness!

Ada understood the loss of her voice as punishment for having lost Philip. On top of sorrow came shame; she believed illness
and death were moral failings. The shame flooded down through
the generations, "a thousand deaths," her daughter writes. My
grandmother never told my dad there was glaucoma in our family,
as our tendency toward glaucoma could mean we'd done something to deserve it. My grandma discreetly nestles her own grief in
parentheses when she writes, "(I understand)," because Marcella
lost her own child, Charles, when he was eight years old, and like
her mother, Ada, she did not speak of him after.

One of my daughters developed tics from a strep infection. In
researching tics, I learned they once were thought to come from
having a cold mother. Like the refrigerator mother theory that
blamed autism on lack of maternal warmth, or Freud's theory
that women he labeled "castrating mothers" had made their boys
neurotic. How much of women's reluctance to speak of children's
illnesses is because the medical profession is likely to blame them?
How much guilt because in making life we also make death?

Are there parts of our bodies unfit for our bodies, a hierar-
chy of bodily functions that cast death with the greatest shame?
There's humus (the ground, the soil) in the word "humiliation."
There's death (the mort) in "mortification." Etymologically, it is
embarrassing to die.

Katha Pollitt says, "Storylessness has been women's biggest

problem." There are very few Western stories about the glories of aging. My friend Alida recently corrected me. Her mother and I were joking about the saggy upper arms of older women, a trait Alida admires. More than once she's wanted to compliment an older woman for her soft and beautiful pouches of skin. Alida told me these arms are like the bellies of older cats, a clever mechanism of self-defense. If an older cat gets in a fight and is grabbed by the extra skin and fur of her belly, she's unharmed. Alida's story made me wonder if arms that jiggle could be the start of wings.

I need better stories. Or I need to listen more to the better stories being told. One of my daughters, resting in my lap when she was younger, said, "Mama, you're so nice and chubby and your beard is so soft."

She recently asked about menopause. I told her it's the time when periods stop and wisdom flourishes. I told her about Darcey Steinke's book *Flash Count Diary*. Steinke went looking for species besides humans who outlive our reproductive years. She found killer whales. "The older females not only live thirty to fifty years after menopause, but they also lead their pods—complex cohesive family groups—particularly in times when salmon, their main food source, is scarce." Steinke draws from an article in *The New York Times* that cites the work of Darren Croft and Emma Foster on Southern Resident killer whales when she writes, "Elder females hold ecological knowledge and all whales, even younger males, prefer to follow the older females."

My grandmothers needed better stories, something to replace the brutal calculations they arrived at as Christian women who loved God and had lost their children. God hadn't listened to their prayers. God had forsaken them and judged them. They must be bad people, their badness evidenced by the death of their

children. A shame everyone could see, a shame that met a sorrow
so terrible it was already beyond words. What a compounding of
pain—to lose a child and then feel one shouldn't or couldn't ever
speak of him or her because the world would judge you harshly.

When I was a young mother I met a woman at a yard sale who
wore a large medallion with a photo of a child around her neck. I
asked and she said it was a photo of her dead son. I apologized for
being nosy, but she stopped me. She wore the necklace because
she wanted to talk about him. She hated feeling like she was not
allowed to speak of her child since he had died. No guilt or shame
in having a mortal body.

The fear of death that grips some parents has created a fantasy that one might stop death with the proper restraints: the hell
that is helicopter parenting, choking controls on children's lives
enacted by out-of-control parents attempting to suppress the lone
certainty that comes with the gift of life.

After my essay about One Direction was published, I heard
from more readers than I ever had before: young women from
Tehran, Australia, Brazil, people all over the world, some who had
never listened to 1D. It was thrilling to connect, but one letter
in particular struck me, a note from David Wheeler, the father
of three boys. Wheeler's six-year-old, Ben, had been murdered in
the school shooting in Newtown, Connecticut, three years earlier.
Like most of the world, I'd been immobilized with fear and grief
by the unimaginable events at Sandy Hook. My oldest daughter
was in kindergarten at the time. My mind got stuck in a terrible
rut, imagining the halls of my children's school, everyone's children's schools, imagining our principal, imagining children hiding across America because adults were too stupid, too greedy to
do anything to fix our gun laws.

David Wheeler and I struck up a correspondence. In one reply I wrote: "In trying to write a response to your kind letter, I found myself grappling with your very materiality. Forgive me, but if you are real, then your dear boy really was killed and this is a truth I still, these years later, cannot fully reconcile." What a terrible thing to put on him, but it was not untrue.

Wheeler's response was beautiful, through so much pain. He wrote:

> If I've learned anything through this harrowing theft of part of my life, it is that the daily navigation that allows one foot to be placed in front of the other requires the ability to hold two entirely contradictory ideas in one's head and heart at the same time without reconciliation or even the hope of it. A necessary close embrace of polar opposites of every kind. Refutation of this duality is an open door to a very dark, painful and remote place.

I think of David Wheeler as someone who has had to explore emotions most of us are too frightened to even approach. His wisdom is a gift, and I am grateful he did not opt for silence. The reconciliation he navigates could move us beyond any too-simple idea of opposites. Not life or death, black or white, male or female, future or past, sound or silence, us or them, but both, all. How to make room in our bodies for these "polar opposites"? How to take a narrow space and make it wide? As Wheeler suggests, perhaps a first step toward this understanding might come in recognizing that broken means open. Broken doesn't need fixing, but rather courage to remain open to emotion. After my dad got sick, I went to a therapist for the first time. I'd always avoided therapy. I was wary. When I met her, I said, "Don't cure me." I was afraid she might take something from me, like a lobotomy. I was worried I wouldn't be able to write anymore if she fixed me up. "Don't cure me," I said, as if she could apply Krazy Glue to my broken parts. She got a good laugh out of that.

David Wheeler writes of walking, stepping forward. In Janet Cardiff's sound walk *Her Long Black Hair*, she says, "One step after another, one foot moving into the future and one in the past. Did you ever think about that? Our bodies are caught in the middle. The hard part is staying in the present. Really being here." Championing one side of a perceived duality, we miss being here. We miss a fullness, we miss being open to all we've been given, not just our lives but our deaths too.

This piece seems to be written in the voice of someone who believes she's okay with death, as if I have calmly meditated on our mortality and risen above the fear. That is not true. I want to find a new story for dying.

Sebald's *The Emigrants* begins with an image of a graveyard, then a character who lives in a house with a façade made to look like Versailles. The fakery of identity is rooted in our reluctance to accept death. Sebald's most loquacious character, Dr. Henry Selwyn, speaks for pages, describing his life, home, travels, garden, childhood, pets, and more, barely stopping for paragraph breaks. Selwyn says many words, a flood of language, without telling a reader much about who he is, until finally he arrives at this: "The years of the second war, and the decades after, were a blinding, bad time for me about which I could not say a thing even if I wanted to." Sebald makes a wall of language with this character in order to permit the horror of his one silent moment. This silence makes me think of Ada. Selwyn, depleted by the horror of World

War II, lives behind his own façade, albeit one that's crumbling as he ages. Selwyn has changed his name, anglicizing Herschel to Henry. He's nearly buried the truth of the pain he carries.

What secrets of identity are so dangerous, shameful, or painful that we hide them behind a fake wall? When my friend Laura's mother died, Laura found an actual fake wall in her mom's closet and inside, photos and documents of two aunts Laura had never heard of before. One aunt had been institutionalized, one had died young. Illness and death shoved into the back of a dark closet.

At the end of Dr. Selwyn's chapter, the body of Johannes Naegeli, a man Selwyn loved deeply, is found in a glacier, his boots poking out of the ice, seventy years after Naegeli was lost. A truth that was hidden, but could not hide forever: We die.

The first American women's rights convention was held in Seneca Falls in 1848, during a time when American women were subservient to their husbands, lost their wealth at marriage, had no claim to their children, and could be pursued as runaways if they fled an abusive marriage. In celebration of the Nineteenth Amendment's centennial, my friend Suzy Pelosi introduced me to the work of Dr. Sally Roesch Wagner. In her book *Sisters in Spirit*, Wagner teaches a quiet history of the suffrage movement. She writes that the suffragettes "believed women's liberation was possible because they knew liberated women, women who possessed rights beyond their wildest imagination: Haudenosaunee women." The women of the Haudenosaunee, or the Six Nation Confederacy, lived in a matriarchy. These women nominated and removed their chiefs, held political and spiritual offices, and controlled property. Their children belonged to the mother's clan. Matriarchy is in the very soil of the state where I live, though it is sometimes hard to feel it. The damage of patriarchy is so entrenched in our land. Stories that make sense—stories of brave women, wise children, nonbinary beliefs—are often suppressed. So it is like stepping into Technicolor to find a historian or a writer who tells a different story.

In her book *If Women Rose Rooted*, Sharon Blackie writes:

In Scotland and Ireland, the Cailleach—the Old Woman— made, shaped and protects the land and the wild things on it. In these and other Celtic nations, Danu gave birth to all the other gods and was mother to the people who followed. Women: the creators of life, the bearers of the Cup of knowledge and wisdom, personifying the moral and spiritual authority of this fertile green and blue Earth.

Do you remember those days?

Me neither. Other indigenous cultures around the world may still respect and revere the feminine, but we Western women lost control of our stories a long time ago. The story which I was given to carry as a very young child . . . accorded no such significance to women. In this story, woman was an afterthought, created from a man's body for the sole purpose of pleasing him. In this story, the first woman was the cause of all humanity's sufferings: she brought death to the world, not life.

In her book *Wayward Lives, Beautiful Experiments*, Saidiya Hartman calls it "critical fabulation," her process of re-fleshing women who have been lost to history. Using legal documents and the historical records of rent collectors, prison case files, and psychiatric interviews as skeleton, Hartman gives bodies and full lives to Black American women of the early twentieth century through a process of informed speculation. Alexis Okeowo's essay "How Saidiya Hartman Retells the History of Black Life" asks, "Can stories fill in the archive? They might provide comfort, but to whom? For the dead, it is too late. In the end, Hartman decides that the goal is not to 'recover' or 'redeem' the dead girls but to create a fuller picture of their lives." In answer to Okeowo's question, stories provide me with tremendous comfort. Stories make reality. As I try to wash away the Western world's terrible, narrow, fearful stories of mothers, women, children, and bodies, the lesson from Wagner, Blackie, and Hartman is keep digging, keep looking for stories that reflect the truth. Often the truth is well hidden and often the truth is hideous. I don't mean to suggest that we dig looking only for the beautiful stories. When we dig, we are certain to find histories that say people are bad, people are ignorant and cruel. My intention is not to dig past these truths looking for a better story or a story that doesn't hurt. Once I had a student tell me they wouldn't read Ali Smith's novel *How to Be Both* because one of Smith's characters uses a hateful word for her gay brother. This reluctance to engage with human ignorance worries me, as if a world without cruelty exists if we only keep our blinders on. My intention is to find as many stories as I can to create a truth that feels whole.

The constellation Pleiades is sometimes called the Seven Sisters. In Japan the stars are called Subaru. To the Celts they are Tŵr Tewdws. Hawaiians call them Makaliʻi. Māori people call them Matariki. Aboriginal Australians, Persians, Arabs, the Chinese, the Quechua, the Maya, the Aztec, the Lakota, the Kiowa, the Cherokee all include this prominent cluster in their mythologies. The Greeks named the nine brightest stars for Atlas, the Titan charged with holding up the sky; Pleione, an ocean nymph; and their seven daughters. Sometimes the sisters have been pursued into the sky by a man. Sometimes the sisters have killed themselves in grief over the death of their other sisters. There are so many stories and the Pleiades contain so many stars, far more than seven. There are thousands, in fact. But only those stars bright enough for the naked human eye to detect are called sisters. What are the untold stories of the other stars? The stars we can't see?

I come from women who wrote a lot down. Ada's youngest sister, Vera, wrote a history, *The Mills Family: Twelve Generations Descended from Pilgrim Simon Mills I from Yorkshire, England 1630*. In my grandma Marcella's memoir, she warned us about her aunt Vera. She wrote that Vera "married money and became to my mind insufferable." My grandma was an Iowa farmgirl. She thought many people were snobs. She was wary of the lies people tell to puff themselves and their identities up. She wrote to us, "Read the family history by Aunt Vera with a wary eye—It is embellished beyond imagination in places."

Vera wrote exhaustive accounts of her sisters, or the sisters she deemed worthy, like Ada, a bright star. Clubs and society memberships, marriages, honors, children. But beside third-born Ella Mills's name, Vera records only one terrible, short entry.

Ella Mills, Sept., 1869. A precocious child. Died young.

This cruel blank in Vera's book made me curious. What did "precocious" mean in 1869? Bold? Intelligent? Mature? The Jefferson, Iowa, graveyard presents an alternate story. Ella Mills's complete dates, carved in stone, are 1869 to 1891. Twenty-one years old. Young, but not a child, and so perhaps also not precocious? What was Aunt Vera trying to hide? My great-aunt Barbara provided a copy of Ella's dramatic and tenderly compassionate obituary published in *The Jefferson Bee*. It strikes a very different tone than Vera's account, Vera, who was only six years old when her sister Ella died.

AND SHE FELL ASLEEP.

DIED.—At Independence; Monday morning, March 2, 1891 of brain derangement, ELLA MILLS, daughter of Mr. and Mrs. A. R. Mills, of this city, in the twenty-second year of her age. To the home wondrously saddened by this bereavement, in the spirit of trust that pervades the household, there must come the words of Him who said: "What I do ye know not now, but ye shall know hereafter." Past finding out are the ways of the Infinite One, when we seek to measure them with eyes covered by the film of tears and decay. And so those who sorrow most for this dear daughter and sister find best comfort in saying "He knows best!"

It is not a long story that tells how Ella Mills followed the shadowy pathway that led from the health and strength of girlhood down into the valley of death, and yet the decline was so gradual at first, and the stealthy approach of the messenger so guarded and gentle, that we venture an introspect, briefly of intervening days. While Ella was at Ames some two years ago, she suffered severely from an attack of German measles, and never fully recovered from the effects of this scourge. As her family now remembers her condition after this sickness, they note a definite change in her interest in what was going on about her and also, as to her general demeanor. Nearly a year later she had an attack of the "grippe," a great burden to her already broken health. She seemed to recover from the disease, but those who knew her best saw that it had served to lessen her waning ambition and led to a marked indifference concerning material things. Slowly and surely the mind and strength were yielding to the inexorable decree "thou shalt surely die." Our readers are aware how under a strange, unaccountable hallucination this daughter who loved home better than any place on earth, boarded a moving freight train about six weeks ago bound for Council Bluffs; how she was intercepted at Scranton and brought home; how the light of reason flickered so dimly that at last it was deemed best to try the benefit of an Institution founded in a spirit of helpfulness to such unfortunates; and how at last the tired spirit was loosened from its earthly home, and went to the loving care of Him whom she loved and trusted.

Ella Mills was born in this city September 16, 1869, and she has never known any other home than Jefferson. Her entire life has been lived here, except the year and a half she was at Ames, and the time she spent in teaching school. Hence it is not necessary to speak at length of her worth as a loyal daughter, sister and friend; of her Christian virtues that shone with the radiance of a perfect trust; of an integrity of purpose concerning what she thought was right that nothing seen or unseen could shake; of an influence for good that followed her everywhere, an influence that was not lost upon the great congregation who yesterday looked upon her calm, sweet face in its final resting place among the flowers that bedecked her narrow house. She was a girl of unusually bright mind. She graduated at fourteen in the first class of pupils under Mr. Hammond who paid a fine tribute to her scholarly attainments. She excelled in mathematics and no question seemed obtuse but that her mind had for it a clear, accurate analysis. As a reader, she made marked progress, and gained many honors.

Her funeral was held at the M. E. church which she joined when but twelve years of age. The house was crowded to overflowing although the services were held during the busy afternoon. The services were conducted by Pastor Everly, who preached a very impressive sermon from the text "Her sun has set while it was yet day." A quartette choir—Mrs. LeGore, Mrs. Gallup, Mr. J.A. Henderson and Will Simmons—sang some touchingly beautiful anthems. At the conclusion of the services a large procession followed the remains to their long home in the city of the dead.

And so we all, with bowed heads, render our last earthly service of love to this pure, bright girl. The hand that led her through devious ways and in gathering gloom, gives her the greeting of welcome fellowship in "the better kingdom." The sincere sympathy of our people is for the stricken family who will always cherish in their garden of memories loving remembrances of the child and the sister who has gone home.

The state hospital at Independence, Iowa, was built in 1873 because the Mount Pleasant asylum was overcrowded. Independence continues to operate today as the Independence Mental

Health Institute. When I wrote to request Ella's records, I had little faith that the paper archive remained. To my astonishment, the hospital mailed me copies, as her next of kin. Dr. W. S. Schermerhorn, an expert on placenta previa, admitted Ella to the hospital in the winter of 1891. "I hereby certify that according to my judgment, said person is insane." The document goes on to ask and answer a number of questions as part of Schermerhorn's examination of my great-aunt, an event conducted with Ella in physical restraints, as his notes specify.

When were the first symptoms of this attack manifested, and in what way?
    The first volatile change in her condition was about three weeks ago. She ran away and got on a freight train; was carried to the next town and removed by force.

Is the disease variable, and are there rational intervals? If so do they occur at regular intervals?
    She is rational on some subjects, irrational on others at all times. There are no regular intervals.

On what subject or in what way is derangement now manifested? State fully.
    She insists that she is an adopted daughter and an alien in her family. She wants to travel and will run away when not constantly watched.

Has the patient shown any disposition to injure others?
    No.

*Has suicide ever been attempted? If so, in what way? Is the
propensity now active?*
   No.

*Is there a disposition to filthy habits, destruction of clothing,
breaking of glass, &c.?*
   No.

*What relatives, including grandparents, and cousins, have
been insane?*
   None.

*Did the patient manifest any peculiarities of temper, habits,
disposition of pursuits, before the accession of the disease—
any predominant passions, religious impressions etc?*
   Always disinclined to associate with others of her age
or go in society but not in such a degree as to come under
notice.

*Has constraint or confinement been employed? If so, of what
kind and how long?*
   Only for a short time on this occasion, but constant
watchfulness has been necessary.

State any matter supposed to have bearing on the case.
   Her friends think there is painful menstruation but she
has been unwilling to admit it.

There's a frightening refrain I hear after reading Ella's admission
papers. The refrain comes from her obituary: "He knows best!"

Darl Bundren's family commits him to an insane asylum at the end of William Faulkner's *As I Lay Dying*. On my first reading as a high school sophomore, this sudden institutionalization came as a huge surprise. Darl had shepherded me through the book. Of the fifteen narrators, Darl's voice is the one I listened to and trusted because he sees more than the other characters. Unlike his siblings, Darl had left Mississippi. He fought in World War I. Darl had seen death, and, while his siblings and father do all they can to fight it, Darl tries to let his mother's body return to the earth. In knowing death Darl sees so much, he sometimes even sees without his eyes. He's intuitive, reading the world and reporting it. He's institutionalized for that reading, seeing, knowing of death. His brother Cash says, "Sometimes I ain't so sho who's got a right to say when a man is crazy and when he ain't. Sometimes I think it ain't none of us pure sane until the balance of us talks him that-a-way."

I know a person who looks like Hedy Lamarr. They feel the presence of the dead. They feel places where tremendous violence has occurred. They were institutionalized when they were younger. They make me wonder, what and where is the difference between remembering, dwelling in the past, staying open, being intuitive, seeing ghosts, suffering from mental illness, being awake to beauty, wonder, tragedy; and being someone who knows death. Hedy's last name, a chosen name, means the sea, *la mar*, a place that knows no binaries. It is *el mar* really, but in Spain, if someone loves the sea, they call her *la mar*.

I have Ella Mills's obituary, her admission papers, her death certificate, an 1885 census that records fifteen-year-old Ella as head of that very large household, though both her parents were still alive, and I have an account from *The Aurora*, the newspaper of the Iowa State Agricultural College, that tells me Ella, as a student there, took fourth place in the freshman-sophomore declamatory contest with the repellent poem "Whistling in Heaven." This poem tells the story of a pioneer woman terrified when her husband, off to restock provisions, leaves her home alone with the baby in their cabin. The woman trembles, fearful of wolves and "savages." The fear that lives in maternal minds feeds on stories of women's weakness, dependence, precarity. The mother in the poem hears a whistle in the night that turns out to be a neighbor's boy. Knowing she was alone and thus terrified, he arrives to accompany her through the dark hours. "And now, my kind friends, do you wonder / since such a good reason I've given / why I shan't care for the music / unless there is whistling in heaven?"

These are the only documents I have to rebuild Ella Mills's life. Anyone who might have known Ella, or stories of Ella, is long deceased. My sister Amy and I speculate how Ella came to board that freight train bound for Council Bluffs. Was she pregnant? In love? In love with the wrong person? Disappointed by the idea of marriage and motherhood as her only option? Was she running away or did she simply long to travel, as she told Dr. Schermerhorn? How much of Ella's "insanity" is based in the hateful word "hysteria," from the Greek for uterus? Ella and Ada were only a year apart. Was Ella tired of being compared to Ada, being in opposition to Ada, whom Vera describes as:

The "belle" of Jefferson from the time she was voted, age 16, "the most beautiful girl in High School". Her charm, her warm personality held an inimical streak of individuality. With a talent for leadership she seemed able to achieve

anything she attempted. No one possessed more diversi-
fied talents. Listing her natural gifts, her accomplishments
can scarcely be over-rated. She was artistic, literary, poetic, musical, dramatic as well as being domestic, and an
ideal mother. With it all she was a delightful person to be
with—witty, clever and brilliant. With all her strength of
character, she symbolized superior womanhood.

With such brightness nearby, I wonder, did Ella find it difficult to define herself as anything but the anti-Ada, a dark sister to
counter Ada's lightness in a society that believed in opposites and
binaries? Did Ella's younger sisters offer Ella companionship and
love? Did Ada? I wish I could ask them.

In his *Dictionary of Word Origins*, Joseph Shipley writes,
commit, *See* mess; **looney**, *See* pants. Shipley lets oxygen into
language, making space for difference, for ecstasy, being, and
freedom: Ella riding into the fresh air aboard her freight train.
Shipley's dictionary is a rare one, a work of reference that permits
roomy interpretation rather than seeking to carve narrow and
forced definitions. There's no Ada *or* Ella, Life *or* Death, Good *or*
Bad. Naming under Shipley does not feel like a coffin or a narrow
house, it does not feel like Cinderella's sister slicing off her heel to
make that slipper fit.

In *Labyrinths*, Borges tells the story of fabricated reference
books—encyclopedias of the created world Tlön, a place crafted
over years by a secret society. A reader is asked to speculate, what
reference book is not fabricated? The very word "reference" implies a mirror, fun house or not. All reflections bear their own dis-
tortions and subjectivity. Just because something is alphabetized

does not mean it is true. Though this ought to be plain, it often isn't. Borges reminds us that the observable orders of our world, outside of nature, are created by "chess masters," not "angels."

Ten years ago any symmetry with a semblance of order—dialectical materialism, anti-Semitism, Nazism—was sufficient to entrance the minds of men. How could one do other than submit to Tlön, to the minute and vast evidence of an orderly planet? It is useless to answer that reality is also orderly. Perhaps it is, but in accordance with divine laws—I translate: inhuman laws—which we never quite grasp. Tlön is a labyrinth, but it is a labyrinth devised by men, a labyrinth destined to be deciphered by men.

Having children who are in middle school has been an education in the workings of fascism. I ask my girls to ignore the kids who enforce conformity or the ones who use narrow definitions. Silence can be powerful as it challenges the desire to classify, define, and commit. To normalize. However, silence has its own dangers, like Ada and Marcella's never speaking of their dead children. That silence might come from a grief beyond words, but what if their silence was something else, something fearful? Asking the universe "Why is my child gone?" questions and pesters the contracts of men, the works of reference that attempt to create a human-scaled sense of order on our non-human-scaled universe. When my friend Patchen was murdered, my grandma Norma told me, "God must have needed him." I didn't buy that. Isn't God here with us, among us? Isn't God us collectively? *What I do ye know not now, but ye shall know hereafter* is another way of saying, Don't ask why. Don't ask where we go when we go is a fiction made too simple. It is a rebuke against reading our world, against detection, complexity, science, wonder, and all the puzzles I like to assemble, even if I assemble them very badly.

"That's fine, Mr. Katagiri. It's better that you don't remember. The whole terrible fight occurred in the area of imagination. That is the precise location of our battlefield." In Murakami's short story "Super Frog Saves Tokyo," Mr. Katagiri falls into a coma. During his unconsciousness, he and Frog, a six-foot-tall, *Anna Karenina*–loving amphibian, fight Worm, big as a locomotive and angry enough to destroy Tokyo with a wriggle, with an earthquake. Katagiri and Frog manage to temporarily thwart Worm and his anger. As our beaten amphibian hero, our beacon of light, is disappearing at the end of the story, really just dissolving into a pile of dark, crawling, holy bugs that emerge from his wounds, Frog takes a moment to reflect on literature he has loved. "Fyodor Dostoevsky, with unparalleled tenderness, depicted those who have been forsaken by God. He discovered the precious quality of human existence in the ghastly paradox whereby men who have invented God were forsaken by that very God."

When I attempt to fill in the blanks of Ella's history, I imagine how she felt when her mom and dad dropped her off at Independence. How they drove away from that asylum without their daughter, a woman who was committed because she had a hard time being social, because she wanted to travel and didn't want to be restrained. Much of my interest in Ella's life is because she sounds a lot like me at twenty-one. But when I was a young woman building my life, finding new families with the Stacys; Linda and John; Brian and the Annies; Pamela and Paula; Joe and the Hagans; my birth family loved these new people and places I came to call my homes. My birth family made room.

I imagine the quiet in the Jefferson house that greeted the telegram declaring Ella's death at Independence only five weeks after
they left her there. I imagine her mother's hands on the telegram,
her father's breath, the family's guilt and grief. Did the remaining
sisters climb into their maple tree to remember that limb of their
family now buried underground, a root crossing the mycelium
that turned their sister's body back into earth? What pressure,
what true horror, told these sisters to never speak of Ella? To bury
the shameful record of her life? Was it because no man would
want to marry the remaining Mills sisters if they knew Ella had
been driven "insane" by the strictures of patriarchy? Or did the
Mills family hide Ella's life because they felt somehow responsible
for her death?

Christina Milletti's novel *Choke Box* is dedicated to "all the
madwomen in their attics" and begins with a woman attempting
to convince a psychiatric board of her sanity. Milletti invited me to
read at the University at Buffalo. I drove the back roads, passing
through Candor and Bliss, New York. I stopped to visit a nearly
frozen Niagara Falls. Arriving, at last, in the city, I could scarcely
believe my eyes. The university had booked me a room in a hotel
that appeared to be a castle. It was tremendous, glorious, soaring.
No building nearby matched its majesty. I stood awed before the
woman who worked in reception. "This place is crazy," I said,
meaning gorgeous, huge, surprising.

She soured at my unprecise turn of phrase. "Yes. This is the
former Buffalo State Asylum for the Insane." The hospital in Buffalo, as well as the asylum in Independence where my aunt Ella
was sent, were both Kirkbrides, buildings designed by Thomas
Story Kirkbride, b. 1809, a physician and superintendent with the

radical idea that asylums should be filled with sunlight and fresh air. I can't help but love his middle name.

I'm embarrassed to say I was frightened that night. Despite the beauty of the Hotel Henry, I hid my head under the covers. In the morning, I called my sister-in-law Kristina and told her I'd been frightened. I told her I was embarrassed by my fear. "I'm not scared of dead people and I'm not scared of the mentally ill."

"No. But you're scared of what might have happened to them while they were there," she said.

In "Sex and Death to the Age 14," Spalding Gray writes of the connections between desire and death.

> I found two erotic pictures in *Life* magazine that I kept going back to. One was of Prince Charles jumping over hurdles as a young boy, which I kept under the bed and used to look at every time I was anxious. The other was of the collapse of Rome, with everyone crawling around in the streets half naked. Maybe they had the plague. I thought, this is really sexy.

How much of Ella's perceived illness was the tidal wave of desire—for touch, for experiences, for life, for self—that most twenty-year-old bodies feel? How much of Ella's perceived illness was really about the way we've learned to hate our bodies?

In the early days of the Covid-19 pandemic, some young people ignored the mandate to social distance as the virus spread. They crowded spring break beaches in Florida and Mexico, unable to imagine or believe that death is real. The photos show young people dancing close. Women in bikinis riding on the

shoulders of tan football players, women the same age Ella was
when she died. Some of these people, of course, soon after, were
dead. Desire and death twist into one strong vine. The nature of
desire is fleeting, *to love that well which thou must leave ere long.* I
had a life-size poster of James Dean on my bedroom wall as a girl.
I'd kiss it, coming into and going out of the room, like paying a
toll. I thought he was perfect. I didn't yet realize that part of his
perfection was that he was dead. Dean was the first dead boy I
fell in love with. Some of these dead boys (the damaged, the drug
addicts, the abusers and the abused) were breathing still when I
fell for them.

In a small theater in New York City in the fall of 2001, a human who glowed as if they were a sea anemone began to sing.
"Should I call the doctor? For I fear you might be dead." Then
the song takes a pause, a silence held so long that many of us
in the theater that night felt we too might expire by the sheer
extent of our longing and delight at dwelling in this in-between
place of silence. Eventually the song began again, but the silence
had made its wound, its womb. Antony and the Johnsons made a
song about falling in love with a dead boy. The song, like a storm
on the ocean, started low and slow and built to a rolling place of
unstoppable waves.

My friend's sister died two years ago, leaving behind a teenage daughter. My friend has more than once mentioned her intention of buying her niece a vibrator, intending the device as a
prophylactic against bad choices made based on bodily desires. I
wonder, with desire and death such close bedfellows, if a vibrator
might also be a prophylactic against our walk toward death. Fill
the holes. Stay alive.

The permeability of our bodies is at the heart of desire. We are so full of holes. The biggest holes are the ones left by death. Do we love one another because we know that one day we will be dead? We are well versed in *la petit mort*, the French euphemism for orgasm, but we fail to consider all the other small expirations, tiny deaths we suffer: trimming our nails, scratching dry skin, crying, spitting, peeing, farting, bleeding, birthing. And what of the more complex unravelings of our minds, those thoughts that spin away from us? Sometimes I can't stop talking, letting my insides out. Sometimes the reason I write is in order to get the language out of my body. We are always dying a little bit and these little deaths humiliate us, return us to the humus. We lose small parts of ourselves—teeth, minds, dust, gas, salt. Perhaps we are wrong to think those parts belonged to us in the first place—the façade of identity—when they are only borrowed from the earth. I think we are even more wrong to suffer humiliation as if our bodies' functions are a failure of virtue. Our small deaths—balding, depression, sneezing—prepare us for the big one, *la grand mort*. If we were less humiliated by our bodies and greeted the small deaths without shame, we could come to the big death easier, with less fear.

One of my exes died young. We hadn't seen each other for years. We'd married other people and grown distant. When I heard he was dying, we started up a correspondence again. He'd always been beautiful. He looked like Samuel Beckett, prematurely silver-haired, tortured muscles in his face. He had marks all over his body: a gunshot wound, a brand he'd given himself, and various other scars. When I was with him, I was interested in pain. He was good at providing it, dragging my heart through many sharp jealousies. Our relationship ended right as my father got sick and died. The grief of death trumped any of the pain he and I could conjure for each other. The grief of death made me less interested in pain. Some species of desire had been consummated and extinguished.

My ex had been very physical, very strong. I think that is why a few months after he died, I really wanted to know what had become of his body. Was he interred? Was he cremated? I texted an old friend to ask. "Hi. Apologies for a strange question, but I'm wondering, do you know what Diane did with Matt's body? I've been thinking about it a lot. Sending you love." And then the reply, "Sorry wrong person. Don't know who Diane or Matt is. Must have been an old phone number for the person you are trying to reach."

The playwright Suzan-Lori Parks says of her characters' speech, "It's, you know, blah-blah-blah doin diddly-dip-da-drop. It's just sound. It's the sound of the dead, and the dead don't make living sounds."

A number of years back, the writer Diamond Sharp screened Flying Lotus's "Coronus, the Terminator" video for me. It was an experience of being suddenly cracked open by art. I have since watched this video, directed by Young Replicant, hundreds of times. A man lies dying in bed, surrounded by family. They wash his body. They lay their hands on him. The muted sounds seem underwater. His child, missing a forearm and hand, looks on from the doorway as the father slips away from life. A car arrives, a human-like shadow is cast on the laundry line. Someone approaches. The beat begins and the dying man, the dead man, now clothed, walks downstairs. In his living room he finds three strangers assembled. Those who arrived. They are dusted in ghostly white powders. They begin to move in a way that is irresistible. The beat is hypnotic and unstoppable. Its slowness speaks

of confidence, certainty. The man, recognizing why the strangers
have come, flees. He runs through the city, trying to escape death.
The figures both follow and lead him to an underworld, the Los
Angeles River. The tempo is aching and at moments in opposition
to the dancers' movements, which are sometimes smooth, sometimes jerky, a rigor mortis of sorts, a reconciliation of opposites.
It's impossible not to follow the dancers, not to want to go with
them, sirens leading us to wreck our ships on the rocks. The man
kneels in the river and his son stands behind him. With a mechanical arm now connected to his body, the child fires a gun into his
father's head, an explosion, an eruption of rose petals and birds.

Chickadees' hearts beat 480 times per minute. My dad's Blackwing pencils say, "Half the pressure, twice the speed." Which
makes me wonder, if I write something fast will it make sense
when read at a slower pace? It's taken me forever to write this piece.
Read it slowly. Read it fast. Perhaps the meaning will expand at
different speeds. Chickadees are an LP recorded at 33 spinning on
78, too fast for me to understand what they are saying. But what
happens when we change the scale, change the speed? In "Good
Picker," Stephen Vincent Benét writes, "If you took it about three
beats slower," in regards to trying to understand a line in a play.
Aging changes our tempo. When exercising, older hearts cannot
beat as quickly as younger hearts. During the Covid-19 pandemic
my mom's life really slowed down. She stopped going out. She
told me that each day she'd unearthed some new memory by simply slowing down. She told me the story of a small man she met
on an Austrian mountain trail who sold her a number of colorful
stone eggs. "I haven't thought of him in years." In "Two Heartbeats a Minute," an episode of the podcast *Invisibilia*, the host
Hanna Rosin tells how a handful of people—one with an interest

in microscopic pond scum, one with an interest in whale songs, and two who work with machine learning—are using ideas of scale and tempo to decode the languages of nonhumans. They've found that whale and human languages have similar shapes, like Mandelbrot's fractals. They're building a Rosetta Stone to translate the languages of animals, trees, anything into the languages of humans. How long then, I wonder, will it be before we can talk to the dead in words we all understand? How long before we recognize that some people already do?

"Coronus, the Terminator" is from Flying Lotus's opus *You're Dead!* Out of the intensity I felt and still feel in that song, I began to build a device in my head I call the Mourning Machine. It doesn't work yet. That's not a problem. I'm still not even entirely clear what the machine looks like, but I know it is dark inside, a place for transformation, a place where skin is all pores, all holes. The Mourning Machine is not made out of new things but contains a junkyard of devices other people thought too old to function anymore. It contains forgotten engines and tools that have been liberated from serving capitalism. *See* Ghosts in the Machine. There will be old train cars, old record players that spin not only at 33, 45, and 78 but other tempos as of yet unheard, 12, 9, -4, 111. The Mourning Machine involves being drenched in sound, words and songs that take our breath, translate other frequencies to our human ears, sounds that stop our hearts just enough so that we, the living, can approach a place where it might be possible to speak with, sing with our dead, even if that singing sounds a lot like silence.

Freighters were the only trains that passed through Jefferson, Iowa. Though Ella was removed from the train at the next town, having traveled only ten miles, I wonder what she saw on that journey, crossing over the North Raccoon River. I wonder what senses she let enter into her thinking. My sisters and I planned a trip to visit Jefferson and Magnolia. The Covid-19 pandemic put these plans on hold. In the meantime, I've taken Ella's rail journey myself via Google Earth. It's not a long trip and the landscape varies little. It's a railroad not for humans, but freight. Farms and fields in winter. Trees without leaves make a blur. Mostly, the experience of trains is an experience of sound, a sound so loud that it comes close to silence. Benét asks, "I wonder what sound they listen for now at night, in the small towns sunk in the wheat of the mid-continent—the young and ambitious, the ones who mean to get away? The drone of the mail plane, I suppose . . . In our day, it was the long, shaking whistle of the Limited." The Limited, indeed. Who pulled Ella off her train?

My grandparents were high school sweethearts. He went to college a year before she did. My grandma writes:

> Walter entered Ames that fall . . . The dreadful flu epidemic of 1918 where thousands died was at its height and he almost immediately contracted the dreaded disease— The huge gym at the college was made into an overflow hospital . . . his family was called. Mother Hunt decided she must go to his side immediately and I asked to go with her! Everyone agreed for we were all terribly worried. I'll never forget that trip from Logan to Ames on the local train for at every stop we would watch them unload caskets of the victims. A heart rending sight. As we pulled into the Ames station Mother Hunt was being paged with

the news that under no circumstances would she be allowed to come to the campus to visit Walter because of
the strict quarantine rules. However he was still <u>alive</u>. We
could do nothing but board another train for home.

I live near the tracks. I hear the trains at night and wonder
why they are louder in the dark. I wonder where they are going
and who is living in those terminal lands.

Frog has gone to battle with Worm, large as a locomotive;
"with all different kinds of hatred he has absorbed and stored
inside himself over the years, his heart and body have swollen
to gargantuan proportions." And Frog, dying from his wounds,
recalls his beloved *Anna Karenina*. "My enemy is, among other
things, the me inside me. Inside me is the un-me. My brain is
growing muddy. The locomotive is coming."

From Shipley:

locomotive, *See* mute.
(L. *movere*, whence *move*.) (L. *loco*, from a place to a place.
Emotion.)

loco, *See* yokel.
(Sp. *loco*, stupid, from It. *locco*, a fool, from *alocco*, an owl.)

Was Ella cold on the train? Was she beyond cold? Where
was she heading? Had she read *Anna Karenina*? The first English edition was published four years before her death. Was she
a reader? Was Ella's journey hopeful or was she fearful as the pioneer woman who needs companionship to sleep at night? Or did
Ella find freedom on that freighter? Riding with her un-me? Her

history becomes mine to imagine, so I do. I see Ella breathing the air that grew fresher and more foreign with each inch of journey gained. She makes up her own definitions for what she is doing. She finds new words as the train moves her into a place where one definition indicates many things. Ella, like the ones who mean to get away, listens to the sound of that train, so loud it makes silence, makes room for all, riding forever, each car its own narrow house, linked to the others, a locomotive without end, a thousand deaths and even more.

Re-Vision

I found my dad's eyeglasses in the compost pile fifteen years after
he lost them. He'd been bending over to empty a tarp-full of leaves
and the glasses had slipped from his shirt pocket into a mountain
of yard litter. He looked for hours but they were gone, for good,
he thought. It made him so mad. He'd just had them, then gone,
completely gone. Things, he thought, don't just disappear.

In his introduction to Sergio Pitol's *The Art of Flight*, Enrique
Vila-Matas writes:

> I remember the day because there was a pounding rain and
> Sergio was constantly losing his glasses; the latter was not
> at all unusual, his penchant for losing and then finding
> his glasses being legendary. That day he lost them several
> times, in various bookstores and cafés, as if that were a
> perfect antidote for not losing his umbrella. I recalled the
> day Juan Villoro had found in Pitol's tendency to lose his
> glasses a clue to illuminating new aspects of his poetics:
> "Sergio writes in that hazy region of someone who loses

his eyeglasses on purpose; he pretends that his originality
is an attribute of his bad eyesight."

My husband asks, "Do you have the car keys?" And I'll say,
"What? The carcass?" It drives him crazy because he thinks I
mishear things on purpose. Maybe I do. Maybe that's how I shift
what's boring and domestic to life in a crime noir. Mishearing is
how I love the world.

Years after he died, I pulled my father's eyeglasses from compost that had become the darkest dirt. Black gold, my brothers,
sisters, and I once called it, imagining the fortunes we'd make sell-
ing our fine, rich soil. Money from nothing is a game my siblings
and I enjoy playing. In a testament to the superpowers of plastic,
neither the lenses nor the frames had suffered more than a minor
rotting, something like the delicate tracings worms sometimes
carve on wood beneath the bark.

I keep my dad's glasses on my bookshelf now. He'd like it there.
His vision was worse than mine and the glasses make me dizzy,
but my daughters enjoy try-
ing them on. They never got
to meet their grandfather.

I bought my house from
a man named Les Moore.
Honest to goodness. He
didn't show up at the closing. He didn't want anything
to do with me. The house
had belonged to his parents.
Les grew up here. I understand. I'll be troubled by the

person who buys my mom's house someday. Even if I like them, I won't believe they are real. How can they live there when my family will forever be living in that house?

After I moved into my own home, I became friendly with a couple of sisters who grew up down the street. "Ooo!" one said. "You live in Butchie Moore's house." I didn't understand their excitement. It's a very modest, vinyl-sided home. I love it, but it is really nothing fancy. I was happy to learn Les's father's name. "When we were kids Butchie had that house so stuffed with junk, our mom said if you cut the house at the corners and peeled back the walls, the house would still stand."

"He was a hoarder?" That made sense.

"Oh, yeah. He had barns all over the lot filled with junk. You should get a metal detector," she said. "I bet there's stuff all over your yard." The house was empty when we moved in, besides some stained carpeting and a wagon wheel chandelier.

Sebald writes, "And so they are ever returning to us, the dead. At times they come back from the ice more than seven decades later and are found at the edge of a moraine, a few polished bones and a pair of hobnailed boots." There's an echo of James Joyce's "The Dead," which is an echo of *The Iliad*, which likely is an echo of something that's fallen out of view to the living.

I haven't gotten my hands on a metal detector, but I do a lot of gardening and often find treasure Butchie Moore buried: rusty scissors, Listerine bottles, corroded metal pots. I'm glad to find these signs of the feet that trod here before mine, but recently I've started leaving these treasures underground. That's someone else's dead. I already have enough of my own.

We donated my dad's eyes. They were very pretty. What eye

isn't? Somewhere, I suppose, my dad's eyes are still very pretty. The eye bank sent a note thanking us for our "gift," creating an idea of a gruesome present with ribbons and pastel wrapping paper. The bank wrote that it is not allowed to share the name of the recipient. A good policy, as chances are high that I would try to find the person who got my dad's eyes, catch a glimpse again, probably even tell that person the things my father saw with those eyes: the Minnesota railways, the Korean War, two marriages, six babies, lots of drinks, lots of smokes, cancer, and so many books.

On a trip to California I convinced myself that a stranger's damp blue eyes had originally belonged to my dad. I followed the stranger around the vineyard where he worked for a couple of hours. It's less creepy than it sounds. He was a tour guide, so I alone knew I was stalking him.

I looked for my dad everywhere right after he died. I even looked for him on the internet, a place that often troubles me, as I still can't tell whether or not the internet is where the book dies, or where it goes to live forever. Borges writes, "I declare that the Library is endless," and the internet sometimes fools me into thinking it is too. In reality a good number of volumes are missing from the internet. When I looked for my dad there, I found little to no evidence of his full life. He hadn't survived long enough to make a dent in the digital realm. He was a much more material man. My father's absence from the internet seems a good indicator that the internet sucks. One of my favorite mistakes is when I read the word "internet" as "internment."

In *The Book of Nightmares*, Galway Kinnell writes of wearing secondhand shoes, of reanimating the foot smells of the departed. In the tenth nightmare, 1 + 0, the final section of the book,

Kinnell writes that the 1, a figure I understand to be him or me, takes a walk off the end of the book with the 0, a figure that seems to be death.

one creature
walking away side by side with the emptiness.

Death as a perfect 10, a real beauty. The book ends. *The Book of Nightmares* was published in 1971, early in the technological takeover, so I don't imagine Kinnell was thinking about this, but the 1 and the 0 are also, of course, binary code. That other place where the book ends.

In college I convinced my best friend John to drive a handful of hours with me to Sheffield, Vermont. We parked outside Galway Kinnell's house to see what he was up to. Kinnell fascinated me. The white linen suits he wore, his salt-and-pepper hair, his life in a small town, away from the world. Mostly I admired the way Kinnell wrote about death. Nothing happened outside Kinnell's house. I think there was a sheep nearby. Eventually we drove home. You say stalker, I say writer.

On Wings' *At the Speed of Sound*, Denny Laine sings that he read a note "you never wrote to me." The song refers to the mayor of Baltimore, bottles floating out to sea, and governments galore. It's a complicated, fluid, melancholy song I've always loved without fully understanding its meaning.

One day I had the strange experience of reading such a note, one that the filmmaker, actor, and writer Miranda July never wrote to me. Before she performed at the Whitney and the Guggenheim, before she appeared at the Cannes Film Festival radiant in a peacock-colored dress, I sent her my book *The Seas*. It's a book about falling in love with a dead boy. The only other stranger I sent my book to was Antony (of Antony and the Johnsons). In reply July sent me a postcard with a puppy on it, telling me that her new film would be premiering soon and she'd be giving a talk afterward. Would I come? Yes, I would. I bought my ticket, found a seat near the front, enjoyed the film and talk, but afterward, when it came time to begin our friendship, I couldn't find her. She'd disappeared into some backstage green room because in the weeks between the puppy postcard and the premiere, she'd become famous, and I am too shy to chase a famous person backstage.

Months later I received another letter written by her, though she never sent it to me. Technically, it was not a letter but a draft of a story July had titled "Dear Samantha Hunt." It had been submitted to her publisher as part of her new short story collection. Someone photocopied it and faxed it to a friend of mine, who then dropped it in the mail and sent it to me. I mean to say, I read the note she never wrote to me.

The letter/story "Dear Samantha Hunt" tells of how July came to read my stories and of her embarrassment at being stalked by a tan man, a hippie. Stalkers, she thought, should be pale and unhealthy nerds. In the letter/story she wrote of her father and a man who owns a gas station in Portland, Oregon. The letter/story was full of potential energy. This, mixed with the unauthorized photocopying, the circuitous route it took getting to me, the creaky reproductions made by fax machines, thrilled me. This was fertility. This was compost. The letter/story had come into my hands via possibly illegal and certainly unethical means. I have always liked this about the letter and keep it in a paper file with other documents I hope will last.

Then, like someone who awaits a no-longer-surprise party

held in her honor, I awaited the publication of July's first book, *No One Belongs Here More Than You*. I was excited to be implicated in her fiction, drawn into the wake of her fame. My ego thrummed. I tried to tamp down my excitement, but between the direct address of the book's title and the fact that the collection was to be published on my birthday, it was difficult to keep my ego from running wild.

I bought July's book on my birthday, but the story "Dear Samantha Hunt" had been cut from the final draft. July had made a revision, seeing things freshly, with new eyes that maybe even felt like a gift. "Dear Samantha Hunt" did not exist. If not for the paper copy I possess, I might even begin to wonder if "Dear Samantha Hunt" was ever real. How many potentialities disappear each day? Re-visions blurred and hazed into something that looks like nonexistence, but isn't quite that.

In 2004, the artist Janet Cardiff made a work of art that changed me forever, *Her Long Black Hair*. It's a sound walk through New York City's Central Park, completed with headphones and a small packet of photos. Cardiff's voice leads the way. "Try to walk to the sound of my footsteps so that we can stay together. And then go down the stairs. All the way to the bottom. There's a woman below talking on a cell phone . . ." Because of the binaural recording system Cardiff uses, a walker always hears Cardiff's footsteps following right behind, just at the back of the walker's brain. "I keep thinking I hear someone behind us," Cardiff says after a silence. "But we can't look back. It's one of the rules of today." Every time I took the walk, despite the sunshine, despite the crowds of the city, this moment chilled me. I always looked back. And every time no one, everyone, was there.

Cardiff follows the path once walked by a woman with long

black hair, a woman who exists in three photographs taken in the park and tucked into the audio set the walker wears. Cardiff later followed this woman's walk. Then I, and thousands of other New Yorkers, followed Cardiff. The piece is built in overlapping layers, like memory, like thought. The walker keeps walking, keeps listening through them all.

> CARDIFF'S VOICE: Go to the left . . . We're following the course of an old stream that they put underground when they began building the park. They uncovered human bones buried a hundred years before.
>
> BAUDELAIRE: You will come to this, my queen, after the sacraments, when you rot underground among the bones already there. But as their kisses eat you up, My Beauty, tell the worms I've kept the sacred essence, saved the form of my rotted loves.
>
> HARRY THOMAS: The spring afterwards, in 1850, I escaped again. Chased by dogs. Hiding by day in the bushes and moving north by night. After three months walking I made it across the border into Canada.
>
> CARDIFF: Follow the road to the right. While Harry Thomas made his epic nighttime journey across America, Baudelaire walked the streets of Paris. I like to imagine that at times their footsteps lined up as if they walked together.

I've taken Cardiff's walk multiple times, laying down tracks on top of my own histories even. Imagine one day my walk was dark blue, another day yellow-green. Kevin Henkes, in his book *Birds*, writes, "If birds made marks with their tail feathers when they flew, think what the sky would look like." What if each revision we made remained? My father saved each new draft of his book in a fresh file, and really, things do start to get crowded that way, even if it is true that no matter is ever created or destroyed. I write longhand in notebooks and revise once the writing is on the page, adding material in margins. Once it goes into the computer, I try to keep only one draft. The one time I remember saving all my drafts was for "The Story of Of," a piece about procreation by division, like the amoeba. Things swiftly got out of control and I began to feel like versions of the story were dividing and reproducing on their own. I ended up with two different stories, the bookends in *The Dark Dark*, "The Story Of" and "The Story of Of." I still feel grateful that I managed to escape saving multiple drafts with only two finished pieces that are the same/different story.

Somehow, I started to believe that Cardiff found the photos of the black-haired walker in a junk shop. Now, so many years later, I wonder where I got this idea. Did Cardiff make it up? Did I make it up? Could it possibly even be true? Do I care? I can't say any longer what's Cardiff's and what's mine. An intimacy so tangled with a woman I don't even know. The best metaphor is ashes, dirt. (The Baudelaire is from his poem "Carcass," or "Carrion," an astonishing work, a love poem that imagines the decomposition of the beloved's body. That's some revision.) Sergio Pitol says he is the sum of "the books I have read, the paintings I have seen, the music I have heard and forgotten, and the streets I have walked."

When I was looking for my dad on the internet I found another Walter Hunt, the man who invented the safety pin. Somehow, I'd never known my father shared a name with this essential inventor. I'm sure my dad knew even without the ease of internet search engines. It is the sort of alignment that would have tick-led him.

Walter Hunt of the safety pin is buried in Brooklyn's Green-Wood Cemetery, not too far from Elias Howe, inventor of the sewing machine. The safety pin and the sewing machine. It makes me laugh every time I visit beautiful Green-Wood, which I do rather frequently, as my brother Andy lives nearby and twice yearly I go to the cemetery with my writing students.

Now when one of my daughters asks for help pinning an item of clothing, I take that ingenious tool invented by Walter Hunt in hand. Piercing P (the past), I (me), and N (now) with a sharp stick, trying to keep these opposites, the differences, together. He holds on to the granddaughters he never did get to meet, even if, with eyes and eyeglasses elsewhere, a re-vision, he can't quite see them.

twang and a tang

Picasso in the ladies' room I remember a Modigliani at my dad's office. I loved its blank eyes even before I learned that two days after the penniless, alcoholic Modigliani died from TB, his love, Jeanne Hébuterne, eight months pregnant with their second child, jumped out a window to her death. What is preserved in oil paint? What emotions harden there? And how odd for these bits of feeling to be exhibited now in wealthy palaces where people might feel very little of the original, possibly painful impulse that made the art.

Chapter 2 (cont'd)

"This is my assistant," Colonel Law said, "Miss Phoebe Poon. Say hello, Phoebe." Phoebe did so, and she was introduced to John and me. We had both stood up, although the officers remained seated. I extended my hand, which seemed to take her off-guard. As we shook, I said, "Miss Poon, is it?" She gave me back a soft "yes," her drawl breaking the word into two syllables. Miss Poon had a **twang**.

First thing, B. V., send her up to the new-name department. Then get her a voice coach. Baby, we're gonna make a big star out of you.

She spoke to the two officers. "You all know there's a **Picasso in the ladies' room**? In the LADIES room!" She addressed John. "Mr. Gilchrist, this must be the most *beautiful* place to work! What do you have in the men's room?"

John—Mr. Gilchrist—was smiling like a circus clown. He didn't seem to have heard her. He stared at her happily.

"What?" he said, slowly realizing she had asked a question.

I felt it necessary to jump in. "I think they pay a bit more

the standard accoutrements of a men's room When I was a girl, my dad once said something to me about "urinal candies." He meant the briquettes of room freshener common to men's lavatories, locations I had never visited. "What?" I asked. "Are you telling me all men's rooms have candies in them?" Rather than clearing up my confusion, he reveled in it. "Yup," he said. And—because I love candy—the gendered injustice I already felt at a young age really hit home.

knock the coffee table askew These observations of Ken (John) are keen if my dad really wrote this in 1981. Ken developed Parkinson's disease and would die from it in 2006. This manuscript, read in hindsight, makes Ken's illness plain, though for years none of his colleagues knew he was ill.

red-breasted humming-birds While there is a ruby-throated hummingbird, the red-breasted hummingbird does not exist. This seems a genuine mistake. My dad was not good with bird names. He knew the trees, but birds individually, specifically, were not his strength.

attention to the ladies' lounges around here," I said. "The men's rooms are pretty basic."

She looked at me and blushed. I was going to go on and enumerate the standard accoutrements of a men's room, but I saw something in her eyes, and didn't. Instead, I said, "Did you see the Van Gogh?" and indicated with my arm the fireplace wall in John's office. She rewarded me with a smile of gratitude and turned to look.

"Gosh," she said, "a Van Gogh. It's beautiful."

"Pull up a chair, Phoebe," Colonel Law said, "and sit down. You don't mind, John? Phoebe knows everything that goes on in my office. Probably better than I do."

John didn't answer. He was trying to get out from between the sofa and the coffee table to get a chair for Miss Poon. He didn't make it in time, although he managed to knock the coffee table askew, which Colonel Law promptly squared up again and opened the file that had been given him.

"Let me preface my remarks," he said, "with a little history of how we're thinking. We have a lot of problems that we're facing. We're going to have a fight on our hands when we bring some of our programs to the Hill. We have to deal with all the handwringers in State. We've got the anti-nukes, and all the other cry-babies. These are normal. N-O-R-M-A-L. Normal. If it isn't a Senator yelling about infringement of his legislative powers, then it's some flake with a beard yelling about the threat to the red-breasted humming-birds. But we've got more problems than that, and we're thinking about them. CINC is thinking about them, and we've got a mandate to do something about them, whether Congress goes along or not. Let me overview you. You all know we've lost our moral fiber. Result of Viet-nam, plain and simple. People don't

first water The expression "of the first water" is not one I was familiar with before this. It comes from the gemstone trade and means something of the greatest purity or clarity, i.e., a diamond of the first water. My dad had a lot of expressions that were unfamiliar to me. This one interests me especially because soon after he died I realized his name is only one slim "l" away from the word "water." How easy for a lowercase "l" to erode, to slip away. I mentioned this at his memorial, how the dead are like water, become water. Stranger still, my dear friend Linda Krantz had brought me a hanky, a navy square with white flowers and a beautiful, Laverne-like, cursive "l." I keep that hanky with me in the room where I write.

how important that could be for spying on the Russians Paul Collins wrote a magnificent story about François Sudre, the man who invented the language SolReSol. What makes Sudre's language so special is that it is truly universal and can be expressed as music, touch, color, writing, or manual signs. While Sudre thought of SolReSol as a universal point of connection, it turned out that the most interest he received in his careful, thoughtful, inclusive language came from the military.

want to fight any more. Now, gentlemen, that's a disaster of the
first water. Seeing corpses makes people sick to the stomach. But
that's what war is about. Corpses. But what if we could develop a
pill that cured the sickness? A pill that removes fear? Let me tell
you, we're working on it. That's just one thing. You know what
ESP means? Extrasensory perception. I don't believe in it myself.
But what if it works? What if there really are people who can see
across geographical barriers? Do you realize **how important that
could be for spying on the Russians**? We could know everything
they're doing, everything they're thinking. It may sound crazy, but
we're working on that, too. And that brings me to the reason I'm
here."

He had been talking directly to John. But now he looked at
everyone, and his gaze came to rest on me.

"Do you know what SOI means?" he asked.

He seemed to be asking me. "No," I said, almost automatically.
Then I remembered Mr. I. Crane. I hadn't thought of him since
our meeting. Wasn't that the name, the initial letters, of his organization? I thought so. Society of Icarus. But I didn't really know
that. It was just a guess. Colonel Law was still looking at me, as
if giving me time to change my answer. "No," I repeated. "I don't
know what it means. The British had something during the war,
didn't they? SOE? Something like that?"

"Special Ops," Law said. "No, this is different." He continued to look at me as if expecting the right answer to come forth.
My eyes dropped; I saw the pad I had put on the coffee table,
leaned forward, picked up the pencil and began to doodle. I drew
a square, then put it in perspective to make it a cube. I remembered reading somewhere that the principle of perspective hadn't
been discovered until the Renaissance. It seemed odd to me that

cube My dad specialized in making one sort of origami. An empty paper box. *See* Empty Boxes.

him In wondering whether or not this "nut" was based on someone real, I found instead the sad story of Albert Birney Seip, a World War I veteran and student at Cornell who jumped from the Washington Monument to his death in 1923. Seip suffered from PTSD.

executive From Shipley's dictionary: **executive, execution**, *See* refrain.

I could almost unconsciously incorporate this elusive idea into a casual doodle, as if I had been born understanding it—the obviousness of the unknown, once it is known. I tried to put an open lid onto the **cube**, to make it into a box, but I got it wrong; the way I drew it, the lid didn't fit the box. Still, the idea was there, and what had been a solid cube, now appeared to my eye to be an empty container.

I looked up. Colonel Law was still fixedly staring at me. I shrugged my shoulders. "You got me," I said. "What's SOI?"

Law relaxed and leaned back in his chair. "Let me put it to you this way," he resumed. "Do you remember a month or so ago a story in the papers about this nut who climbed the Washington Monument?"

John broke in. "Yeah, I remember that. They had to take **him** off in a helicopter, right?"

"Right. Normally that's not something we could be expected to be interested in, but, you see, I realized that there's a beautiful firing line straight from the top of the monument into the White House. A sniper could sit up there and take a pot shot at the President any time he passed a window."

It occurred to me that the sniper would have a rather hard time escaping detection in such a spot, but I said nothing.

"So we got interested in the case. In fact, I sent Phoebe down to police headquarters to check it out. You know we're not set up for operations. I want to talk about that later. There are only a few of us in Westhem, and we aren't supposed to be in operations anyway. We're **executive**. Don't forget that."

I could see that John was mulling that over seriously, flagging it as a piece of deep wisdom. "They're executive," he would say, "not operations," and the vacuity of the statement would

Leonard Park Leonard Park is the name of a city park in Mount Kisco, New York. My dad passed it every day on his way to work. I never thought of it as a man's name before and can imagine the laugh my dad had when he realized Leonard Park was his character. Now I wonder if Leonard Park might be related to Ed Park. Ed is also an editor. Do all editors fly? Do editors dream they are flying? Lila Wallace built a Japanese pagoda in Leonard Park. I would go there after doctor's visits and a trip to Friendly's for ice cream. I was born a block away from the park. My dad died a block away from the park. Four of his grandchildren were born a block away from Leonard Park years after he was dead.

lame in one leg Possibly based on my dad's friend Edward Ziegler, a very witty and kind man who had had polio as a child. He was an editor too. Did Mr. Ziegler know how to fly without wings? He was the ghostwriter of *Word Power*, *Reader's Digest's* vocabulary and etymology section. Imagine, a vocabulary section in a magazine! Mr. Ziegler worked on the Philippe Petit story, played and built harpsichords, and wrote five books. One story I remember being told is that his wife, Sally, also an amazing person, gave birth in the car on their way to the hospital. I wish I knew whether or not Mr. Ziegler had had flying dreams.

momentarily suck the air out of the room he was in, stupefying all in attendance.

"Phoebe did a good detective job." He shot a glance in her direction. "She found out the man's name. It's **Leonard Park**."

Yeah, I thought, it was in the paper.

"She found out what he does, and oddly enough, he's in your line of work, yours specifically, Sam. He's an associate editor on Publisher's Forum. You heard of it?"

"Yes," I said, "we're subscribers."

"Good," he said. "That gives us an inside track."

"A lot of people subscribe," I added. "It's a trade magazine about books and publishing and book marketing."

"What I mean," Law said, "is that you would have a perfectly normal reason to be in touch with this Leonard Park, right, to call him up, have lunch with him and so on. Because, you see, it turned out Mr. Leonard Park couldn't account for how he got up to the top of the Washington Monument. Couldn't account, or wouldn't say. He insisted that he just found himself up there, didn't know how he got there, and sure as hell couldn't get himself down."

"I thought he climbed up like a mountain climber," I said.

"That was what the papers said," Law reminded me. "But Phoebe found out that the police hadn't found any climbing gear, no ropes, no pitons, no special shoes, nothing, and when they checked out Mr. Park's background, he had no history of mountain climbing, or even walking up hills. For one thing, he's sixty years old and **lame in one leg**. The police think he was flown in, heloed up there, same way they got him off. And that's what I tend to think too. But there wasn't any proof, and finally they had to let him go."

Bulgaria Shout out to Dimi, friend of my dad's, born and raised in Sofia. Also an editor. Did Dimi know how to fly?

Easthem Adopting the language of the enemy.

West Eighties My sister Lizzie's old neighborhood.

bright and early The "girl" Phoebe does all the work. A real Nancy Drew. While I was able to stop the narrative earlier so that Phoebe did not have to do the men's bidding, here comes the truth: Phoebe does all the work and gets no credit.

"Did he have a gun?" I asked. "A rifle?"

"Not on him," Law answered. "But, of course, first thing he'd do, he'd drop it, let it fall, and a confederate would pick it up."

"Oh," I said, "he had confederates?"

"Of course. How else? These people are very slick. Probably trained in Moscow, or more likely, Sofia."

"In **Bulgaria**?" I asked.

"You got it."

"Jesus," John exclaimed.

"But that's **Easthem**," I said. "How does Westhem come into it?"

"Smart boy," he said. He looked at John. "You got one smart boy here, John." He turned back to me. "It's like this. I asked Phoebe to keep our Mr. Park under surveillance after the police let him go. Well, he went down to Dulles, got himself onto the shuttle for New York, came up here and went back to work. He lives alone in the **West Eighties**. Rides the subway back and forth to work. Doesn't see anybody much. Doesn't have many friends, doesn't eat out, doesn't go to the theater. He took in a movie one night, then went back to his apartment. And in the lobby of his building when he got back, there's a man waiting for him. They go up together, and as far as Phoebe can figure out, he never left. She never saw him anyway. Probably he went down a back way. Phoebe was there **bright and early** the next morning to pick up on Mr. Park. He went to work as usual. It was Friday. She waited around. At quitting time, he came out, went to a restaurant, had dinner and then afterwards he just sat there. Right, Phoebe? Every once in a while he looked at his watch, but otherwise he sat there. He had to be expecting a meeting, a drop, some message from someone. But nothing happened. About seven-thirty, he got

ll5 115 might have been closer to my brother Andy's actual address on Watts. It was a wonderful apartment back before that was a fancy part of town, though, in truth, it was already heading that way. We would dim the lights in Andy's place so we could better watch Bette Midler in her apartment across the street.

indulgent My father is making fun of people who draw absurd conclusions from a bunch of random evidence. He is making fun of my purpose and process for this entire book. He is also making fun of the way his mind worked. One of his favorite driving games was assigning meaning to the letters of strangers' license plates, as if the random letters revealed deep truths. For example, FCPB 637 ahead of us at a stoplight might swiftly become Fast Car, Pea Brain to my dad.

up, left a tip and walked out. But he didn't go home. That was unusual—unless he was going to a movie. But he didn't. He got on the subway and rode downtown. He got off at Canal and then walked down to Watts. He went into number 115."

Colonel Law was retrieving this information from the open file before him, to which he made frequent reference, occasionally flipping a page over. "Inside, he rang a mailbox buzzer, was admitted, and went upstairs. Phoebe waited. In about five minutes, a man appeared, the same man she had seen meeting Mr. Park in his apartment lobby. He went in and rang the same buzzer, was admitted and went up. Phoebe waited some more. Half an hour, right, Pheeb? But no one else showed. She went into the little vestibule where the mailboxes were and checked out the name slot. It didn't have a name. Anyway, we don't think it's a name. The paper in the slot read SOI."

"Maybe it stands for Sofia," John said.

The colonel gave him an **indulgent** look. "Maybe. We don't think so. Phoebe tried the door. It was locked. She didn't want to ring the buzzer. Too dangerous. But as she was looking around, she saw a card on the floor. A business card. She picked it up. It read, I. Crane, Consultant."

"I suppose anybody could have dropped it," I said.

"Wait," the colonel cautioned me. "Phoebe went outside again, took up her post. In about half an hour two men came down the stairs. It was our Mr. Park and his unknown friend. They were looking for something in the entranceway. They scouted all around the floor, opened the outside door and looked there, then went back inside and upstairs again. Whatever they were looking for, they didn't find, and the only thing that was missing was the card that Phoebe picked up. Ergo, one of those men is named

Ima Hogg Whenever we talked about people with unusual names, my mom told me a story about a father who wanted boys so badly that he named his daughters Hell and Damn. I have three daughters. People sometimes say to me, "Keep trying," or cluck their disappointment at my girl-heavy family. These same people ask me how I will afford three weddings. I wonder if these people actually know any girls.

Chitzen-itza My parents were once invited to visit Chichen Itza with friends. My father, who was terrified of heights (how does that relate to his flying dreams?), was dizzy and trembling at the top of the Mayan pyramid. My mom had to sit beside him, calm him down, and slowly walk him back to the ground. This same trip, they had come to know the musicians at the restaurant where their friends ate dinner every night. As their friends sat down to eat, they were surprised by a most unusual floor show. My parents, somewhat disguised in dancing costumes, having no idea what they were doing, began to perform.

I. Crane, and we know it isn't Mr. Park. Does the initial I. suggest anything to you?"

"Ivan," John said.

"Yes," the colonel said, "or Igor. How about you, Sam?"

"Well, given the last name, I'd guess Ichabod. But who the hell would name his kid Ichabod Crane?"

"People are pretty strange," the colonel said. "What about **Ima Hogg**? But you're right, it isn't Ichabod. We ran a check on Mr. I. Crane. Turns out his name is Icarus. The FBI had a file on him because he once got into trouble in the Yucatan, and the local consulate had to bail him out and get him back to the U.S."

"What kind of trouble?" I asked.

"Odd case. He was trespassing on the pyramid at **Chitzen-itza**. They're very fussy about that sort of thing. He was up on top of the thing—someplace he wasn't supposed to be, and got arrested. The consulate managed to smooth it over."

"Is that the connection with Westhem?"

"Exactly. You ever look at a map of the Carribbean? Most people here in the United States don't realize how far out the Yucatan sticks. It's in the Central Time Zone. Guess who its nearest neighbor is."

"I take it you mean off-shore?" I said.

"Yes. Off-shore."

"I don't have to guess," I said. "It's Cuba."

"Exactly. Suggestive, right?"

To the suspicious sort, I supposed it was suggestive. Actually, the fact that Mr. I. Crane had been found trespassing on a Mayan pyramid—trespassing up on *top* of it—was a whole lot more suggestive to me. But I didn't say anything about that.

"The F.B.I.'s been keeping an eye on Mr. Crane ever since.

You begin to see how it fits together Me, right now to you.

Actually, I didn't You, right now to me.

divided the world into two camps, those with him, those against him. *See* Citizens of the Peace.

sodomize all children below the age of eleven Forty years before Pizzagate—the conspiracy theory that Hillary Clinton's campaign manager's emails contained coded messages revealing a Democratic Party–led child sex ring—my dad saw where America's divisions were heading.

Funny thing. He keeps showing up in the Yucatan. He's been spotted there several times. Coba. Uxmal. Tulum. Those are all sites of Mayan ruins. So they ran a check on the airlines. No Mr. I. Crane listed on the manifests. No one matching his identity, even when the airline people were alerted to his identity, given a photograph of the man. You know what that means?"

"No," I said.

He viewed me with disappointment. His voice took on a hushed tone. "Clandestine," he said.

I must have looked stupefied.

"You begin to see how it fits together," he said with a smile of satisfaction.

Actually, I didn't. Probably that's why I looked stupefied. I was astounded at the stupidity of his whole edifice of conjecture. At my age I could look back a ways and, looking back, it seemed to me that I had always distrusted those who had substituted a dogma or an idea for the infinite variety of human motivation and action. Colonel Law **divided the world into two camps, those with him, those against him.** When people manifested their differences with him, or even their indifference to his fervid ambitions, he imagined a cabal, secretly dedicated to his destruction. If, to take the most mundane of examples, he found himself frustrated by those who opposed building the B-1 bomber, he was unable to grant to his opponents any but the most vile and, at the same time, grandiose motives. They wished to raze the foundations of democracy, abrogate all religious and spiritual tenets, and, probably, **sodomize all children below the age of eleven.** His enemies had no individual coloration. They were all the same. That what he feared was what he wanted had never occurred to

Cocaine. Marijuana. My dad's addiction helped him be nonjudgmental. Everyone had troubles. Everyone was good and bad. Years in twelve-step meetings and rehab introduced him to people from every walk of life. Some of his friends were addicts and drunks; all of them, as he came to know, were human.

natural connection The ever-present danger in making connections between unrelated things, as I do, is that a person might draw conclusions that are wrong, hateful, and bruising.

worlthey, betw I don't know if this abrupt and disturbed language is because the digital file had not been updated in many years and crumbled when I opened it—like Chuckie's Funnies Book—or if this is simply where he one day stopped work on this chapter, right in the middle of a word.

him. His mission was to safeguard the world. Once he controlled everything, only then would the world be safe.

"How does it fit together?" I asked.

"Drugs," he replied. "**Cocaine. Marijuana.**"

"Yeah," said John, "I see." And I suppose he did. As I've indicated, he was an ideologue himself, although not as smart nor as dedicated as Colonel Law appeared to be. In the mental world that they occupied there was a **natural connection** between Cuba, drugs, Bulgaria, rock-and-roll, SALT II, Darwin, and the Sierra Club.

Lieutenant Noble, the colonel's aide, had scarcely said a word so far. Now he stirred in his chair, and leaned forward. Enemies had no individual coloration. They were all the same. That what he fear. But in the **worlthey** occupied there was a natural connection **betw**

Ghosts in the Machine

Only the second chapter and things are starting to break down. I didn't alter that last sentence. I'm pretty sure my dad wrote this book after he got sober, but maybe not. My mom only vaguely recalls him working on this book, so it's hard to pin down a date. When he was still drinking, I'd find pages of text rolled in his typewriter in the morning. The words on the page were filled with typos and holes. Hard to read, drunk. But a lot of the writing I do stone-cold sober is filled with typos and holes. Maybe the typos and holes in his manuscript are because I was careless about bringing his digital files into the future with me, through each new software upgrade and technological improvement that makes our original digital files unreadable. Did I miss a few years of updates in my software? Yes, I did, and now a number of his files crumble into nonsense words. Or maybe that's how they always were. It's hard to write a book.

I inherited a hand-me-down electric breast pump from my friend Jenny. I'd wager I'm not the only new mother who heard her breast pump talking to her. In the machine's whirl—a tight system that relies on boob suction to create a vacuum—the motor spoke to me. It said, "Meat tower," over and over again. Robotically. "Meat tower. Meat tower. Meat tower," while I harvested four to eight ounces of breast milk from my body. I'd picture a skyscraper-sized hunk of gyro meat roasting on a stick, or a mile-high pile of thinly sliced prosciutto, a pastrami sandwich from Katz's. A meat tower. Was I the tower of meat my borrowed breast pump referred to? The inventor Nikola Tesla called humans meat machines, and certainly I'd never felt this assessment to be more accurate than during the period of my life when my body made food to feed three other humans.

Why, of all the messages the ghost in this machine might have to relate, was "meat tower" the one I heard? How is "meat tower" different from the message in your breast pump? Or the words your elderly dishwasher says to you each night after supper?

The ghosts in my machines speak a lot because I have an affinity for aged devices. I don't really like new things. Waste is a design flaw and capitalism is a sick system. I don't like to make trash. I had a college crush on a man who produced only one small paper bag of garbage over an entire year. I thought that was extremely sexy. Old things are usually made better and more interesting, even if some of the machines in my life suffer from dementia or hearing loss. I have an EarthLink email account, got it in the nineties. It delivers about 90 percent of my emails. It's like the Pony Express of emails. It's exciting. Will my messages make it through? Maybe. Maybe not. My email address practices the Japanese principle of wabi-sabi, an aesthetic that finds beauty in the imperfect, impermanent, and incomplete. People tease me about my email address and I think, Oh, you poor follower of the new, surfer of trends.

My phone is ancient; my laptop is old; my car is geriatric. I hate putting tools out to pasture when they still have usefulness. My daughters are embarrassed to arrive at school in our old jalopy. They groan when I tell them the real shame is people who buy new cars before they've used up the ones they already own. They can't believe that I still wear clothes I owned in high school. But I hate our disposable way of life. Plus, I respect a device that acknowledges its mortality, shows its age. Faulty devices are porous and allow space enough for difference and different outcomes. They are anti-bureaucracy. In that way, I think aged devices can help us be anti-fascist too, can help us stay open and nonjudgmental as they remind us that the only certainty is the cycle of decay. *See* A Thousand Deaths.

My dad smoked cigarettes most of his life. He carried with him little packages of death, memento mori. He kept his smokes close, as if they were his dearest friends, until those cigarettes finally did what they had always promised they would do: They murdered him. People do have to die. I understand that. In what way do you keep death and decay present? A rotting tree? A rotting tooth? A torn shirt? A broken machine? A broken mind?

Thomas Edison tried to invent an electronic megaphone for talking to the dead. I wish I had one. With all these older tools and devices around, maybe I do. Maybe it's just a little bit broken, and in that brokenness the dead, or at least the death inside us, is able to speak.

Citizens of the Peace

I took my kids to Del's Dairy Creme for milkshakes. They ate their food on the hood of our car, and afterward they did a little dance on the roof. I'd been alone with them all week. I could see them well enough from where I was sitting at the picnic table, but I needed a break from the constant watchfulness expected of mothers.

Almost immediately, two nurses in bright medical garments showed up. "Whose kids are these?" one asked.

"Mine." I didn't look at her.

"They're climbing on your car."

I had a direct view. "They do that all the time." I wouldn't look at her. The hormonal brew occurring inside my skin made me feel a touch Bruce Banner, thinking, Please, Hulk, don't hurt her. I packed up my family. The nosy nurse had spoiled this small pleasure.

Later, at home, my kids were upstairs and I was out back when someone knocked. A sheriff, six feet tall, with a shaved head and a Kevlar vest, a few lethal weapons, and wraparound shades he didn't remove when he spoke. "Ma'am, were you at Del's?" That nurse had called the cops on me.

As a girl I thought "cops" was an acronym for Citizens of the Peace. I don't know what gave me that idea, but I believed there was a force of people, Citizens of the Peace. Now I see the word "force" is tricky and "cops" is no acronym. New York City police once wore buttons made out of copper.

If my daughters saw a person dressed like a storm trooper in our yard, it'd be months of nightmares. I tried to say the right things to make him leave. "Yes."

"Were your kids on the roof of your car?"

"I didn't know that was illegal." I kept my voice low.

"It's not." Then a spontaneous investigation into my parenting. "Do your kids have proper car seats?"

There's got to be someone better we can call than this scary creature if a person needs help taking care of their children. Did his visit make me a better parent? Not at all. It stressed me out. I bet I even yelled at my kids that night.

At a 1974 show at Don Cornelius's Soul Train nightclub, Richard Pryor told the story of a man on a date who gets pulled over by a white cop. Pryor noted that a white man getting pulled over might say, "Hey, officer, yes, glad to be of help," while a Black man must say, "I am reaching into my pocket for my license, 'cause I don't want to be no motherfucking accident." The audience laughed, familiar with the scenario Pryor sketched. The insults and injustices pile up. "All right, put your hands up, take your pants down!" The audience laughed even louder as the scene he described grew more and more inhumane. Just when Pryor had his audience rolling in their seats, he landed the brutal truth quietly, the cycle of violence that is unleashed by white fear on Black communities. "You go home, beat your kids and shit. You going to take that shit out on somebody."

I convinced the cop to leave. I used my whiteness, my male spouse, and a yard that had recently been mown to get rid of him. It felt like crying uncle to a bully. It also felt like protecting my daughters. I'm good at pretending to be a female who is tolerable, digestible to sexists. A survival skill I've worked on over the years. I can pretend my life aligns with the narrow parameters of normal the cop was there to enforce, even if it makes me feel like a coward afterward.

Silla, the immigrant mother in Paule Marshall's *Brown Girl, Brownstones*, works tirelessly to buy a brownstone, to have a house, in order to shield her two daughters from racist, sexist America. She wants to keep their bodies hidden and thus un-abused. Silla participates in that American word, "safety." But her daughter Selina does not want to be hidden in such narrow confines. She has done nothing wrong. She wants to dance. She wants to be seen.

Debra Harrell, a South Carolina mom, left her nine-year-old with a cell phone at a very popular playground where shade and water were available while Harrell went to her job, a shift at a restaurant nearby. Another adult at the park called the cops. Harrell's daughter was temporarily placed in foster care and Harrell was arrested. Harrell's Black. Her story is not unusual. How many times each day does normal mean white? Male? Wealthy? I send my daughters to the park all the time. Isn't that what parks are for? Places for children to play? Last night I was out walking just before dark. The park was full, but full of boys. Harrell made the healthy choice for her daughter. Rather than staying home fixated on a screen, hidden away, Harrell's daughter could be outside, in nature, with other people near in case of the very slim chance her daughter might require adult assistance.

Madeleine L'Engle writes, "Stay angry, little Meg. You will need all your anger now."

Harrell's story haunts me in a thousand ways. I am particularly chilled by how we tell our daughters they need to hide, that the outdoors is dangerous, that nature is no place for a girl.

My village does not have a police force. That doesn't mean we don't have cops. My village pays sixteen thousand dollars a year for outside officers from three different entities to come through on patrol. One winter in a blizzard, eighteen inches of snow, my three daughters and I went out for a walk. The streets were empty as everyone knew better than to drive in a blizzard. What freedom for us to walk down the middle of the street, a freedom not always available. Theodore Kaczynski writes in his manifesto:

> A technological advance that appears not to threaten free-dom often turns out to threaten it very seriously later on. For example, consider motorized transport. A walking man formerly could go where he pleased, go at his own pace without observing any traffic regulations . . . But the introduction of motorized transport soon changed soci-ety in such a way as to restrict greatly man's freedom of locomotion.

In a blizzard, the streets were ours, freed from the tyranny of cars. At least until, from a long way off we heard a vehicle approaching. We made our way out of the road in plenty of time. It was a cop. We kept walking, but I heard him slow as he approached. He rolled down his window and told my daughters that it was not safe for them to be outside in a snowstorm. The officer was twenty years my junior. Kaczynski writes "walking man," not walking human, not walking girl. Kaczynski also, of course, stayed so angry he turned himself into an explosive murderer.

Knowing this officer would never say anything so idiotic and fear-laced to a group of boys, I snapped. "You, Officer, are the only dangerous thing out here." He spewed some more fear and stupidity on my daughters and me. We kept walking, and eventually he drove off, but the damage was done. My oldest said, "Ma, let's just go home." I refused, and our nature walk through wonder became a forced march ruined by male fear and control.

My daughters often play "What would you do if you had a million dollars?" I know my answer. I'd make a place in nature, in the deep woods, where girls could stay outside as long as they wanted, a place where girls could be with trees and moss and rivers. Where they could walk alone at night through woods reserved for girls.

I did nothing illegal at Del's, but as the cop left my house that day he issued a warning. My name would be added to a watch list. I didn't ask, "A list of overwhelmed working moms who go out for milkshakes?" Instead I spent the next few months scared he'd show up again and try to talk to my kids, armed with further fabricated reasons why I'm an unfit mother in his universe. A good friend is undocumented. What if she had been at my house? Had I endangered her life by taking my kids out for shakes? The nurse who reported me didn't consider the web of connection between lives: the three-day walk through the desert (water gone after day two) that our friend had survived in order to escape her town in Mexico, where her brothers and cousins had already been murdered.

Years later we had to find a new pediatrician when ours moved. And there she was, the nurse who had called the cops on me. She was taking my daughter's blood pressure. I see Molly the nurse at least three or four times a year now and I never say anything. I stare at her with a creepy eye, a look that means, I remember you and I know what you did. She probably has no idea that we are the same family she called the cops on. What angry filter was she looking at us with that day at Del's? Eyes that read me as a child abuser. Sometimes I think we should switch doctors, but in truth, I relish the moments in the exam room with Molly. I sit silently, smiling, taking a read on her righteousness, trying to understand where it comes from and how she divides the world into good over here, bad over there.

We forgot how to speak to each other. How to say, "Are you okay? Do you need some help? I am worried for your safety." We are sunk in a me-first mindset where the only code of conduct remaining is, Me and mine and to hell with the rest of you.

Why do we call the cops on each other? What does this have to do with my dad's book?

People call the cops as if calling on God, believing in a force that is bigger and stronger than the individual, one that enforces some sort of universal law, moral reason, or code of conduct. But what arrives when people call the cops? An individual with his or her own deep faults and biases. We call the cops looking for some way to rein in our fear without ever examining what it is we are afraid of. So, what are we afraid of?

Mostly, I think people are afraid to die. That's how this relates to my dad's book. I return to James Baldwin again and the problem that white Americans do not believe in death. Or at least we want to pretend that it can be thwarted. That it is not part of our perfectly designed lives. Why did we take my father to the hospital when he was getting ready to die? Because we believed that hospitals stop death. My dad should have died in our house. He'd lived there so long and loved it, but we were scared of death. We thought hospitals could stop death. So, when he collapsed in our house, we brought his body to the hospital. They kept him alive a few days longer, a few days filled with the anxiety of a family trying to stop death. Nurse Molly works in a broken health care system. One that very often helps people and that I am grateful for, but one that also sometimes floods our bodies with drugs that do more harm than good. Still, Americans love going to the doctor. *See* Queer Theorem.

Our dread of death gets twisted into wild ministrations of anxiety and fear that manifest in the cruelty of control. Think of the model of agriculture that applies killing pesticides or plants monocrops that deplete the soil in the pursuit of higher yields. An agriculture so controlled that it kills humans, animals, and ultimately our planet.

Like Nurse Molly—who, in pursuit of some idea of safety, forgot our web of connection—our fear of death turns other humans into an anonymous cloud of otherness and difference, a place to put the blame. Policing, control, and classification deal in binaries: good guys or bad guys, dead or alive, right or wrong. They work with a notion that there is one concept of normal to be upheld. In 1995, members of the Aum Shinrikyo cult killed thirteen people and injured thousands by releasing sarin gas in the Tokyo subway. A few years later Haruki Murakami published *Underground*, his meditation on the attacks. The book collects

Murakami's interviews with people affected by the sarin, both victims and perpetrators. In the essay "Blind Nightmare: Where Are We Japanese Going?" Murakami writes that after the terrorist attack, "people all jumped onto the 'right,' 'sane,' 'normal' bandwagon. There was nothing complicated about it." He writes, "We crane our necks and look around us, as if to ask: where did all *that* come from?" The answer, of course, is "Not me."

In his story "CivilWarLand in Bad Decline," George Saunders assesses the truly paltry options for being an American man that binary thinking produces. There is the warrior, the worrier, and the capitalist. Saunders labels the amorphous and shifting cloud of fear white Americans carry. The amusement park CivilWar-Land is being attacked by "gangs." A reader never fully sees these gangs, but a shapeless fear of them hangs over the story like a dark fog, a worry that a gang might attack paying park visitors at any moment. The narrator, a middle-management sort, sees the absurdity in the word "gangs," but lacks the courage to make change. He worries he'll be fired if he speaks up. That ever-present fear of not being able to provide the American Dream (whatever that is) for one's children. "Mr. Alsuga believes the solution to the gang problem is Teen Groups. I tell him that's basically what a gang is, a Teen Group." They hire Quinn, a "world-class worrywart," to meet "force with force." Quinn's "dirt poor, with six kids." In other words, he needs the money. Throughout the story parents excuse horrifying behaviors, including murder, in order to provide for their children. "Is this the life I envisioned for myself? My God no. I wanted to be a high jumper. But I have two of the sweetest children ever born. I go in at night and look at them in their fairly expensive sleepers and think: There are a couple of kids who don't need to worry about freezing to death or being cast out to the wolves . . . They may not know the value of a dollar, but it's my intention to see they never need to." By the end of the story, the Vietnam vet hired to deal with the "gang" problem, Sam, has murdered a teen group of bird-watchers (I think of Chris Cooper being accosted by Amy Cooper) and a high school student who stole a handful of penny candy. Saunders's story is drawn with the blood of America's many wars. I feel the poisoned land underfoot and all the violence America tries to bury underground. We rarely catch sight of these purported "gangs" outside of the ones created in our own fearful minds. They are wisps and figments, ghostly bodies seen from the corner of an eye.

This sort of fear, the fear of the parent, the fear that you made your children's deaths, can be crippling. See A Thousand Deaths. One night, when my daughters were still babies, I heard a buzzing. All three girls shared a bedroom. In the morning the buzzing was even louder. By the end of the day, the ceiling above their cribs and bed had begun to melt, like some possessed and slimy monster from a horror film. Or that's the way my sleep-deprived mind saw it. The wallboard dissolved into pulp. The buzzing got louder and louder. My mother arrived. "Yellow jackets," she said. My husband tucked his sweatshirt into his pants, his pants into his boots. He went to the attic with a can of poison but came flying, actually flying, back down the stairs when he pulled up the insulation to reveal a hive of yellow jackets as large as a re-frigerator. That night I believed in evil. Yellow jackets became a repository for all my fears and hatreds. Why does life come with death? That night I also believed that somehow, maybe with a can of poison, I might be able to control death, to fight a war with the yellow jackets, or Lyme ticks, or car crashes, or fill-in-the-blank.

In *River Dreams*, Barry Lopez asks the cottonwood trees about
the heron's dreams. He is aware that these "too young trees" will
lie. Lopez tells the heron what the cottonwood said. "You had a
premonition in a nightmare. An enormous owl arrived while you
slept and took your daughter away, pinioned in his gray fists.
You woke, bolt upright, in the middle of the night to find her
there, undisturbed beside you. You aired your feathers, glared
into the moon-stilled space over the water and went uneasily
back to sleep. In the morning—your first glance—the limb was
empty."

The soil of our land bears the stain of our violent history of
fear and control. Dr. Adrienne Keene writes, "The system in what
is currently known as the US isn't 'broken.' It was designed by
male white supremacist slaveowners on stolen Indigenous land to
protect their interests. It's working as it was designed."

In Tobe Hooper's film *Poltergeist*, a wonderfully American-
named family, the Freelings, move into a home built over the
remains of a graveyard. The developer moved the headstones,
but not the bodies, a cover-up that feels so true to whitewashed
American history. In the film, a spiritual medium, also exuber-
antly named, Tangina, helps the family escape, but the house itself is doomed and eventually swallowed up by a muddy sea of
coffins and angry skeletons that erupt from below.

Isabel Wilkerson's book *Caste: The Origins of Our Discontents*
is an unblinking look at America's violent history that makes me
long for such a *Poltergeist*-ian eruption, a bring-out-your-dead
eruption. Wilkerson's book *is* such an eruption. Here, she ex-
humes the bodies and the truth of those bones. Wilkerson lays
clear the bloody and unstable surface on which America stands.
She writes of our "belief in a human pyramid as willed by God."

Americans have taken that firm and hateful belief and constructed systems and architectures based on the evil stories we tell about the other, fabulist tales that reduce human lives into punching bags for white fear.

Europeans might have believed they were buying the land from the Native people living here, while Native people already understood the absurdity of ownership, particularly the absurdity of imagining that a life-form as minor as a human could believe he owned a mountain, a stream, a meadow, or a beach. I think about my mom's house, so full of objects, and how that fullness is somehow related to an idea that if she owns all these things, she will not die.

When was the last time you asked the soil who owns it? What did it say?

I know people who live on a mountaintop, in a gated community, in a house with multiple guns, guarded by an alarm system. They are generous people. They love making friends and traveling. They help strangers. They welcome all people into their home. They serve their community. I don't understand what they are protecting. Capitalism has sold an idea that one might purchase protection without regard for whether we have anything to protect. My daughters play "How will we protect ourselves from the zombie hordes in the apocalypse?" They don't like it when I say, "What if we just shared what we have with the zombie hordes?" I'm not really sure I believe that, but I'm just putting it out there as one option. In a Möbius strip of fear, do people have guns in order to protect their guns? The message in the marketing of alarms and security teams is, Buy this, pay for it, and you won't have to die. Good luck with that.

In *Underground* Murakami invokes a comparison between the

Tokyo subway attacks and the Kobe earthquake that struck two months later. Calamities that arose from underground. "Common to both was an element of overwhelming violence . . . a tenuous parallel perhaps, yet to those most affected, the suffering was frighteningly similar." In America we could compare the sky-born violence of Hurricane Katrina with 9/11 to ask, Is violence natural? To ask, Where does violence come from? Are we violent because we are scared to die? Is there violence in the earth-crushing pressures of colliding tectonic plates? Is violence man-made or natural as a hurricane? How man-made are our hurricanes? How man-made are men, humans? In what ways are we collectively responsible for each shooter, rapist, abuser, racist, terrorist? For each tornado, fire, and flood? Do you feel the violence of storms in your body?

Back to Frog and Worm. Mr. Katagiri asks Frog why Worm is angry.

> Nobody knows what Worm is thinking inside that murky head of his. Few have ever seen him. He is usually asleep . . . his brain has turned to jelly as he sleeps. If you ask me, I'd guess he probably isn't thinking anything at all, just lying there and feeling every little rumble and reverberation that comes his way, absorbing them into his body and storing them up. And then, through some kind of chemical process, he replaces most of them with rage. Why this happens I have no idea.

Worm and Frog are thin-skinned creatures. One might say they are insecure, without security. They serve as an early warning system. Consider the surging numbers of mutant frogs with too many limbs, or too few. The U.S. Geological Survey, Department of the Interior, writes:

> Amphibians are good indicators of significant environmental changes. Amphibians, unlike people, breathe at least partly through their skin, which is constantly exposed to everything in their environment. Consequently, their bodies are much more sensitive to environmental factors such as disease, pollution, toxic chemicals, ultraviolet radiation, and habitat destruction. The worldwide occurrences of amphibian declines and deformities could be an early warning that some of our ecosystems, even seemingly pristine ones, are seriously out of balance.

In Toni Morrison's *Beloved*, the white slave owners are "men without skin," horrific, desensitized monsters who appear to feel nothing as they torture other humans.

Like Worm, America absorbed the violence and anger of 9/11 and unleashed it on Iraq, a country that had nothing to do with the attacks of 9/11. Did that relieve our stress, the way an earthquake releases the stress of the land? The way yelling at your kids releases the stress of not having enough money, of having suffered abuse? I don't think so. Was Molly better off after she called the cops on me?

Department of the Interior: What happens to the dirt, the trees, the birds, the people of a place where violence and war have raged for centuries, where people have been slaughtered, where people have been enslaved, brutalized, impoverished, incarcerated, and controlled in order to deny death? What happens to land that has been stripped of its riches, polluted by an uncaring populace? Where does the land hold its fury, its contamination of cruelty and injustice? When you drink the water that has coursed through these damaged places, what part of that anger and violence do you consume? Does America's kindness, which is large and local, ever balance out the cruelty?

In *The Kept Private*, a play written by Jeremy Davidson of Storyhorse Documentary Theater, Davidson digs deep into the soil of the Hudson Valley. The text and story are drawn from interviews Davidson conducted with the Earth scientist Brian McAdoo, as well as from historical documents, letters, and the Revolutionary War pension application of Andrew Frazier of Milan, New York. Frazier was a free Black man who enlisted with the colonial army and then fought a bureaucratic battle to prove his service for the rest of his life. No one believed he was a free Black man. Like the finest American ghost story ever written, Toni Morrison's *Beloved*, Davidson's play is punctuated and haunted by the holes in our violent history, particularly a history that Americans cover up: the story of slavery in the North. McAdoo's involvement is striking to me, an admission that we need geologists to know our history, to look deep enough into the dirt and read the rocks. The play ends with a search for the burial grounds of enslaved people and these lines from McAdoo:

> One of my students did a course on tracking. So she's really good at seeing things most of us don't. And one of the things she pointed out was that when the wind blows . . . the leaves will collect wherever the ground is just a little bit lower. And you can see it—sometimes there will be three headstones . . . but then right next to those, will be a fourth spot, with leaves collecting in the shape of a 2ft wide 6ft long rectangle. Where someone else was buried . . . without a marker . . . just . . . leaves.

Can poisoned land be redeemed? Maybe, but first listen to the urgency, know what happened there, read the land where you live. Keep digging. Who planted that tree? Who built your apartment? What stones did they use? Where did those stones come from? Where does your electricity come from? Your water? What is underground beneath your feet right now? Once we understand that, then maybe we can begin to feel less terrified about the day we will return to the soil.

Danielle and Greg, friends from my village, were visiting Canada and drove into Rousseau, Ontario, another small town. Oddly enough, Rousseau had been cast to play our village in a television show. There in Canada my friends found a re-creation of our own American bakery and general store, our parking regulations, and even our zip code on the Rousseau post office. All of it reproduced for television. The crime show *Eyewitness* thought our hometown was perfect to tell the story of a triple murder, but it's cheaper to shoot television shows in Canada, so they built a fake New York town in a real Canadian town. The most haunting and silently unmentioned part of the whole strange construction is that my village did suffer a crime in the 1990s, not a triple murder but one so horrible, few people here speak of it.

There's a nature preserve near my house, 1,722 acres of land. It's an intertidal marsh. The Hudson River abuts the preserve. The Catskill Mountains are in the distance. Two bays, fed by Stony Creek and the Saw Kill, are home to cattails, wild rice, water celery, and abundant moss species. The biodiversity of life supported in this land is staggering: ospreys, snapping turtles, muskrats and beavers, Virginia rails, black ducks, flycatchers, and bald eagles, to name a very few. One might find Tawny Emperor, an uncommon butterfly; the short-nose sturgeon; estuary beggar-ticks (*Bidens bidentoides*), a flower most rare; golden club, a water plant; and a moss called fissidens that makes its sole New York appearance in these preserve lands. To list these few species is absurd, a bad attempt to capture a staggering diversity using only a handful of life-forms.

When I was new here, my sister Katy and I hiked the bays. We each carried one of my twin daughters as we walked along a tributary that empties into the Hudson. We were stopped by strange cries, like those of a woman or child in pain. The squawks were coming from a great blue heron and an owl fighting. We observed the birds for a moment before hiking on, making it home just before rain.

The day after, my friend Lisa joined us for dinner. I told her I finally explored the preserve and loved it. "You know what happened there, right?" she asked. "Some guy raped a mom and her seven-year-old daughter. They never caught him."

I look at the poison ivy growing near my house, and the ticks that carry Lyme disease, and I shudder. Bad nature, I think. Stay away from my family! Poison ivy, I think, is not like me. I am good. It is bad. I am Murakami's blind nightmare, craning my neck, looking around and asking, "Where did all *that* come from?" and the same rotten answer, "Not me." Not me. I create Us vs. Them. I create more hateful ideas of normalcy, instead of asking what part of each rapist, each act of terrorism belongs to us all. What part of poison ivy, Lyme disease, and coronavirus is me? My friend Gian Carlo Feleppa once wrote, "I found a baby deer tick and its mother might be dead. What should I do?"

It took me five years to return to the bays after Lisa told me what had happened there. During those years, the mile that separated my house from the preserve was not enough of a barrier to protect me. The rape of that child kept me awake for years. Barry Lopez writes, "I think of standing beside you when you have died of your own brooding over the water." This passage was the first time I noticed the connection between fear and mothering in the word "brood": n., *the offspring of egg-laying creatures*, and v., *to meditate over anxiously*.

A friend of mine woke in the night and found a young man downstairs in her home. She lives in a very rural area, alone with her young son. She asked the man what he was doing in her house and then she asked him to leave. He was confused. He had taken way too much Xanax and didn't fully understand where he was. He left her home, got into a neighbor's car, and smashed that car into another car, so the police showed up and the young man was taken to the hospital. When my friend talked to her neighbors later, one commented on just how lucky that young man had been in choosing my friend's house. Every other person who lived on her road owned multiple guns.

Toni Jensen's *Carry: A Memoir of Survival on Stolen Land* underscores this soil-deep knowledge. "Everywhere we live, our neighbors may commit gun violence on us or on our neighbors." One night last year I arrived home from work after dark to find my house blockaded by crime tape. Every police officer from within a twenty-mile radius had their lights flashing. My daughters were in their bedrooms thirty feet away from and looking out to the bloodstained spot where a seventeen-year-old boy had just shot a twenty-year-old in a battle over drug territory.

I still think about the child rapist who committed such terrible violence in my town, to my town. But now when I think of him, I think he must be dead, not only because I hope he is, but also because how could he go on living after he treated other humans,

a child, that way? With time, it became easier for me to walk again
in the woods. Each spring the bays birth trillium, trout lilies, and
jack-in-the-pulpits. I still think of the land, though, the ground
where violence occurred, as a toxic site in the nature preserve. In
Owls and Other Fantasies, Mary Oliver writes, "The world where
the owl is endlessly hungry and endlessly on the hunt is the world
in which I live too. There is only one world." I don't know where in
the 1,722 acres this horror took place, but I think about the flowers
in that anonymous spot, the mosses, rare and common.

So, where are our Citizens of the Peace? How do we help each
other or help ourselves without the threat of violence and control,
without letting fear overwhelm our judgment? What might such a
civil servant even look like, dressed in cruelty-free clothes, armed
with books, healthy food, drug counseling, social resources, and
calm intelligence? Imagine a force intent on peace, one that dis-
regards our fantasies of good/evil binaries and refuses measures
of control that increase anxiety, violence, or cruelty. Maybe it is
a force made up of postmenopausal women, those wise enough
to be calm. Imagine a Citizen of the Peace who helps us accept
the fact that one day we too will die, a citizen who helps us see the
death in others and love them just the same, love them and the
soil to which we will all one day return.

Queer Theorem

HAUL

It can take many years to understand the truths of a single moment. Our dates were older fishermen. If I hadn't been young and dumb, I would've understood that our dates were also drug dealers. That the reason for this fancy meal far from our town was to celebrate getting away with it all, breaking the law in a big way. I was a gangster's moll who didn't know my date was a gangster. I didn't even know he was my date. I thought he was a friend of my cousin's. Courses and cocktails kept coming.

"Dumb" is not a fair adjective when I think of the places "dumb" and discovery intersect: teenagers, new parents, failed experiments, sick people, luck. At fifteen I was so curious about the world, I was blind to danger.

How many truths can exist in one small space? A kiss, a meal, an occupation, a body, a bomb, a desire, an illness, an essay, an experiment. Camera A. Camera B. Camera Z. Camera 533.

FLOWERS

Science is observational and evidentiary. Please accept this wild bouquet of evidence I have collected.

WOLVES

I had three babies within three years' time. A huge and somewhat sudden change in my life, as if a tidal wave surprised me and deposited these small humans in my lap. Having a baby is not unusual, but that doesn't mean it isn't the strangest thing ever. The shifts are tectonic and often obscured.

If I wrote the full truth of what I was thinking during the first years mothering three girls, a reader would wonder why no one dropped me off at a sanitarium, that place where they keep all the sanity. I don't wonder anymore. I was not relieved of my mothering duties, because there was no one else to do them. My mom tried, but she was already getting tired by the time I became a mother. My dad died young. My husband was also fighting to stay afloat as a father of three and a human with a full-time job. My siblings have their own lives and children. So, another idea of truth was accepted: Samantha is fine. This kind of fine: I told my husband he was having an affair with my best friend. I told my mom I had cancer. I told my best friend wolves were circling my house and wanted to eat my babies. I told my sister there was a man living in my basement.

None of this was empirically true to anyone but me. I believed it because I felt it.

I told the lady who owns my local veggie restaurant that I was afraid the shaggy twelve-year-old foster kid down the road from my house was evil because he asked me if he could hang out with me and my three small children. He was huge and con-fused. I could not mother another and didn't want him near my children because I couldn't read his intentions toward them. His eyes roamed everywhere. Instead of putting me to bed, saying, "Shush," the vegetarian told me, "You need to buy some Mace. You need to buy a gun." I wasn't alone in losing sight of sanity.

What makes a new mother experience such an expanded reality?

Proximity to death, proximity to life. God, the abyss, the enor-mity of science and nature is right there in front of our sleep-deprived eyes, but no one miraculously appears to explain the mystery of birth or even the mystery of hormones. In fact, all the world wants to know is: *Boy or girl? Breast or bottle? Cloth or disposable? When will you go back to work? How did you lose all that weight?*

Normalize what's astonishing. Categorize and get back to work. Create capital. Ignore the beautiful abyss.

I'd growl, saliva and blood dripping from my jaws, my hair as matted as any beast's. I just made three deaths. I just made six eyeballs. I will never lose this weight.

ELECTROCUTED

From the outside, it didn't look like a great center of healing. Sleet was falling on top of old snow. Abandoned cars, trucks, tractors, busted refrigerators, and tools were strewn about the driveway and yard. A handful of metal utility sheds were stuffed with bits, bolts, and broken-down things.

The man who lived here had an interest in reproducing the

inventor Nikola Tesla's work. Lately he'd been focusing on Tesla's ideas about healing the body with electricity. I'd been invited to this house and laboratory because I'd written a book about Tesla. Though the place looked a bit like a junkyard, a friend with cancer had been receiving treatments here. He was also doing chemo. He was getting better. I was not sick, aside from the postpartum madness no one would acknowledge.

Two men met me in the driveway, or three men. I don't remember how many men met me in the driveway. I don't remember how I got inside. I worry these holes will make you doubt the truth of this story. These holes are the truth of this story. We are mortal. We are porous.

MORTAL BLUSH

What do you know? I mean, what do you know without your cyborg parts attached?

Brian Blanchfield wrote his 2016 book *Proxies: Essays Near Knowing* using no outside sources. He wrote what he knows in his body. The book contains essays on owls, peripersonal space, *locus amoenus*, sardines, confoundedness, tumbleweeds, and Man Roulette. *Proxies* makes a person feel human again. It's a corrective for a post-truth, technology-choked era because *Proxies* is really about what it means to have a body that is mortal, to live with our own damaged selves and the places where we falter. Blanchfield has included a twenty-page endnote amending, confessing, and celebrating the facts he got wrong. Here are the faults, the flesh, the holy wonder of our undigitized minds. Here's the truth of our wrongness.

What do I know? I know my memory is flawed. Or not flawed, but familiar with both decay and the imagination. I also know that one day when my children were babies, I drove to a scientist's house where I willingly, intentionally entered a room filled with two hundred thousand to three hundred thousand volts of energy. I let the electricity touch me. I'm not sure if the electricity healed me in some way, its intended purpose, but I know that it didn't kill me.

GUY

I was invited into his large garage. It was like the truck room of a fire station. Every bit of space, except a number of cleared paths, was filled with bits of projects in process. Spools and tools, rolls of wire, metal, saws, circuits, all the materials a modern inventor might require. Dashing up and down the aisles, leading me from one project to the next like the most knowledgeable docent and overly excited child, was a man, healthy seventies, casually dressed, bald and shining, talking a blue streak like one who rarely receives visitors and must use this opportunity to fill me up with all the latest reports of his work.

TESLA

When I wrote my book about Tesla, I thought he belonged to me alone. I had never heard of him before. No one had ever taught me about him in school, and certainly no one had ever named a car after him, or put him in a film. I knew only of Tesla the hair-metal band. When I discovered Tesla the poet-inventor, who built a motor powered by june bugs at age nine, and later harnessed Niagara Falls, and later imagined ways to photograph thought, it seemed I'd dreamed him into existence. Thus, he belonged to only me.

Tesla worked independently in laboratories he built himself with little corporate or military interference. He invented radio. He invented our modern AC electrical system. But as he often failed to protect his patents—not believing a person could own thunder and lightning—eventually he could no longer afford a proper, independent laboratory. He then made his inventions in his New York City hotel rooms, in his mind.

What's the difference between invention and discovery? Is it just a question of ego? Or is it one of money?

I lived with Tesla's legacy and papers for years. During that time, one hard thought kept cropping up. Everywhere I knew people who were making buildings, mugs, plays, paintings, sweaters, chocolate, operas, but I didn't know any people, except children, who were trying to fly, who were grafting DNA for wings. I didn't know anyone with a basement lab made for playing with protons. I wondered why we are well acquainted with the phrase "starving artist" while the term "starving scientist" is one I've never even heard.

A PRINCE IN A DEAD MONARCHY

Guy began by telling me he is a prince in a dead monarchy. He produced an issue of *Paris Match* to prove it. He told me that when he was a child, he was visited by the ghost of a guru. Guy strolled me through his workshop, where I saw moments of small obsessions: a copper coil he'd been winding for months, freshly machined silver filings. Guy was beaming; it seemed like it had been a long time since someone had taken him seriously. I had told him many times I was not a journalist, but still, he behaved as if I were there to finally make him famous for all the work he'd done. Though his excitement was contagious, it did little to convince me of his stability. But who was I to ask for stability? And what if stability is just another awful way of saying normal? Of saying sane? Then, who built the borders of sanity? Who decided where those walls should be?

How often was Tesla greeted by people who smiled at him as if he were a damaged child?

Then Guy said, "It's time to see the machine."

TRAILWAYS

That same fifteen-year-old summer of my fisherman/gangster date, I took an eleven-hour bus ride on a Greyhound alone. A woman seated in front of me turned back to confide, feeling she could trust me, that I might be able to help her. She said she had stumbled across a ring of Nazis. At first, I thought she meant jewelry. She wondered if I might have some connections that could expose this hate group. As an early introduction to the paranoid mind, this woman carved out a new skepticism in me. It wasn't that I didn't believe Nazis were active here. I didn't believe she was turning to me for help.

A few years later, in the early 1990s, the psychiatrist and Harvard professor John Mack published accounts of his patients' alien-abduction narratives. The narratives shared common themes: sudden appearances, large eyes, beams of light, a spaceship, a physical examination, and, afterward, increased spirituality and environmental concern for our planet. When Mack was asked whether he believed his patients had been abducted by aliens, he told the BBC, "I would never say, Yes, there are aliens taking people. I would say there is a compelling, powerful phenomenon here that I can't account for in any other way, that's mysterious. Yet I can't know what it is, but it seems to me that it invites a deeper, further inquiry." While Mack wondered if these experiences were visionary or transcendental in nature, he also believed they were no less real in their immateriality.

The dean of the Harvard Medical School recruited a committee to investigate Mack's clinical practice. The committee was chaired by Dr. Arnold Relman, the editor of *The New England Journal of Medicine*, an esteemed, peer-reviewed publication dating back to 1812. The committee found Mack to be professionally irresponsible for giving "credence whatsoever to any personal report of a direct personal contact between a human being and an extraterrestrial."

When the existence of the committee was made public, the academic community questioned the validity of the investigation. People began to worry that their own academic freedom could be questioned. After plenty of shaming, Mack's academic freedom was reaffirmed by Harvard.

THE INTERNET

I now receive email from men who also believe that Tesla belongs to them alone. Some of these men are angry that I, a woman, a non-engineer, speak for Tesla. Some of these men host ideas about life on Venus, the spirit molecule, free energy, government cover-ups, and conspiracies. Some of these men are just glad Tesla has finally been recognized. I like the nutty men the best. I imagine they have good dreams. And no, none of the emails ever come from a woman.

MORPHIC RESONANCE

In April 2008, the British biologist Dr. Rupert Sheldrake was stabbed by a paranoid schizophrenic. The knife cut into his leg, very close to the femoral artery. He had just finished delivering a talk about the "Extended Mind" at the International Science and Consciousness Conference in Santa Fe, New Mexico. This brush with death, with the body, makes a metaphor for the controversy and criticism that buffet Sheldrake's career.

Sheldrake's theory of morphic resonance explores the biological dimension of our connectedness. He studies telepathy. There's a humility and democracy to his experiments. Why do people know when they are being stared at? Can you wake up a sleeping dog or cat by staring at it? Why do pets know when their masters are returning home? How do murmurations of starlings function? How do crystal formations know how to grow? How do we explain the sensation in phantom limbs? Why do you sometimes think of a friend right before she calls you? How do homing pigeons find their way home?

Interviewed in *The Guardian*, Sheldrake described these phenomena as those "which people are generally fascinated by and made to feel stupid about." Sheldrake studied biochemistry at Cambridge, where he won the university's botany prize. He's been a researcher at the Royal Society, a Harvard scholar, and a fellow of Clare College. Nothing to feel stupid about. Still, in battles waged on his Wikipedia page, he's been called a parapsychologist and a pseudoscientist. Some critics have said his work lacks evidence, is inconsistent with established scientific theories, and contains magical thinking. He has even been called a "former biochemist," as if a person could awaken one day having forgotten all he knows from the field of biochemistry.

Sir John Maddox was Sheldrake's most adamant critic. Maddox served for decades as editor of *Nature* magazine, yet another esteemed publication founded in the nineteenth century. In *Nature*, Maddox wrote a review of Sheldrake's first book, *A New Science of Life*, published in 1981.

Even bad books should not be burned; works such as *Mein Kampf* have become historical documents for those concerned with the pathology of politics. But what is to be made of Dr. Rupert Sheldrake's book *A New Science of Life*? This infuriating tract has been widely hailed by newspapers and popular science magazines as the "answer" to materialistic science, and it is now well on the way to becoming a point of reference for the motley crew of creationists, anti-reductionists, neo-Lamarckians, and the rest. The author, by training a biochemist and by demonstration a knowledgeable man, is, however, misguided. His book is the best candidate for burning there has been for many years.

On the BBC years later, Maddox again attacked. "Sheldrake is putting forward magic instead of science, and that can be condemned in exactly the language that the pope used to condemn Galileo, and for the same reason. It is heresy."

Galileo is a curious choice if Maddox aimed to delegitimize

Sheldrake, because Galileo, the heliocentrist, was, of course, right.
It's hard not to read all this as schoolyard taunting, and surely the
process of critique is beneficial for both sides to reconsider where
they might be too attached to their preconceptions. But Maddox's
narrow-mindedness feels so inconsistent to his job as an editor
and a scientist that I have to wonder if perhaps he intended this
provocation to fire up controversy in order to bring *attention* to
Sheldrake's work, an act that the mantle of his prestigious post
forbade. That is, ultimately, what his review did.

Richard Dawkins, the evolutionary biologist, atheist, and author, is another Sheldrake critic. The preface to his book *The God
Delusion* quotes the philosopher Robert Pirsig: "When one person
suffers from a delusion, it is called insanity. When many people
suffer from a delusion, it is called Religion."

As much as I enjoy pondering the idea of group insanities, a
more helpful way to think about organized belief systems is to
consider how people are linked by the stories they hold close.
What is it specifically in a person that might draw them to stories
about snow or fairies or floods or fire or fathers? Stories imbue our
every cell. Lives are ruled by fictions, such as memories, broad hatreds, anticipated social narratives of gender, paradigms, politics,
and time. The people in my family told me stories about the goodness of this world and I believed them. I still believe them. The
trouble comes when people insist there is one truth, when people
won't listen to truths of others.

BAAL

I make a distinction between truth and facts. Facts are singular,
truth can be multiple. A strict adherence to any belief is the

same as wearing blinders, some avowed insistence on a singular narrative and a disconnectedness from other narratives. While being a skeptic means being open to all, not looking for the answer to How should I think? but instead asking, How should I know?

Edgar M. Welch, a young father and an adherent of fake news, luckily did not kill anyone when he showed up at Comet Ping Pong pizzeria heavily armed, ready to liberate the phantom children who were being held in the restaurant as sex slaves for Hillary Clinton. Welch told *The New York Times* after his arrest, "The intel on this wasn't 100 percent." The intel on anything will never be 100 percent, except, of course, for the truth Eva Müller broadcasts in the title of her graphic short story collection *In the Future We Are Dead*. To respond to one's beliefs, to one's truth, with anything as solid and factual as a gun is to make a dire, deadly error.

MAGIC

Science is threatened by fakery and alternative facts. It is threatened when people say "magic" or "angels" or "intelligent design," as these are code words for *Don't ask further questions. Wonder can't be explained.* But still, things happen that we cannot explain. The unexplainable needs to be where science begins. Rebecca Solnit, in *A Field Guide to Getting Lost*, writes:

> Certainly for artists of all stripes, the unknown, the idea or the form or the tale that has not yet arrived, is what must be found. It is the job of artists to open doors and invite in prophesies, the unknown, the unfamiliar; it's where

their work comes from, although its arrival signals the beginning of the long disciplined process of making it their own. Scientists too, as J. Robert Oppenheimer once remarked, "live always at the 'edge of mystery'—the boundary of the unknown." But they transform the unknown into the known, haul it in like fishermen; artists get you out into that dark sea.

Maybe telepathy will one day seem as mechanistic as the moon. Maybe one day we will photograph thought or record the energy released by the dead, and even if we never do, I hope leagues of scientists and artists spend their lives trying.

The problem I have with the supernatural is in the "super" part. Describing phenomena as supernatural robs the natural world of its due. With Dr. Ágnes Mócsy, I visited Brookhaven National Laboratory, where she and other scientists create "little bangs" inside the particle collider that can teach us much about the Big Bang. Mócsy studies our universe when it was microseconds old, not an easy task because, as Mócsy says, "the matter they [the little bangs] create only exists for one thousandth of one billionth of one billionth of a second, and it's also only one thousandth of one trillionth of a meter in size." Mócsy is also an educator at Pratt, where she brings physics to the artists who are her students. The work Mócsy does is absolutely super. It is even beyond super, but it is never supernatural.

A promised idea of perfection in a removed heaven is hard to swallow when faced with the crystallization of snowflakes; the decomposition of dead leaves to humus, dead mammals to dirt; and the birth of our universe. What further heaven could people want than to become part of a tree? Distant heavens are a terrible threat, granting permission to destroy the heaven we already have here.

LEGOS

What is to be gained in fundamentalist thinking, materialist science, and binary divides? What are the benefits in a slash-and-burn, mechanistic approach to science that says: If it doesn't fit, if it is inconsistent with established scientific theories, get rid of it? Dawkins writes, "We are survival machines—robot vehicles blindly programmed to preserve the selfish molecules known as genes." Speak for yourself, Richard. This idea of human machines has had devastating repercussions in the health-care industry.

I went to a specialist for headaches. He told me that he could help me with the pain in the back of my head, but when the pain was in the front of the head, I would have to visit another doctor, as if I were built of Legos. In his science, my head looked like a beef butchering map. I conjured an image of Steve Martin's medieval barber, Theodoric of York. "Why, just fifty years ago we would have thought your daughter's illness was brought on by demonic possession or witchcraft, but nowadays we know that Isabel is suffering from an imbalance of bodily humors, perhaps caused by a toad or a small dwarf living in her stomach."

I believe what I can feel, and I don't feel like a machine. Sometimes I wish I were, but I'm not. I am affected by fictions in very real ways. The novels I inhaled as a girl, stress, the conversations of birds, and even here, the smallest example: last night I tossed and turned because my grandmother Norma died recently and I miss her. I had been cleaning out her condo and had been stopped cold by the finality of her enormous stamp collection, a work she compiled from ages 5 to 101. I woke that night with such heaviness, worry, and dread of death. I blinked in the darkness. But in a matter of moments, I heard small footsteps coming down the hall to my room. One of my daughters climbed into bed beside me. There are multiple reasons why this might have happened, but I choose to believe my granny sent my daughter to comfort me. That reason feels best, most right, most kind. It is the finest story I can tell myself. I fell back asleep with her warm body beside mine.

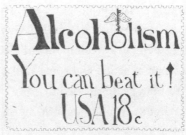

FRIDAY THE THIRTEENTH

"Okay. Where is the machine?"

I followed Guy outside.

What kept me moving forward in that moment? Was I operating under the influence of some entrenched horror-movie narrative? Had I become that girl on the screen who passes through one dark door and then the next, and everyone at the cinema is screaming, "No! No!" because the audience realizes the psycho killer is behind door number three waiting to chop our heroine to bits?

In a small house at the back of Guy's property, there was yet another man, pale, with long white-blond hair. He looked a bit like Edgar Winter. He smiled. Guy smiled. I was led down into the basement, to a small room built within the larger room. There was a wooden bench and some wall pegs, as one might find in a spa. "You can get undressed here."

Both Guy and Edgar Winter headed back upstairs.

WITCHES

In *Witches, Midwives, and Nurses: A History of Women Healers*, Barbara Ehrenreich and Deirdre English explore contemporary health care and the dangers in professionalizing the crafts of nursing and doctoring. They write, "We are mystified by *science*, taught to believe that it is hopelessly beyond our grasp. In our frustration, we are sometimes tempted to reject science, rather than to challenge the men who hoard it."

I'm chilled by the accuracy of the word "hoard" here. Almost every scientist I've mentioned above is a white man. "Hoard,"

Ehrenreich and English write, as if science were the property of a few, languishing in formaldehyde on a high shelf where a stasis of pre-proven ideas is promoted. Dust settles. Science withers and superstition takes root among the uninvited, the non-peer-reviewed, the un-funded. When they are told their observations and evidence are not science, they will instead call these wonders magic.

An amateur painter produces a watercolor, and we name this person an artist. When I watch snow melt in the forest, am I not a practicing scientist? And if not, why not? Is science afraid of the amateur, the nonprofessional, the unmoneyed? Amateur, from *amor*, one who works from love.

My daughters' backyard science experiments are strong and magnificent—they magnify our experience of the natural world—but these experiments often border on the poetic and imaginary. This morning one daughter asked, "What does the sun smell like?" Her research might include smelling the same areas in darkness and light, sunshine and clouds. To me, the nonprofessional scientist, this exploration of the sun's odor seems vitally important. What will happen when dumbness and discovery never have the chance to meet?

LIGHTNING ORCHESTRA

I undressed. Mildew, odd men, icy rain. I was about to electrocute myself. Why? I felt no more naked than I do already, which is to say, very naked, because with me in the basement, with me always, is the vulnerability my daughters brought into my life. Their reckless little hands control my happiness and being. I am in love. I am at their mercy.

Yet here I was. I saw the door to the small room where the Tesla device of electronic healing was beginning to hum. I opened the door. If, as Dawkins says, my goal as a machine is to protect my genes, why was I there? Why can I not even remember who was taking care of my children that day?

I stepped inside the room. I didn't want the vulnerability of mothering ever to equal fear. I wanted mothering to be open. After all, my children had opened my life, so what if I didn't collect the parts? What if I just found peace in remaining open, broken, scattered, roomy?

I closed the door behind me. A machine would go home and protect her gene pool, her progeny. A machine intent on survival wouldn't walk into the unknown. Clearly, we are so much more than selfish gene machines. Or, Mr. Dawkins, at least I am.

The room was totally dark. Real darkness erases the border of a body swiftly. I was uncertain where I began or ended until a rich light dawned. In front of me, behind a small safety railing, was a glowing violet mushroom-shaped device. As I bathed in it, the light grew stronger. Eventually I walked closer to the light and the noise it made. I went hands first, as one might approach an edge. As I advanced, blue lightning bolts shot from my fingertips; with them I could paint the air, lightning as pigment. I'll never forget the beauty of what Guy created in a basement.

The room became thickly charged. Closer still, tiny baby-blue bolts shot not just from my fingers but from multiple neural pathways, like a map of acupuncture points. In people who have suffered electrocutions, their bodies afterward are often marked by tree-like burns, due to the arboreal structure of our blood vessels. Blood is the greatest conductor in our bodies because of its iron content, and in cases where electricity enters a body, the burns happen from the inside out. Electricity goes to our hearts. I am a simple being, yet so totally complex that after fifty years living in this body, I still don't fully know how it works. I also still don't understand the intricacies of electricity.

My hair, long and heavy, blew behind me. A strong wind was somehow gathering in that closed space. I don't pretend to understand the engineering of the device or how that much power, two hundred thousand to three hundred thousand volts, was channeled into a basement. Something to do with sun flares? I don't know why it didn't kill me. Maybe it had to do with high voltage/low current, or with being insulated, or with the skin effect, that tendency of alternating high-frequency currents to crowd toward the surface of a conducting material. I don't know. I do know that I felt lucky to be there, an explorer seeing something very few people will ever get to see.

After fifteen or twenty minutes, the amount of time Guy had allotted for me in the chamber, I left the room and got dressed again.

A MONARCHY OF A DEAD PRINCE

Did two hundred thousand volts of electricity change me?

If my body were made of rigidly packed sand, Guy's machine inverted me, held me up by my ankles, so that each grain seemed subtly shifted, shaken, awakened. But subtlety is a problem when it comes to Western medicine, to Western farming practices, to Western everything. How often we use a sledgehammer where a love tap would suffice. We wonder, Did it work? We want our results to be dramatic, devastating even.

From a report in *The New York Times*: "Prescription fentanyl is used to treat cancer pain and as an anesthetic for surgery. Even small amounts of it can be deadly. The drug is so powerful that law enforcement officers have to wear gloves when searching for it, as just a tiny bit can get into the skin and, depending on the amount, be fatal." When my seven-year-old, thirty-nine-pound daughter broke her arm, the anesthesiologist, assisting the orthopedic surgeon, said, "Is it okay if I give her something for the pain?"

"No," I said. "Don't give her anything." She'd already refused my offer of Tylenol. "If she's in pain," I told him, "I'll give her something when we get home."

Fifteen minutes later, in the recovery room, the nurse told me, "She was given a Tylenol suppository, and the Fentanyl shot should wear off in an hour." That ancient physician's credo, *Do no harm*, is a joke under capitalism.

I wrote a very angry email to the anesthesia group. I cc'ed *The New York Times*. The anesthesia group, a huge corporation, called me almost immediately. They asked me what I wanted. I told them I wanted to attend a board meeting where I could tell the story of what happened to my daughter, how their pharmaceutical-crazed doctor dosed my seven-year-old with poison, against my wishes. I wanted to tell her story alongside the story of a local father of three who died from an overdose after becoming addicted to opiates following an orthopedic surgery. They did not invite me to speak. Instead, they canceled our bill, telling themselves a story, and by story here, I mean a lie. They thought I was upset at being asked to pay for a drug I'd refused, when really I was upset that our healthcare system is so dangerously broken and twisted by big pharma and the love of money that some people who believe they are doctors are actually injurious, harmful, and a danger to well-being.

When I left Guy's house, it was still an awful day, freezing purple rain.

QUEER SCIENCE

One inquiry I get from Tesla fans is, "If Tesla were alive today, would he be medicated?" And the continuation of that thought, sometimes unspoken, is, "If he'd been medicated, would he have invented all that he invented?"

Tesla manifested a handful of conditions we might now call mental illness. Despite intentionally housing a large population of New York City's pigeons in his hotel rooms, he had terrible germ phobia. He feared pearl earrings and human hair. He was also obsessively, compulsively controlled by the number three, always living in rooms divisible by the magic number—3327 when he was at the Hotel New Yorker, 207 in Colorado Springs' Alta Vista Hotel. In all my research, I found no record of Tesla ever seeking mental help. Tesla simply withdrew into his laboratories and spent more time with only pigeons. The question of a medicated Tesla suggests a swiftly narrowing, choking idea of that noxious, cruel word: "normal."

Queer theory is a field of critical inquiry commonly applied to politics, anthropology, sociology, philosophy, and the arts. There's no black and white. No binary positions. What if we applied queer theory to science and health care? No on or off, sick or cured, normal or deviant, failure or success.

Computers are binary. Machines are binary. Humans are not.

What would be lost if we accepted a spectrum of science where the mechanistic and the materialistic existed at one end and utter mystery at the other? Or rather than a spectrum with ends, what if science is a Möbius strip? Queer physics, queer healing, queer chemistry conducted by starving scientists and mad artists.

RANDOM-ACCESS MEMORY

Tesla failed a lot, probably more than he succeeded. He forecasted Beckett's "Ever tried. Ever failed. No matter. Try again. Fail again. Fail better." After Tesla claimed to have spoken with Martians, much of his financing dried up. What might he have discovered had he had access to greater resources, if funding ever flowed to the extremes? J. P. Morgan, in his bloodred library, stopped funding Tesla. Interesting to consider what Elon Musk's wealth—money made under Tesla's name—might have paid for. For Tesla, it was never a lack of imagination but rather trouble convincing others that all the unseens—dreams, fantasies, fictions—made material effects in the material world. His best inventions, including alternating current, which continues to drive our modern electrical system, came to Tesla in a flash, as a vision painted on the air.

FAIL BEST

I had a digital recorder running on the day I spent with Guy. At home I transferred the data to my computer, and a month later I spilled a cup of coffee on that computer. One truth forever erased. One more beautiful failure on my way to finding my truth. Alexis Guy Obolensky died on January 9, 2018.

I'm left to rely on my own original random-access memory.

So. That's what I did, that is what I do. I asked the foster kid down the street, What do you know? I asked Lamarck and the paranoid woman on the Greyhound bus. I asked the mad scientist and the thirty-nine-year-old mother of three. I asked the mother of the mad scientist, What do you know? And Steve Martin. And you, I ask you, What do you know?

And Barbara Ehrenreich and Deirdre English and all their fellow scientists. What do you know? What do you know? What do you know? I asked the people on the internet. They know a lot. A different lot, but a lot. I asked my daughters. I asked the aliens. I asked the vegetarian and Maddox and Dawkins and Galileo and Sheldrake. I asked the man I imagined in my basement, and I asked the fifteen-year-old girl I once was, What do you know?

She said, "I know a lot more than I did before." Then she told me a story about the night she went on a date with a fisherman who turned out to be a drug dealer who turned out to be a fifteen-year-old boy who turned out to be a memory and a time traveler and a chemist and a biologist and the child of some mother who one day asked herself, What do I know? What do I know?

he said When we last left off, the words in my dad's book were crumbling some. This picks up chapter 2 where the file is less disrupted. Lieutenant Noble is speaking.

Free World Or War Us vs. Them. *See* Citizens of the Peace.

Chapter 2 (cont'd)

"It's the airfields that we're primarily interested in," he said. "These people have airfields all up and down Central America, small clandestine landing places that could be invaluable if trouble comes in Nicaragua."

"And we expect it will," Colonel Law interjected.

"The colonel and I have spent some time putting this together. It seems to us a great opportunity. CINC wants to close down the drug routes. He also wants to prepare for the coming trouble in Nicaragua, and maybe elsewhere. He wants to deny Cuba the opportunity to help out their commie brothers wherever they are. But just yet we don't have the strength—the military strength—and we don't have the budget. All that will come, but it will take time. So the colonel and I, here, we put our heads together and came up with FWOW. That stands for **Free World Or War**. And those are the stakes, gentlemen. You better believe it. FWOW is the umbrella organization. Most of what we are doing is secret. I'm sorry I can't go into detail. But one of the sub-headings under FWOW is SUB, Small Unit Base, and that's where we think Mr.

clandestine drug fields Noble and Law connect Crane's flying to drugs. That must be the hardest part of getting sober, finding another way into those lovely states of mind we easily access with a glass of wine or a toke.

some drugs This reminds me of one frequently heard tale of my youth, told like a legend or fairy tale in school, from cousins, whispered at slumber parties, I don't know where I heard it, but its intention was clear: to instill a fear of drugs. My dad never talked to us about the danger of drugs and drinking. I have to imagine that he felt he'd waived that right. The story concerned a young woman who, after ingesting angel dust (the deliciousness of that name to my child ears), believed she could fly and jumped out the window. But she didn't fly. She died. My dad was writing this book to remind himself he could fly without drugs also. That's never been my problem. We always lived in the same place as my grandma Norma and my auntie Pat. I grew up in a matriarchy of women who took flight all the time, who talked to me of angels and birds, fairies and love. And my mom, lover of Chagall and Matisse, filled our home with her tremendous paintings of floating people.

I. Crane and his SOI come in. It's clear to us that SOI is involved
in something clandestine, else why the secrecy? How does Mr.
Crane get to the Yucatan if he doesn't fly on commercial airlines?
We've tracked his schedule. The trips don't last long enough to
allow for surface travel. Does he sneak out to Cuba, then hop to a
secret field in Yucatan? Does he use one of the **clandestine drug
fields** in Florida, or Louisiana?—and they're spreading, you better believe. There are fields in Texas and California, in Georgia
and Mississippi, and those are just the ones we know about. We
want to find out. If we busted up one of the SOI meetings now, we
might find **some drugs** around, but we wouldn't find the fields,
especially the fields we suspect they are using in Central America.
And those are the important ones. Once we locate them, we can
interdict the drug traffic at mid-source. The drugs will never reach
CONUS. But that's just the beginning. When we get budget approval, we plan to set up a Southern Narcotics Airfield Fighting
Unit, a guerrilla force that can go in, probably by parachute, take
the fields, hold them, keep them out of Cuban hands, and prepare
them for eventual use when it becomes necessary to launch incur-
sions in the area. Almost as important, if Mexico should go down
the drain, we will already have our SUBS in place, and that's what
we need if FWOW is to be a success in Westhem—hegemony
from the Arctic to the Southern Straits. In other words, we got 'em
by the ASS. Get it, gentlemen?"

"Thanks, lieutenant," Law said. "That's a sketch of the operational side. But at the moment we are not operational. In fact, as
I've pointed out, we don't have the authorization to become operational. That's White House SOP. We get to think about things,
but we don't get to do anything. I think CINC is going to change

in place I have to believe all of this is true. I have to believe it is part of why my dad wanted to write this story down, to record the dangers of a media that's in bed with the government. If he could see where America is now, he'd be horrified. Odd to think of *Reader's Digest* as the place that might have once had the potential for spreading government propaganda. Who reads the *Digest* now? It seems as benign as *The Old Farmer's Almanac*. Perhaps that's what you get for cozying up to the CIA.

Bay of Pigs In case we need any reminder about the power of fiction, the U.S. government's conspiracy against Cuba reads like a gritty pulp. Next time you fly through Dulles Airport in Washington, D.C., remember Allen Dulles (though the airport is named for his brother John, a former secretary of state). Allen Dulles, the head of the CIA under Eisenhower and JFK, authorized Robert Maheu (CIA middleman and Howard Hughes's [talk about flying!] fixer), in secret meetings held at Miami's Boom-Boom Room, to pay $150,000 to Sam Giancana and John "Handsome Johnny" Roselli, Chicago mafiosi, in exchange for killing Fidel Castro. The mobsters declined payment, saying they'd do it for free, citing their patriotism, though more likely they were hoping for future get-out-of-jail-free cards and a hand in controlling the Havana casinos Castro had shut down. State-sponsored assassination, American-style. Despite their Mafia chops, their multiple attempts on Castro's life failed, prompting RFK, then the attorney general, to ask, "Why can't you gentlemen get things cooking the way 007 does?" 007 who was, is, of course, a fiction.

that. Meanwhile, we have to make do. And that's where you come in, John. You're in place, ready to go."

That was the second time he had referred to John being "**in place**," as if someone had "placed" John in his position as Editor-in-Chief. I had read stories in the Times and elsewhere of individual journalists being co-opted by the government, principally central intelligence, or at least I had read of attempts to do so. It made me wonder. Did John owe his job to behind-the-scenes string-pulling by what forces I could not even imagine? If he did, it seemed to me, he was not aware of it himself. But the possibility made me extremely nervous. I leaned forward again, and began doodling on my pad. I drew a big X and began to embroider it with curleycues.

"What we have here is a terrific magazine story," Colonel Law said. "We are giving you a tip-off. What we expect is that you will look into the story, and when it jells, write a book about it for Talbot's Monthly. Meanwhile, we'd like to be kept informed of what you uncover. The place to start is with Mr. I. Crane and his organization SOI. We need to know a lot more about how and where they operate. That would be a very useful service to the President, and might make a story in itself. Down the road, it could be a very big story, maybe as big as BOP."

"BOP?" I questioned.

"**Bay of Pigs**."

"But that was a fiasco," I said.

"Yes," he said, suddenly sobered. "But we've learned a lot since then."

"Where do we start?" John asked.

"The opening wedge has to be Leonard Park," the colonel said. "First of all, Sam here has a natural reason to get to know him

What cover? Do we devise jobs that mimic the games of our childhood, create codes and rules? Or do we play games as children that prepare us for jobs?

better. The book connection. Wouldn't it be natural, Sam, to ring him up and suggest a lunch to talk over the publishing scene?"

"I suppose it would," I said. "Although probably not too helpful."

"But that doesn't matter. The idea is to get to know him. After that, he may lead you to SOI. That's the goal: to infiltrate SOI and find out what's going on, how they transport themselves to the Yucatan, where the drugs come in, where the airfields are."

I noted that the existence of these things had moved from supposition to reality. I had a question. "Sir," I asked, "what does SOI stand for?"

"That's for you to find out. We don't know."

"So basically, what you want me to do is telephone this Park guy and ask him to lunch."

"That's the beginning."

"Do I mention the Washington Monument?"

"Play it by ear. It might be a way of heading him in the right direction. You could pretend you're interested in it as story for the magazine."

"Why don't I just go down to Watts Street and walk in?"

"Sam, I'm surprised at you. That would blow your cover."

"**What cover?**"

"That you work for a magazine and are interested in a story."

"But that's what I do."

"No, Sam, you're working for the Free World. Don't forget it. This is bigger than Talbot's. This is bigger than Time, Inc. This is even bigger than the Reader's Digest. CINC wants it. I want it. You're serving your country."

I said nothing. I guessed the meeting was about over. Unless

patriotism When Biden and Harris won the election, my daughter said, "Now we can hang an American flag again." Under Trump we'd been embarrassed to be Americans. Our flag had been turned into a symbol of division, bypassing the United aspect of the United States. I do love much about my country, mostly the birds, the trees, the rivers and land, the national parks, New York City, and, often, the people here. When my daughter said this, I thought, Yes, a patriot again, until the root of that word struck me and I realized, No. Not a patriot, a matriot.

brighten Phoebe is starting to sound like my mom, who did briefly work at the *Digest* too before they were married. The *Digest* had a policy: no married couples, though my mom says it was rarely enforced. She had already quit before they got married.

John had something to say. But he didn't. He was beaming in the glow of his **patriotism**.

"Sam," the colonel said, "I want regular reports. Say, once a week, oftener if you've got something urgent. Don't send them to me. Officially, this has nothing to do with me or the White House. We'll give you a mail drop."

He stood up. "Pheeb, take Sam back to his office and give him what he needs."

Phoebe was on her feet also. We all rose.

Colonel Law pointed at my note pad. "Sam," he said, "I'll trouble you for that."

I was dumbfounded, but I held out the pad to him. "It's just some doodles," I said.

He took the pad from me and pointed at one of my scribbles. "What's that?" he asked.

"It's an X with some curleycues."

"Looks like an airfield to me," he said. He displayed it for Lieutenant Noble to examine. "With jungle around it." He signaled to John with the pad. "You got a shredder, John?"

John didn't quite understand. "A what?"

"A shredder."

"No." A pause. "Well maybe somewhere down in accounting, they might have."

"Forget it," the colonel said. He nodded toward me. "I'll just confiscate this, if you don't mind. Take it back to Washington."

John was looking at his watch. "Colonel," he said, "it's about eleven o'clock. If you'd like, we could lay on a tour of the office. We have quite a bit of interesting art. You could get a feel for the place. Then we could all have lunch." I saw Phoebe **brighten** at this prospect, but Colonel Law was looking glum. "Sorry, John.

No time No time for art.

"That's our A box," **she said.** **"That's for secret stuff."** I'm reminded of the moment in Louisa May Alcott's *Little Women* when Laurie repurposes a former birdhouse into a forest mailbox in thanks for being made a member of the formerly all-female Pickwick Club. "As a slight token of my gratitude for the honor done me, and as a means of promoting friendly relations between adjoining nations, I have set up a post office in the hedge in the lower corner of the garden; a fine spacious building with padlocks on the doors, and every convenience for the mails,—also the females, if I may be allowed the expression. It's the old martin-house; but I've stopped up the door, and made the roof open, so it will hold all sorts of things, and save our valuable time. Letters, books and bundles can be passed in there; and, as each nation has a key, it will be uncommonly nice, I fancy."

No time. Duty calls. We have to get back to the salt mines. Semper Paratus, you know."

The Boy Scout motto, I thought.

Phoebe's face had unbrightened. We shook hands all around. Colonel Law dispatched Lieutenant Noble to scout up the cars. Phoebe and I moved toward the door. Law remained. "Give me a minute more, will you, John?" He turned back to Phoebe. "I'll meet you in reception."

We left the room. I had the distinct suspicion that Law was remaining behind to double-check my reliability with John. I feigned light-heartedness and pointed out a few paintings in the halls as Phoebe and I made for my office. I saw one or two secretaries giving her a thorough up-and-down appraisal. I surreptitiously winked at one of them, and she shook her head in mock disapproval.

In my office, I asked Phoebe what I needed, and she produced a memorandum from the briefcases she carried. Carefully printing, she wrote down an address and handed it to me. "**That's our A box**," **she said**. "**That's for secret stuff**. If you just want to check something routine, you can call me on this number." She handed me another slip of paper.

"I'm sorry you can't stay for lunch," I said.

"Yeah," she said, "so am I. It must be really nice working around here. We're stuck in a dumpy little place down in the basement."

"But it's exciting, I imagine," I said.

"Sometimes," she said a little wistfully. "But we spend a lot of time drawing up plans, and not much else. If Colonel Law could just get to see the President, maybe we'd get some action. He's full of ideas."

Flying Without Wings Yes. Let's get back to flying.

brightened Any more brightening and she'll start to glow.

I'm always late. Phoebe is my mom with blond hair. My daughters complain if I'm five, ten minutes late picking them up. My mom would sometimes be forty-five minutes, an hour late. There were no cell phones. I became accustomed to waiting.

"Oh, doesn't he see the President?"

She looked guardedly at me. "Not too often," she said, which I took to mean "never."

"But now maybe things will heat up. What with Free World or War, I mean."

"Oh," she said, "that's just what Noble calls it when he's talking to people upstairs. It really means **Flying Without Wings**."

"Really?" I said, feeling the hairs on my arms go erect.

"Yeah," she said. She looked at me earnestly. "How can you fly without wings?"

"Well, maybe in a balloon."

"Yeah," she said. "I never thought of that. Maybe that's what it means. Have you ever been up in a balloon?"

"No," I said.

"Neither have I." She **brightened**. "Well, I think I'd better go. Colonel Law gets mad if I'm late." She looked at me with puppy-dog innocence. "**I'm always late**. Bye-bye. Maybe we'll be talking, huh?"

"Maybe," I said, and she went out the door.

About a half hour passed in which I tried to sort out some impressions. I wasn't entirely happy with the way the morning had gone. I was standing gazing out my window at the rain when John came by my office. That in itself was unusual. We were a pretty chummy lot at Talbot's, dropping in on each other informally to schmooze. But John wasn't that kind. He had spent his younger years in our Los Angeles Bureau, then some time in Washington before coming to headquarters. There was the sense that we didn't know him as well as we might. A basis for idle conversation was

never established. Nor did the women get along with his wife. She was a very insecure woman, and as a result, when they first came to headquarters, she had put on airs about how important John's new assignment was. Not a popular stance, and it had got worse when John was promoted to editor-in-chief. What their private life was like I hadn't an inkling, but in my opinion she was a royal pain.

"What'd you think?" John asked me.

"Well, there may be a story there," I said, hedging. "It seemed, at this stage, a little nebulous."

"Colonel Law is highly thought of," he told me—again. "He's a take-hold kind of person, you can see that. I had no idea about all the airfields. We really should try to do something about that."

"I guess," I said.

"Whattaya make of Miss Poon?" he asked.

"Cute," I said.

"You think he's getting into her pants?"

The way he phrased the question made my skin crawl. It was 1950s slang, for one thing, the sort of euphemism that had been superseded by much blunter talk. It also assumed a greater degree of intimacy than existed between the two of us. With any number of my friends I could joke about who was screwing whom, but not with John. Furthermore, I detected a nuance of male chauvinism in the remark, the expectation that secretaries, especially pretty, young secretaries, cemented relations in this way with their bosses. That bothered me for several reasons, not the least of which was my own involuntary arousal at the thought. I shrugged my shoulders in answer. "Who knows?"

"You're supposed to file reports with them, right?"

"Yup. Phoebe gave me a P.O. box number."

Blackwing 602 My dad wrote in pencil, rather than pen. His pencils were the elegant Blackwing 602s made by Eberhard Faber at the time. Those silver-skinned writing implements whose miniature pink eraser is housed in its own removable chassis. "Half the pressure. Twice the speed." Each pencil's life could be gauged by how much of the embossed message had been chewed up by the sharpener. He bought Blackwings by the case at Fox and Sutherland, the once-great stationery store in Mount Kisco, New York, now another ghost. He used thousands of these pencils as an editor, a writer, and a crossword puzzler. It's still not uncommon to find remnants and stubs of my dad's pencils in my mom's house. The short ones make me wonder what words he wrote. The long ones, what words he didn't. That these pencils are winged creatures, birds, had escaped my notice until just now. These pencils, if well used and sharpened, all reach a point where Blackwing becomes Lackwing, a subtraction that adds much meaning. FWOW, flying without wings, a lackwing bird. If one continues to write, continues to sharpen, soon, Ackwing. Ckwing. Kwing. Until finally, at the end, one is left with very little pencil. One is left with Wing.

"Oh," he said, "that's all?"

"No, I've got a phone number for her if I have routine questions."

"Let me have that, will you?"

I produced the slip of paper with Phoebe's number on it, and John copied it. "Thanks," he said. "I probably won't need it. But if you're not around, I may want to get in touch."

Time for rumination. I have read over the above notes, and in doing so have been impressed, once again, by the element of self-parody in Colonel Law. I was aware of it at the time; putting it down in black and white makes it so obvious as to be unreal. There is, of course, an element of self-parody in everyone. I can, on occasion, slip into the jargon of magazine publishing and begin to sound like Hollywood's idea of that profession. I can imitate the common idea of the busy executive, firing off terse memos to bureaus around the world, arranging lunch dates with prominent authors, waving my hands as I visualize for an art editor my grandiose notions for a two-page spread that will stun the reader with colorful graphics. But all that is bunkum. Ninety percent of my time is spent in laboriously moving words around on a page, taking them out, putting them back in, wearing down a **Blackwing 602** to the nub every ten minutes. And then worrying about what I have done.

So, for myself, I know what is real and what is unreal. But did Colonel Law? Did Phoebe, or Lieutenant Noble? Or did one's visual image of oneself become the only reality? The jargon, the mannerisms, the illusion of power? I was able to work myself into a very cynical state over these questions. And it seemed to me, in

summation, that much of the world I had grown up in, become
middle-aged in, had succumbed to a vision of the world that was
unreal, that was a parody, that was funny—except it wasn't. In
writing down Colonel Law's conversation (actually, at this point,
it came from Lieutenant Noble), I copied out "Southern Narcotics
Airfield Fighting Unit," and not until then did I realize that its acronym was SNAFU. If Colonel Law had been a parody in a satire,
I could have accepted that as a joke. But Law was not a parody.
He was a smart man. He must have seen the meaning of the acronym. He must have made it up on purpose. He had constructed a
parody of himself, which had become real, and then he had begun
to parody even that reality. Following this thought, I made myself
dizzy, almost nauseous.

I am not in a mood, however, to criticize Colonel Law. I think
that people like him can do enormous damage, but I see them as
victims rather than perpetrators. What has occupied my thoughts
is my own position. I suppose the first time I began to think about
it was after Amy's death. That gives me a date and an event to
ascribe my feelings to. But, in fact, I recognize that I had been
inching in the direction of my present slightly depressed state for
some time before her death, and that since then it has simply intensified. At this juncture in the history of medicine we have even
found a name for what I am feeling. It is called a mid-life crisis,
and every popular magazine, including Talbot's, has addressed the
problem. More than once. (Four times, for Talbot's.) In my opinion the articles have all been boring. And that is what the "crisis"
is all about. Boredom. A man or a woman moves words around
on a page for twenty-five years, or he joins dovetails to make cab-
inets for twenty-five years and, in its simplest form, eventually
he has to ask himself, "Is this all there is?" It is a particularly

all the mentors were got rid of My dad took early retirement in order to stay sober. But he kept working for the *Digest* as a freelance editor.

twentieth-century question. The obvious answer is "no." To which I ask "What else?" And the answer seems to be, "Read the article in Talbot's on mid-life crisis." Or, "Watch television." Or, "Go to church." "Get more exercise." "See a shrink."

A friend once said to me, "I used to have terrific days and terrible days. Now I have fair days. Fair! I thought people in Kansas had fair days. Out there somewhere (in the air he drew a square with his hands) they have fair days. In Los Angeles they have terrific days; in New York they have terrific days. In Kansas people have fair days." In part the feeling is a result of aging. One hundred years ago I'd most likely be dead by now. The body and mind are still geared to youthful achievement and by my age most of it has been achieved, if it ever is going to be. So now I have time to sit around and worry about all the things I didn't achieve. (Once I meant to go to sea, like Conrad or Melville, and the maritime still mesmerizes me.) Or worry that what has been achieved was not worth it in the end. One should be allowed to become a mentor, but mentors are out of fashion now. In my youth I admired the men (they were all men then) who had reached positions I wished to reach, and I listened to them when they talked of what they knew. I tried to learn from them, though there is never a substitute for actually doing the job. In the last economy drive at Talbot's, **all the mentors were got rid of**, and no doubt there will be other such economy drives. No more sitting about whittling and spinning yarns for the young. Predictably enough, once the mentors were gone the powers-that-be discovered that the remaining editors were somewhat less adequate than they had appeared to be when their elders were still present. Moreover, the field had been left open to the jargoneers, the priests of mystification, who

Mere mystification is easy; clarity is difficult I really am trying for clarity, but there is so much I don't know or understand.

mystify to mask an absence of thought. **Mere mystification is easy; clarity is difficult.**

The mentors at Talbot's, now vanished into retirement, were devotees of clarity. But because clarity is difficult to achieve, there has occurred a long, slow slide into simplification. The two, simplification and clarity, are not the same. And I guess what I am saying is that I was tired of it. Bored. Under John, the pace has accelerated toward the simple and the simple-minded. Colonel Law's scheme had a surface appearance of complexity. That was because Law had a propensity for complicating matters. Underneath, it rested firmly on his primitive view of the world. It was simple-minded. Indeed, to me, it was moronic.

I cannot say that these thoughts were in my head as I watched John leave my office and return to his own, his hips slightly in advance of his shoulders. Shortly, I went off to lunch, accompanied by two of my colleagues. But I was only partly present during the meal-time banter. Slowly, listening with half an ear, I ranged over the options available to me, sorting through the events of the last seventy-two hours. I was disturbed by Phoebe's parting revelation that FWOW might stand for Flying Without Wings. Was this seriously meant? Or was it an inside joke that she did not understand? Did it mean that Colonel Law had hidden from John and me the true intent of our (my) investigation? That he had concealed information that he already had about Mr. I. Crane? Information that I, in fact, possessed as a result of Mr. Crane's visit to my office? Information which Colonel Law suspected I possessed because he already knew that Mr. Crane had visited my office; information that had made him ask that I, specifically, be present

at the meeting in John's office, but not so specifically (asking for the Book Editor, of which there was but one) as to give away his knowledge that I, and I alone, had been visited by Mr. Crane? And if I followed this train of thought, was I not overlooking or eliding the central question: How serious was all this business?

Trying to evaluate the colonel's true intentions meant that I was accepting Mr. Crane's preposterous hints as fact. And if I accepted that, then the colonel's complex scenario made a sort of sense, too. Whereas I was convinced that both men were lunatics, although of totally different sorts. Of the two, Mr. Crane struck me as being decidedly the least dangerous. Indeed, when I thought of him, an image came to mind of Ferdinand the Bull, indulging in peaceful fantasies beneath his cork tree, about to sit on a bumblebee. Seen in this light, it was my duty, anyone's, to warn him about the bee.

Of course, I had to reason that I might be reasoning just as Colonel Law expected me to. Realizing this, I felt trapped. Perhaps the best course of action was simply to telephone Mr. Leonard Park, who had in some fashion ascended the Washington Monument, and proceed slowly. But that was boring, wasn't it? Instead, by the end of lunch, I had decided to journey into Manhattan, find my way to Watts Street and attend the meeting of SOI that I had been invited to. It was Friday, the day of the weekly meeting. Colonel Law's timing was perfect.

Mediums

Ann's apartment is on a quiet street beside a park. The lobby has marble tiles, prewar. Her office is on the first floor in the front corner, a space usually reserved for doctors and dentists, but unlike a doctor or dentist, there's no delayed billing, no insurance company to obscure the financial transaction at the heart of Ann's ministrations. You give her money, she tells you a story. It does not escape my notice that this is similar to my own job description.

I enter a bright white room, empty besides some artwork on the walls. Ann calls out from the back and I go toward her voice, leaving the sunshine for a dark, windowless office with brown walls. It's like a film noir set; Ann plays a stereotype. Her blond wig is askew. She wears chunky jewelry and has coral lipstick on her front teeth, painted-on eyebrows. Her fake nails are white. The table beside her is covered with odd old lotions and medicines. A small couch is upholstered in synthetic wool, cream and brown.

I brought a few reproduced portraits of Charlotte Brontë. I want Ann to ask Charlotte what she thinks of my new book. I have come here for a blurb. I don't like the process of collecting blurbs for my books—those bits of praise from other authors stuck on the back jacket.

"*Wuthering Heights*?" Ann asks.

"That's her sister, Emily. Charlotte wrote *Jane Eyre*."

"Yes. They made a movie."

"Yes."

"I didn't see it."

"Neither did I." I don't mention the other Brontë sister, though she and my medium share a name. If a person can talk to the dead, they have access to the most voluminous library already. Right?

I settle in for my reading. That term, used in mediumship, turns *me* into the book. How legible am I? Ann tries to collect information about my life. I try to obscure it, as if I'm there to test her skills rather than rely upon them. This is a problem. I don't believe in any of this. Ann asks about my husband. "Is he very romantic?" I stay focused on the blurb. She asks about my novel. I remain vague. I don't want a blurb from Ann. I want her to get in touch with Charlotte Brontë. But Ann is curious. She enjoys a story. "There's a man and a woman?"

"Yes." I speak slowly. "My book has both male and female characters."

"Ah, a romance," she intuits.

I shrug. "Not really."

"Not a romance?"

"Not really."

"So, then there's a murder."

Recently, *The New York Times Book Review* described me as an "established horror writer." Both words, "established" and "horror," were a revelation to me. I do write about death. And perhaps at this time, the die being cast, to write of death is to write horror. It just strikes me as funny because in all earnestness, while I wouldn't file the work I make under the heading Romance, I really do believe that I am writing love stories over and over again. The dead do not scare me. Indeed, many of the people I love most in this world are dead.

Silence ticks between us. What's the difference between fortune-telling and familiarity with genre? When my daughters watch TV, I know how their shows will end. Am I psychic? Can I predict the future? We're all going to die, right?

The first time I paid an older woman to talk to the dead for me, I was at Lily Dale, "the City of Light," a Spiritualist summer camp in western New York. Like nearby Chautauqua, Lily Dale has an antique atmosphere. It's a gated community of gingerbread homes where people focus on communication with the dead. Lakes, forests, and pet cemeteries dot the campus.

My oldest daughter came with me. She was two at the time. We strolled past fairy houses, past the library and museum. We made our way up to Inspiration Stump. The name invokes teenagers and heavy petting, but Inspiration Stump is actually an open-air amphitheater in the woods. Twice daily during the high season, visiting and local mediums contact the dead. Attendees gather hoping for a word from their departed. During my visit, the mediums were joyful, humorous, or New Agey. Some sounded like somber auctioneers. "I'm speaking with Harry. Yes. Anyone here looking for Harry? Sorry, no. Larry. Anyone, Larry? Not Larry. It's Mary. Who's looking for Mary?"

I didn't necessarily feel the presence of the dead at Inspiration

Stump, but I felt their impact on us, the not-yet-dead. Bereaved mothers were there looking for their children. Though I was new to mothering, I knew the loss of a child would mean never fully returning to the land of the living. These women, faced with the impossibility of death, held out hope that, in the woods of western New York, comfort might exist. These mothers insisted on life despite their familiarity with and proximity to death. What bravery they demonstrated. This insistence was what I'd come to Lily Dale to see and feel.

We were given a small room in one of Lily Dale's two hotels. A number of the regulars gathered on the large porch, as folks might gather before dinner in a nursing home. An older woman in a wheelchair admired my daughter and made a gift to her: a very cool, hand-cranked flashlight that advertised the daily ghost tour through Lily Dale. As a Spiritualist tool, the flashlight struck me as odd. Spiritualists believe communication with the deceased is natural and desirable. So, what's scary in the dark? My daughter loved the present.

Our room in the hotel was simple: bed, dresser, and lamp. Communal bathrooms were down the hall past a sign that advised, "Please no readings, healings, or séances in the hotel. Thank you." These quarters belong to the living.

My mother was angry I brought my daughter to Lily Dale. "Why?" I'd asked. "Where's the harm? You don't believe in ghosts."

"Of course, I don't believe in ghosts."

"Then what are you afraid of?"

"Nothing." Her voice was unconvincing. Whatever unnamable thing was frightening my mother was also frightening me. Maybe people who believe in ghosts are scary. I didn't sleep that night. I kept vigil over our room, self-cranking flashlight in hand.

By morning I was ready to flee Lily Dale, head up to Niagara Falls to wash off my ghost hangover. People who'd seemed quirky the day before looked lost at breakfast. Their grief was so heavy. Why was I here? My thinking had shifted in the light of day. Why was any living person here in a town made for the dead? I wanted to take my small, living daughter and run. Despite my ideas about living closer to the dead, some days I just can't do it. Some days I pretend death cannot touch us. I had a ten o'clock appointment for a private session with a Lily Dale Assembly–approved medium. I stayed. Canceling last minute with a person who may have connections to the land of the dead seemed like a really bad idea.

The woman who received me in her house wore polyester pants. She had frosted hair and rouged temples. She invited me into her converted porch. "Women," she said, "come to me on this side of my body, in this ear. Men in the other." That was it for preliminaries. She began. "There is a woman here. She wears emerald rings on her fingers." The medium checked me to see if I knew this ghost. I had no idea who the woman with emeralds might be. I come from Iowa farmers on one side and Brooklyn Irish on the other side. Fingers covered with gemstones seemed unlikely in my family.

But my skepticism, even my outright non-belief, did not matter, because after the bejeweled woman said her piece, the medium, like someone standing before a locked door trying different keys, said, "There's a man here who wants you to know that in life, he never would have passed through these gates." The door unlocked. I was blubbering on her converted porch. She directed me to a box of tissues. She kept on. "Your father?"

I nodded.

"Well, he's here. Is there anything you'd like to say to him?"

I called my mom after it was done. Her take was, "That woman took one look at you and thought, College girl, raised by skeptics who'd never go to a psychic. Anyone could see that about you. She tried a woman first. Maybe she thought I was dead. Emeralds for your red hair. And when the woman didn't work, she tried a man."

"I know," I said.

But the half hour I spent with that woman was time-collapsed therapy, years of work waded through in minutes. And it only cost sixty bucks. She presented my dead dad as a willing participant in conversation and it turned out I had nothing to say. We hadn't left things unsettled or unspoken. He loved me. I loved him. He was a great, mythic, messed-up dad. He told me a lifetime of stories. He made me love books. In one half hour the medium made it clear that even though I miss my dad and wish he knew my kids, it's okay for him to be done living.

Later, standing before Niagara Falls, in the same place where my mom and dad had once stood, I thought, Maybe from here on out I'll be able to let my dead dad be dead.

Back with Ann in Albany, while I hate to admit it, I tell her *Mr. Splitfoot* does contain a kind of murder. Sort of. She's right.

"I knew it! I saw it," she says. "She's lying on the floor in a pool of blood. How did he do it? With a gun?"

I shake my head. There's no blood at all. Still, I like a faulty medium, seams exposed. When Ann calls Charlotte "Jane" by mistake, she marks no difference between fiction and life. Neither do I. I carry each book I've ever read with me, just as I carry my dead—those things that aren't really there, those things that shape everything I am.

I asked Charlotte Brontë for a blurb. Asking the dead felt

much less humiliating than asking a living author. I had a feeling
Charlotte wasn't terribly busy anymore. I didn't even mind paying
for a blurb. Paying for words of praise strikes me as more honest than relying upon the kindness of other authors. Blurbs are
advertising. Why shouldn't I pay? Ann accepted seventy dollars
for her services. A good price, though it was hard not to wonder
what sort of blurb I would have gotten from the man who wanted
to charge me seven hundred dollars for the same job.

Death has been rough on the English language and Charlotte
is less articulate now than when she was alive; still, Charlotte
Brontë blurbed my novel *Mr. Splitfoot*.

> *I get the chills. I see the color of creativity which is a light
> green and then I see yellow or gold. I know it's interesting and
> should be great. Is it a true story? Is it a sad story? I get the
> chills even more. I feel a good vibration. I feel good about it.
> There's this attraction. Yes. It's what people want. Yeah. I think
> it's good. It's good. I think it's a good one. Of course, it's fiction.
> The girl is not real. It's not a true story. Which is good. It has
> a lot of good energy and people, people will like it. They will
> keep reading it until the end. You know what I mean? It's got
> good motion. It's intriguing because a person will know there's
> something two-sided. I like the name, Mr. Splitfoot. It will sell
> because it's good. It's intriguing. Yeah. It's a good one.*

> —CHARLOTTE BRONTË,
> author of *Jane Eyre*

In the psychic's back room, I wrestle with finite plotlines and
every story that's ever been told. Charlotte haunts me with her
eternal, beautiful, ever-unfolding book, and I surrender to the

pleasing limitations of narrative, genre, and theme because even if we know how this story is going to end (and, people, *we know*) it never stops life from filling with fresh wonder.

Ann mistakes my moment of meditation for melancholy. "I'm thinking you might have been Emily Brontë in a past life." She throws me a bone. She offers me a fiction. I love fiction. "Do you really think so?" I perk up.

"Yes," she says. "I mean maybe. Yeah. Sure. Emily or Jane. Charlotte. Why not?"

"Why not," I say, because *Of course it's fiction. It's not a true story. Which is good. People will like it. They will keep reading until the end. You know what I mean? Yeah. It's a good one.*

Ghost Story

Do you believe in ghosts? Do I believe in ghosts?

Near my house, there's a big grocery store, a newer construction on a hill with a large parking lot. It created a new four-way intersection that gets busy by small-town standards. The town installed a light.

A grieving family erected a cross as memorial to a young man killed at the intersection, a roadside shrine. I notice when the fake flowers get refreshed on certain holidays. The cross says "Billy" and has the young man's abbreviated dates. Someone added a "Look Twice, Save a Life" sign, leading me to believe that Billy was riding a motorcycle when he died.

Years back, my family was driving past. My oldest was five. My twins were two or three. No one had started school yet. My kids couldn't yet read. The oldest noticed the memorial and asked, "What's that?"

Are all children interested in death? I know I was. I'd often ask our mother to read one of three poems. Edgar Allan Poe's

"Annabel Lee," Robert Southey's "The Inchcape Rock," or Alfred Noyes's "The Highwayman." I love these poems. Each details a glorious death. Noyes tells the tale of Bess, the landlord's black-eyed daughter. He writes that she "Had watched for her love in the moonlight, and died in the darkness there." Southey writes, "Till the vessel strikes with a shivering shock, / 'Oh Christ! It is the Inchcape Rock!' / Sir Ralph the Rover tore his hair, / He curst himself in his despair; / The waves rush in on every side, / The ship is sinking beneath the tide." And Poe, "Yes!—that was the reason (as all men know, / In this kingdom by the sea) / That the wind came out of the cloud by night, / Chilling and killing my Annabel Lee." These poems give me goosebumps. I remember my mother's delight reading them, her voice paced for suspense and the thrill of mystery.

My children know some things about death. We live in a rural area where people hunt, and we buy meat directly from the farm where it was grown. My girls know the difference between "a milk cow and a killing cow." A handful of moms and dads have died. Still, when my oldest daughter asked about the memorial, I hesitated to answer.

The car was silent. When one of the twins spoke, we heard her clearly. "That's where William died," she said.

Again, she was two or maybe just three. While she knew her letters, she could not read yet. And the shrine says Billy, not William. Even if she knew how to read, which she didn't, she wouldn't know that Billy is a nickname for William. "How'd you know that?" I asked.

She shrugged. "The robot in my head told me."

The next morning at the bus stop I told my friend, a fellow

mother and a scientist, what had happened. She quickly tried to find a "rational" explanation. "Someone must have told her. Or maybe she read it somewhere."

"She doesn't know how to read," I said, but stopped our conversation. I could tell my story angered my friend. She was annoyed I would describe an event that could not be easily explained. I stopped telling people this story for a few years.

All three of my daughters have had moments of eerie knowledge. And when it happens, there it is, the unexplainable. People who don't want to think about this will dismiss me as flighty. Think that if you need to. Flight is a place of freedom and I enjoy considering the idea that new people, young people like my daughters, haven't damaged their sight and hearing yet, haven't shut down some way of knowing the history of a place with their tuned and tender ears, a sound too quiet for the rest of us to detect.

jour Ursula K. Le Guin says, "Magic consists in this, the true naming of a thing."

khakis and a sweater My father had a uniform. He would wear the same clothes until they had holes in them, only then replacing his garments with the exact same items. In his adult life, he probably went shopping for clothes five times.

Old Farmer's Almanac My sister Amy and I both continue to consult *The Old Farmer's Almanac* regularly. We are not farmers.

Chapter 3

MONDAY EVENING, APRIL 27

It still bothers me that this "journal" does not reflect the correct "**jour.**" I cannot seem to catch up with the current day. Thus, to satisfy my desire for currency, I will record what happened to me this morning before going on to relate the startling events of Friday night.

Today, on purpose, I awoke at five o'clock. I do not remember that I was dreaming at all, and the alarm rang for some time, I believe, before it penetrated my deep coma. I threw on my clothes of the day before, **khakis and a sweater**, lying conveniently where I had discarded them at bedside, and went foggily downstairs to the kitchen.

It was still dark, which surprised me. I had pulled out my **Old Farmer's Almanac** last night and found that sunrise was about five a.m. The fact that I even had an almanac to consult was one of those idiosyncrasies of mine that never failed to amuse Amy. The point being, I guess, that neither of us lived in any need of

I had to add an hour This seems a bit of convenient fiction. Why wouldn't the almanac include the time change? It would. Was he looking at the wrong day?

entered the orchard The house where I grew up was once a farmhouse. My parents bought it from an older woman named Mrs. Heerdt. When her son Bruce married, he and his family moved into the horse barn on the property and made it into their home. They were my neighbors for years. I'd often ask Bruce what it was like growing up in the house where I grew up. He told me many things about the old days, particularly things about the one-room schoolhouse he attended. There's an apple orchard out back and a number of chestnut trees that he had planted and we harvested for years. Around the time that my dad wrote this book, Bruce sold off the remaining farmland, twenty-six acres that I'd roamed as a child. A developer began to develop a neighborhood of new homes that wraps around the house where my mom still lives. There are now very few signs of the former farm. A hay mow too rusted to move and a tumbledown stone wall where they cleared the fields. The new neighbors don't farm. One of them hires a yard company to apply a Scotts product to his grass each year that is so toxic, the law requires the company to send out a mailer notifying neighbors of its application, as if a mailer alone can protect the neighbors and their wells from this poison.

knowing when the sun rose and set, nor cared what night the moon was full, or when the planets crossed into this or that area of the zodiac, or depended on the rise and fall of tides. It was the very lack of need, I tried to explain, that made it necessary. Sunrise, sunset, high or low tide were elemental factors in life, and my need for knowledge was the need to be in touch with my past, the past of man. It impressed me that scarcely one hundred years ago, given my mid-western birthplace, familiarity with these heavenly signs might well have determined my survival. Although fully acclimated to an existence that gratefully witnessed the splendors of the stars at night, yet persistently ignored their movements and all else to do with them, I still had to acknowledge the stirrings of a primeval wonder and desire—a yearning, an ache, for wisdom and mastery, which surely is, and has always been, the metaphorical meaning of the heavens.

But it was still dark. No sunrise. Then I remembered that yesterday we had switched over to Daylight Saving Time. **I had to add an hour** to the almanac's calculations. It would not get light until about six. Wrong again. I put the coffee on and puttered about the kitchen and along about 5:30, the eastern sky in back of the orchard began to lighten. I had of course witnessed sunrises before, but never, I realized, in relation to the exact time the sun appeared. It came as something of a surprise to me to discover that daylight arrived before sunrise.

Caught by this surprise, I hastily took a swig of coffee and went outside, crossed the backyard and **entered the orchard**. Here the grass, left at meadow height the previous fall, stained with damp the leather tops of my boots, and I knelt to wrap the untied laces around them. In places the winter had matted the grass, and it had been trampled by deer who came to nibble on the fallen

prominence My siblings and I spent much time on this rise as kids. Bruce's sons, Lindy and Randy, had abandoned an old jeep up there years before I was born. Trees grew through its engine, moss coated its seats, and we thought its rusting carcass made the greatest toy.

a slow rising I can feel this sensation of liftoff, of flight, one or two inches above the ground, though I myself have never flown.

apples. I followed a zig-zag route along these natural paths to the old tumble-down stone wall at the back of my property. From here the land, undeveloped as yet, rose to a slight knoll. The slope had once been farmed and only recently allowed to go back to bushy growth. But the top of the knoll itself, rocky and angular, had never been cultivated, and here a grove of oak and shag-bark hickory had taken root many decades ago. I headed along a foot-worn trail to this **prominence**, made my way into the trees and finally stopped in the lee of a large boulder. Here I was out of sight of my house, of the road that passed in front, and of the neighboring houses on either side.

It was to be out of sight that I had risen early and made my trek.

I looked up. Through the dark limbs of the unleafed trees, I could see above me an archipelago of small cumulus clouds, tinged orange on the underside by the sun. Between these inviting islands, the sky varied from milky blue to a hazy gray where the light did not penetrate. The moment of orangeness passed swiftly, was replaced by gold, and intensified into colorless brightness. The sun was up. The rock nearby emerged from solid gray into a mottled surface of flinty blue and pale lichen-green, flecked with red and black oxidized ores.

I bowed my head and closed my eyes as if in prayer. I was trying to think myself aloft. I had no desire for aerobatics. I wanted only an inch or two of levitation. Even this, I feared, would upset my balance, and like a piling uprooted from its sandy base, I might float atilt into the tide and bang my head on a tree. And so, behind my closed eyes, I pictured that: **a slow rising** into the air, one inch, two, three at most, until I hovered just above the pebbles and grass at my feet. And then I pictured letting myself

A breeze entered the grove Everything in this section is written so close to life, I have to believe that my father did try to fly from the knoll.

crane The machine is named after the bird? Or the bird after the machine? Suddenly I've become suspicious of I. Crane. Maybe he is not a bird but a machine.

slowly descend. Again. I thought myself into the air. I thought
of myself gradually rising. I raised myself on the tip of my toes,
straining. No. Wrong. Again. I tried to relax, to let my weight
drain, first from my head, then my shoulders, then my torso, to
slough off my weight in stages until the earthly bond of gravity
lay at my feet like a slipped garment. I felt my head clear, then my
shoulders. The sensation reached my rib-cage; the upper part of
my body felt as airy as fishnet. My mind leaped, as it were, ahead
or downward to my feet, by-passing my hips and knees. Get the
feet off the ground! And in an instant the heaviness, the gravity,
returned, pushing into every capillary of my brain, making even
my hair feel leaden.

A breeze entered the grove, whispering. I tried to hear what it
said, as if it might speak to me, a message of strength and encour-
agement, of unity in aspiration with those things that soar and
inhabit the heavens. I heard the breeze; I absorbed it in my ears,
nose and mouth, through my closed eyes. I put out my hands and
let it brush my fingertips. I tried again. To rise from the earth.
But I could not clear my mind. I felt the lightness come, but it
seemed to halt at eyebrow level, occlude itself, disappear. I experienced a moment of panic. Don't disappear, my soul cried. But it
disappeared.

Again? I was weary. I tried to think of rising, but it had turned
utterly mechanical, as if nothing would do but to bring in a crane
and hoist me on a hook to twirl gawkily in the air like some unre-
hearsed Peter Pan. Again? I could not even summon the thought.

I gave up. My shoulders drooped, and in the movement I realized how tense I had become, how my neck ached, how knotted
was the small of my back. I experienced a sense of disappointment. I had not expected to rise into the air, even an inch. The

the full limits of failure *See* Queer Theorem.

God, God Leap of logic. Leap of faith.

flying I hope my dad did try to fly. He was often so melancholy and had trouble being free. How do the quiet make their quiet heard when everywhere there is so much noise? The day his brother died, my eleven-year-old dad greeted his parents as they returned from the hospital. He said, "So Chuckie kicked the bucket." My dad was a boy. He didn't have the right words yet. And his father, in a moment I wish could be redone, rather than hugging my dad, crying with my dad, struck him and yelled at him for using such careless language. My father fled upstairs. My dad told me that soon after he thought about killing himself. He was so young that the method he'd devised to end his life was to flush himself down the toilet, as if he might be able to chase after his brother, to follow him to wherever it was that Chuckie had gone.

disappointment was not over that failure. I had been at this foolish enterprise for about two minutes—no more than three at
most—and I was exhausted, both mentally and physically. How
could I hope for success in such a short time? And success is not
the right word. I did not hope for success. But in such a short
time, I could not even expect to have tested **the full limits of failure**. Amy had been right; I needed regular exercise. I had let my
body deteriorate.

I opened my eyes and blinked several times. The sun was now
bright, though still low, a couple of yards above the horizon. My
little archipelago of friendly clouds had drifted by, leaving an un-
charted expanse of silvery blue. I circled the knoll and descended
along the path to my orchard. Here a large flock of crows waddled
about, pecking at the grass. A flock? A herd. They were as fat as
cattle. "Caw!" I cried at them, and flapped my arms. "Caw," they
called back, and flapped, too—hopped, flapped and made it into
the air. "Caw. Caw."

Or were they saying, "**God, God**"?

Such thoughts were pointless and unwanted. Nonetheless, my
mind raced on, forming a mute prayer, "Oh, God, in whom I neither believe nor disbelieve, if **flying** has anything to do with You,
this project will never get off the ground!" I could do better than
that. I tried again, but no thought came. I turned to look back at
the knoll. Had I really—just a few minutes ago—been standing
out there, head bowed, behind a rock like someone sneaking a
leak, trying to fly? Maybe I needed a vacation.

I entered the house by the kitchen door. My older son was up
and staring vacantly into the open refrigerator.

"Watching the ice cubes freeze?" I asked, and was instantly
sorry, because one milli-second before I said it something had

"God," he said, "as I understand Him." "God as I understand him" comes from AA. Sobriety as a great adventure, opening that fairy door to magic, to flight.

Icarus "You need to get as close to death as you possibly can."
         "But there's a danger to that."
         "Like when Icarus flew close to the sun."
                  —Haruki Murakami, *Killing Commendatore*

when I talk of my own experience This is how AA works.

come to me, something that Mr. I. Crane had said. Was it still there, in my mind? What had he said? I remembered the sudden flash of intuition his words had given me, an intuition that in physical form was like a plain stretching to infinity. "God," he had said. Something about God. **"God," he said, "as I understand Him."** And for one brief moment, I had stood like an adventurer coming from the woods to the endless, golden plain, or like a boy in a fairy tale before a magic door.

My mother told me about her flying dreams when I was five or six years old. Whether I myself had had such dreams before this, I cannot remember, but I did afterwards. Few sons are capable of imagining their mothers swooping about above the ground in graceful arcs and loops, but that is what my mother did in her dreams. Oh, not every night—at intervals. And so did I.

We who fly in our dreams, do not fly in aircraft. We are birds of will and ability who soar and bank and hover with no mechanical aids whatever, not even the giant eagle wings of **Icarus** or Daedalus, nor the juddering flappers of a Da Vinci ornithopter.

In the end we are useful to each other only in so far as we can share experiences; repeated failure makes empiricists of us all. I may criticize my friend or partner and advise, cajole, admonish, urge another form of action, but it is only **when I talk of my own experience** that I can be understood. It is the difference between, "Do it the way I say," and, "This is what happened to me."

This is what happened to me. My mother told me that sometimes in her dreams she flew. It had begun for her when she was a child living on a farm in Iowa, and the scenes of her early flight were in the barnyard, the hay loft, the apple orchard, she a little

red-headed girl in ringlets and pinafore levitating among the cows
and performing aerial pirouettes for their astonishment. The
scenes changed over the years: high-school, college, the city she
came to live in and that I was to be born in. She remembered the
time especially that she rose slowly out of her seat at the football stadium at college and flew over the cheering crowd at the
home-coming game in 1921. The gathered heads turned upward
toward her in admiration, not as would no doubt occur in reality,
in amazement or consternation, perhaps even fear, but with ap-
preciation and a gentle accolade.

These were still the days of the lone eagles (it was but seven
or eight years after Lindbergh's solo Atlantic crossing). The buzz
that came to earth from a distant aircraft was not common, and
we stood, hands shading the eyes, in the front yard and leaned
back to fix the solitary aviator in our gaze, and our spirits climbed
the bridge of eye-sight to sit beside the brave pilot in the cockpit.

Minnesota is famous for its lakes and woods, but all that lies
to the north of St. Paul. The southern third of the state, in which
the capital is situated, resembles Iowa, a low, rolling land of corn
and wheat and dairy farms, dotted with lakes, to be sure, but neither a wilderness nor a resort. Here the weather sweeps in out of
the west and southwest and is visible long before it breaks over
one's head. In my youth, a farm was defined by a clump of trees
rising above the fields, nestling in their protective strength and
shade the house and barns. Above these leafy sanctuaries rose the
bleached vanes of a windmill, seldom still in the constant breezes
that blew in from the Dakotas and beyond. From one fortress of
trees to the next measured a section or a half-section, laid out
in geometric rigidity to the horizon, and from any knoll I could
encompass a dozen or more habitations in the twenty-mile circle

of my gaze. Here, on still and dark July afternoons, suffocating in heat and dust, I have watched the thunderheads gather in the west, ominous with rain, tentative fingers of lightning touching the earth, as if the precursors of catastrophe, revolution or magical reawakening. Boom and crackle reach the ears on freshening winds, damp with distant oceans and springs. Rebirth, freedom, baptism sweep across the fields, and the grain bows before a magisterial force. Rain drops explode in the dust, patter through the leaves, drench the aisled corn. Then—gone—racing eastward toward tomorrow, the moment of a miracle. The sun reappears, dimmed by the vapors and mist that rise from the caldron. And through the golden light, my eye reaches out to a world newly green, resurrected.

Here in the east, where I now live, the rain comes unseen in the night, and in the morning, it persists, a gray substance, a film of wetness, which whispers of gloom and death. It is not a place for flying. Nor are the towered cities of the east coast, those nettles of pride that attest to the triumph of man and seem a challenge to the gods. The landscape of my youth was precisely the reverse: a triumph of God and a challenge to man. There, one could fly, if one dreamed.

Perhaps I dreamed flying dreams before my mother spoke to me about them. Who knows? My whole life up to the age of five or six, on the evidence of memory, seems not to have happened. In that sense, life began for me the day my mother told me her dreams.

I did not soar immediately. I had to learn. I found myself on a hill at twilight, a hummocked field of wheat such as I had seen from the car window on Sunday excursions. I was a tousled-haired lad amidst the sheaves, looking to the spirals of cloud above, a

symbol of dreams and hopes. An evening star twinkled on the horizon, just above a forest. I returned to this field for several nights as I slept, and the feeling that lingers in remembrance is one of yearning. I was yearning myself aloft. But for some time I remained rooted to the ground. In my dreams I even took to fluttering my hands in a tentative way, as if this partial concession to bird flight would help. It didn't help. I asked my mother about it. We were in the kitchen where she was making cinnamon buns. She held her doughy hands before her and looked at them curiously. Did she flutter them? No, she didn't think so. She gave them a little flutter. No, definitely not. Then, as if they had a life of their own, her hands bent at the wrists and swung back and forth rhythmically like the hands of a Balinese dancer. That was the motion she used, she said. It gave her control. With little twists of her hands—graceful hula undulations—she could change her direction, or altitude. I tried it myself. I didn't like the effect. And in my dreams, I couldn't remember my mother's advice, anyway. There seemed to be a blocked channel from our kitchen to the windy wheat field where I practiced.

Mr. I. Crane.

Vestry is a short street on Manhattan's lower West Side, in the "triangle below Canal," now called Tribeca, not to my mind a gracious coinage. Vestry runs east and west, more or less, and is made up of dilapidated warehouses, factories and lofts, some now converted to living and working quarters for artists, a few apartments, a few shops, a few bleak and run-down facades of no distinguishable architecture or purpose; in short, it is characteristic of much of lower Manhattan, before one reaches the World Trade Center

low-rise atoll In John McPhee's *In Suspect Terrain*, the geologist Anita Harris explains the saddle of New York City. "The towers of midtown, as one might imagine, were emplaced in substantial rock, Anita said—rock that once had been heated near the point of melting, had recrystallized, had been heated again, had recrystallized, and, while not particularly competent, was more than adequate to hold up those buildings. Most important, it was right at the surface. You could see it, in all its micaceous glitter, shining like silver in the outcrops of Central Park. Four hundred and fifty million years in age, it was called Manhattan schist. All through midtown, it was at or near the surface, but in the region south of Thirtieth Street it began to fall away, and at Washington Square it descended abruptly. The whole saddle between midtown and Wall Street would be underwater, were it not filled with many tens of fathoms of glacial till. So there sat Greenwich Village, SoHo, Chinatown, on material that could not hold up a great deal more than a golf tee—on the ground-up wreckage of the Ramapos, on crushed Catskill, on odd bits of Nyack and Tenafly. In the Wall Street area, the bedrock does not return to the surface, but it comes within forty feet and is accessible for the footings of the tallest things in town. New York grew high on the advantage of its hard rock." This passage taught me that rocks are books.

a magazine That magazine was a Standard Oil publication, one of my dad's first jobs. The founder of the Pratt Institute, Charles Pratt, had a company called Astral Oil that would become part of Rockefeller's Standard Oil in 1874. Astral is Standard.

Varick Street My husband worked on Varick Street for years, at *New York* magazine. My dad called Joe a few weeks before he died. Joe and I weren't yet married, so they didn't know each other well, though they had enjoyed playing banjo (Dad) and ukulele (Joe) together. Joe is a little hazy on what was said during that phone call, allowing me to imagine their conversation, something like, Take good care of my baby. Which, knowing my dad, is definitely not how it went.

disappearance My dad was not very good at day-to-day parenting. He was not much of a cook and not really involved in our activities. My mom did all of that. It wouldn't surprise me to learn that he, father of six, had never changed a diaper. Maybe writing this book was a way to deal with the fear of what he might do in case my mother died before him.

Charley Charley is my brother's name, after his uncle Chuckie. Charley has a son named Charles.

ability "Ability" here is a tricky word, as if women come to parenting naturally, whatever that means. I remember babies being thrust into my arms as a teen, as if I would somehow know how to take care of them because I was female. Parenting well isn't natural, it's a skill that anyone can learn.

and the towers of Wall Street, a generally decrepit, **low-rise atoll**
awaiting the landing craft of a more advanced civilization.

I was vaguely familiar with the area because years before, for
a brief time, I had worked for **a magazine** that employed a print
house quartered on **Varick Street**, which crosses Vestry, and I had
regularly made the trip down from mid-town on the Broadway
IRT, inky proof sheets in hand.

Returning from lunch on Friday afternoon, I had first, however, to make those arrangements necessary to a single parent.
About two p.m. I called home and caught my younger son in that
split second between his arrival from school and his **disappearance** into other people's houses. I told him I would not be back
for dinner as I had a meeting in New York City, information he
greeted with indifference. I told him what he might find to eat
in the refrigerator, how to prepare it, when he could expect my
return, and please, would he leave a note for his brother, passing along this information? He asked if he could have **Charley** (a
friend) over and I acquiesced, seeing already the empty soda cans
and deflated potato chip bags left about the kitchen that I would
find on my return, the only evidence that he had actually eaten.
If he went out, leave me a note telling me where he had gone and
telephone by midnight when I would be back and could come
retrieve him, unless he was staying overnight at whatever friend's
house he had come to roost in. I wished to draw out the conversation to make sure I was covering every eventuality—aware that I
did not possess Amy's **ability** in this area—while my son, obvi-
ously, wanted to terminate the call as quickly as possible. "Okay,"
he said, "I gotta go," as I continued to admonish him, but finally
I put up the receiver, certain that my absence from home would
precipitate some irreversible catastrophe. I then called Mavis to

Pegasus Pegasus is the logo of *Reader's Digest*, but this place he describes, with its proximity to Grand Central, is the Yale Club, where my father was a member for years.

The Pegasus Club A place I would end up years later. *See* The End.

mushroom What fertility there is in fungus.

not yet completed Right.

cancel a tentative date for a quick drink after work—tentative, that is, to my mind, but confirmed in hers. And what vision of irresponsible bachelordom (foxtrotting with a bevy of show girls in the Rainbow Room or some other Gatsbyesque dancehall) I left her with, I do not know. But it occurred to me that I was as impatient as my son, hungry for some undefined freedom which I felt Mavis might deny me.

I rode to Manhattan on the 4:15 with that impatience still barking at my heels, as if my departure were in fact a stealthy retreat and I had nearly made it but for a pesky dog. Detraining in Grand Central, I walked a few blocks north to the Pegasus Club where I still maintained a membership, though I rarely had occasion to use it. Under the circumstances, I was aware of the ability of **Pegasus** to fly, but it was not that art that had given the club its name. The winged horse had struck a rock on Mount Helicon with its hooves and from the spot rose a spring, later sacred to the Muses. **The Pegasus Club**, originally, was dedicated to the arts, principally writing and painting, and was now open to magazine editors, illustrators and advertising executives of every stripe who had the money to keep it afloat. (Pegasus tamed, once again, by a golden bridle.) Although I knew few of the members well, the club was a comfortable oasis for a drink and a meal, a place where I could wash my hands and relax in the lounge before dinner in an unhurried way that was impossible in a public restaurant or hotel.

I made my way upstairs to the club library, a cozy place of wood paneling, leather chairs and quiet. The musty odor of old pages, a **mushroom** scent of things growing in the dark, evoked mystery, secrets, adventures **not yet completed**. I wandered among the stacks at one side of the room and took out the slim

dry martini After my dad got sober he'd tell me how, on nights when he couldn't sleep, he'd think that if he went downstairs and had three shots of vodka, he'd sleep. But he didn't do it. *Just don't drink*, as he told the people he sponsored in AA.

no one had borrowed the book in decades Somewhere is a book that has been sitting the longest, untouched on a library shelf. It almost makes me sweaty with desire to imagine pulling this book off the shelf, opening its pages to the air, to my eyes.

known, but ungrasped *The Rings of Saturn*.

the final pages Did my dad know he was writing his final pages here? Did he know he'd never finish writing this book? I've been working on this book so long, some days I wonder if I'll ever finish writing it. And even if do, I already know I'll never finish writing it. As long as I am alive I will find more clues, more books, more evidence that belongs here. I don't think I've ever really finished writing any of my books. I just stop reading them and so my additions and revisions stop too. I start working on something else. When my novel *The Seas* was republished almost fifteen years after it first came out, I took the opportunity to change and fix many parts of that book.

volume of Wind, Sand and Stars by Antoine de St. Exupery, his last book before he was lost over the Mediterranean in 1944. Then I descended a floor to the lounge, selected a chair, and signaled to the waiter. I ordered a very **dry martini**, which here, at the club, was a beakerful of crisp gin and ice, and settled back with the book. The glue in the spine creaked arthritically as I opened it; apparently **no one had borrowed the book in decades**. I flipped the pages, reading here and there a paragraph, a sentence. De St. Exupery wrote straightforwardly enough, but with just a touch of ellipsis, an element left out occasionally or hurried past, and when he came to the deep truths of his experience, he said it once and not again as if the truth, for him too, slipped away like a will-o-wisp, seen, gone, **known, but ungrasped**.

My drink came. I took a sip and put the glass on the side table. The book in my lap fell open to its last pages. I looked down and read:

Here in **the final pages** of this book, I remember again those musty civil servants who served as our escort in the omnibus when we set out to fly our first mails, when we prepared ourselves to be transformed into men—we who had had the luck to be called. Those clerks were kneaded of the same stuff as the rest of us, but they knew not that they were hungry.

To come to man's estate it is not necessary to get oneself killed round Madrid, or to fly mail planes, or to struggle wearily in the snows out of respect for the dignity of life. The man who can see the miraculous in a poem, who can take pure joy from music, can break his bread with

murdered What murders men? *See* Citizens of the Peace.

breathe upon *See* Spirits.

comrades, opens his window to the same refreshing wind off the sea. He too learns a language of men.

But too many men are left unawakened.

Idly, I let slip a few more pages, and came to the end of the book. Again I read:

What torments me . . . is the sight, a little bit in all these men, of Mozart **murdered**. Only the Spirit, if it **breathe upon** the clay, can create Man.

A shadow darkened the page and remained, and I was aware that someone stood before me. A man. I could see his feet. I did not want to be disturbed. I ached with a need for loneliness, a time of expiation for my sin of discontent. But it was necessary to look up, to acknowledge the presence. It was Mr. I. Crane. My annoyance at the interruption must have showed.

"Is it as bad as that?" Mr. Crane asked. "Just think. I might have been Colonel Law instead."

I closed my book, but otherwise did not move, fearful of betraying any emotion. "You know Colonel Law?" I said as flatly as possible.

"I know *of* him. We have not met."

"Then I suppose that you know that I saw him today."

"I do not know it, except as you tell me now. But I suspected it."

"And why would you suspect it?" I asked.

"Because he has become interested in me ever since the affair of Mr. Park."

I showed no recognition of the name. "Mr. Park?" I said.

deus ex machina *See* Ghosts in the Machine.

pronounce the Latin My mother tells how once she reflexively corrected her Midwestern mother-in-law's pronunciation of the Parisian fashion label Mainbocher. Immediately my mother cringed and regretted the correction, realizing she'd embarrassed my grandma, who responded, "You Easterners pronounce everything differently." In copyediting this book, Greg Villepique informed me that while Mainbocher was a fashion house in Paris, leading people to pronounce the name "Man-bo-shay" (the correction my mother made), the designer Main Bocher was actually an American man from the Midwest whose name is pronounced Maine-Bocker. It's unclear whether the faux French pronunciation of the fashion house was authorized or not. Petra Slinkard, curator of "Making Mainbocher," the Chicago History Museum's retrospective, called the pronunciation of the brand one of the "most controversial topics" in putting together the show. In other words, my mom and my grandma are both right.

"Bring it along," Which made me ask, *Can a person go to an AA meeting when they are drunk?* The best answer I found is that the only requirement to attend a meeting is a desire to stop drinking.

"Leonard Park. The man who was on the Washington Monument."

"Oh, yes. I remember you mentioned a man on the monument. I've wondered since then, is it really possible to stand on top of the monument? I have a picture in my encyclopedia. It looks rather pointy."

"I've no idea," Mr. Crane said. "I suppose for an aerialist, a daring fellow like Philippe Petit, with a balancing pole. Mr. Park was not standing on top of it. He was hugging the stone like a teddy bear, crying out for mercy and succor."

"Oh," I said, and could think of nothing else. I considered "succor" a Biblical word, and that put me in mind of the phrase *deus ex machina*, the machine, in Mr. Park's case, being a helicopter. I would have mentioned this, but I was never sure how to **pronounce the Latin**, so I demurred.

"I take it that Colonel Law did not mention Leonard Park to you."

I could not lie outright. I never could. "Yes," I said. "He mentioned him."

"Are you going in to dinner?"

I was caught off guard. "Yes," I said. Mr. Crane stood back, as if to allow me to rise from my chair. Feebly I sought some delaying tactic which might shake him off. I thought of pleading an engagement, and then realized it was useless, especially as I meant, in a short while, to appear before Mr. Crane again at the SOI meeting. Still, seeking delay and possibly an excuse for not sitting with him at dinner, I gestured in the direction of my drink. "Yes," I said again, "but I uh . . ."

"Bring it along," Mr. Crane said.

Well, shit, I thought, why do these things happen to me?

**honesty, clarity, A tendency to side with those whose innocence had rendered them
eccentric or slightly mad** Yes, he did.

Park Avenue Leonard Park Avenue? Ed Park Avenue?

The whole idea of attending the meeting that night, which I had wrapped in a comfortable sense of adventure and exploration, began to appear a vexation. An intolerable burden. I no longer wanted to go. I wanted to go home, where I could be truly alone with my thoughts. There in familiar surroundings, in the company of my own mind, that was the only comfortable adventure. I missed Amy deeply in situations like this. She welcomed what I shied from, and had made possible for me forays into the unknown—even, I mean, such simple unknowns as attending a cocktail party where the crowd was not "ours." She could talk to strangers, and I, lingering by her side, could join in occasionally, and when desperate for a casual utterance, could turn to her for comfort and a response that need not be regarded as a challenge. And thinking of her, I was given a strength not normally mine to wield.

I had these strengths: an aggressive, even ruthless, **honesty**. A need, a compulsion, for **clarity**. A sense that merely acting in a moral and responsible way was not enough. A keen eye for charlatans. **A tendency to side with those whose innocence had rendered them eccentric or slightly mad.**

So girded, I arose and, taking my drink, accompanied Mr. Crane. The dining room had a high ceiling, decorated with a floral molding from which hung many armed chandeliers. It could accommodate more than a hundred people, but tonight only four tables were occupied. The maître-d gave us a wave of his arm and let us pick our own. Mr. Crane chose a side table, along the windows, looking out over **Park Avenue**.

The End

That is it. That's where my dad's book stops. With a start so well thought out, clear and fully drawn, it is strange to find no end. Why did he stop writing? Lack of time? Concern for the marketplace? Frustration with the publishing industry? What uncertainties stop art? Did he know where he wanted the book to go, what he wanted to have happen? Did he know the ending? Did he write it down? Not even an outline, or at least not one I've found yet. One day, one year, I will have to clean out my parents' house. Who knows what I will find when I do. Maybe my father's book will be revealed to me little by little. Maybe I will learn how to fly. Already, here at the end of my book, I didn't find an end to my dad's book, but I *did* find even more of it.

Peter Sís drew and wrote an adaptation of Farid ud-Din Attar's *The Conference of the Birds*, the twelfth-century Persian poem I started my book with, the poem that tells a story of how the birds of the world set out to find their leader, to look for answers. Toward the end of *The Conference of the Birds*, the bravest birds have crossed the Valley of Quest, the Valley of Love, the Valley of Understanding, the Valley of Detachment, the Valley of Unity, the Valley of Amazement, and even the Valley of Death. They are so tired. They ask the wise Hoopoe bird, "Are we alive or dead? Where is that king with all the answers? We've come all this way. Let us see him! We made it through all those valleys!" The Hoopoe bird answers, "Valleys? Those were only an illusion, birds, a dream. We've been through nothing. We are just now at the beginning of our journey." Then, on the following page, in a circle of text that makes a reader unsure where to begin reading, Sís writes, "Some birds could not believe it. On the spot they lost all hope. They dropped dead and fell from the sky. Some kept flying."

We have come all this way, so many chapters read, some that were perhaps as arduous as any steep valley. *See* A Thousand Deaths. *See* Citizens of the Peace. Please do not lose hope when I tell you we are just beginning.

Perhaps chapter 3 is not the end of my dad's book, just the place where he stopped writing. It's not a terrible place to leave us forever, a grand, empty dining room above Park Avenue, a glass of cold gin. The room he's thinking of is in the Yale Club, a luxurious place we visited as children. The club is steps away from New York's Grand Central Terminal. I remember one meal there, a buffet brunch, ending with an actual silver bucket filled with chocolate mousse. I helped myself to the greediest serving. Then, back at our table, one bite revealed that the dessert had been laced with rum, ruined to my tastes. I burned with shame and disappointment. The pile of brown mousse browned even more, staring me down. Such waste and a newfound suspicion of all good things. I was young when my father gave up his membership. I know he loved the quiet of the library there and its proximity to the trains, but it became an expense a man with six children couldn't justify. And my father, a cardinal among the hawks, his Midwestern, tender heart, stopped looking for a home among the Ivy men with loud voices.

Shipley's dictionary states that "cardinal," the word we use to mean a fixed and unchanging point, comes from the Greek *kardan*, to hinge, to swing. A word that grows out of its opposite. I am alive. I am dead.

After a forty-year absence, I recently returned to the Yale Club with my mom. The class of 1951 invites the widows to attend their gatherings. We went out of curiosity, looking for parts of him. We went to spend a weekend together in the city. We sat in that same large room of the rummy mousse, the room my father described in the book. We had a giddy glass of wine underneath a portrait of Gerald Ford. My mom is game for almost anything. She is fueled by curiosity for the world, and I know how lucky that makes me. We spent the next day listening to the stories of my dad's classmates. As the weekend was coming to a close, a man named Jack announced that Yale does not hold seventieth reunions. In a stark way, this was goodbye forever. The realization settled in the room. Jack didn't find the words to say what needed saying. Maybe this blank was appropriate to the unknown that lay ahead for these men. But the truth was bleak. Jack sat down. The room felt raw. No refreshing wind off the sea. Where was the classmate naked enough to offer a poem of parting? He'd already departed.

Despite my efforts, death continues to hurt me and lace my life with fear. I worry through the night. Sleep like a spotted thing.

I move through the loves death might and will one day take from me. There's a compulsion I feel to do every single thing right: light a candle in the morning when it is still dark, not yell at my children, cook food, serve people, help clean my mother's house, stay off screens, keep myself beautiful and quiet and clean, and if I do everything right, death will pass by me and mine. Even in writing that, I know it to be untrue. There's no right or good that avoids death. The fear and sorrow I blame death for are just another story I tell myself, a story that goes, Death is forever, death is alone, death is destruction. I have always loved stories, even the sad ones, even the bad ones.

The next morning, my mom slept in. She had a terrible hangover. She never drinks, and the catering staff at the Yale Club had been so smooth and professional, I think she didn't even notice they had refilled her glass many times over the course of the evening. She had drunk far more than she can tolerate. Perhaps she'd been nervous. Perhaps she felt the spirits. Most unfairly, her hangover put me in a foul mood, as if finally, here was someone I could blame for all the damage alcohol had wreaked on my family, even though my mom was never the one with a drinking problem. She felt so awful, so sick, and, rather than caring for her, trying to ease her illness, I felt wounded. I was both mad and sad. I had so wanted us to go to the brunch room, thinking that if we were there together, if she helped me remember the way things had been, my dad would have to appear and for a moment or two we'd have him again. We'd eat toast, drink coffee with him. He wouldn't even have to speak if he didn't want to. Instead she was hungover. Too many spirits. The magic of my memories, the fictions I write, often shine brighter than the realities of death and disease. I brought my mom coffee, Advil, a buttered roll. I ate brunch alone, hurt, reckoning the history of addiction in my family and still fearing all that death will take, particularly the loss of human wisdom. I ate quickly, wanting to collect every story before the storytellers were gone. I searched the hotel, but the '51 classmates had dispersed, and honestly, looking for my dad at Yale is as fruitless as looking for him on the internet. The handful of men I had spoken with didn't remember my quiet father. One asked, "Walter Hunt, the architect?" A new story I wanted to hear, but no, he was not an architect. I went to the empty library instead and there, in a display right by the door, just inside, I found Stephen Vincent Benét, the writer my dad's broken book mentioned. I let Benét speak for my dad.

> I came to New York to look up spiritualists and mediums.
> You'd be surprised at the number of practicing ones there
> are. But they're rather dull as a class—duller than I ex-
> pected. And when I found that you were both here—well,
> I couldn't miss seeing you, the last day.

We both were there, Dad. Did you see us? My mom got a ride home from her boyfriend. Though he offered me a ride, I boarded the train instead, for the loud silence of a locomotive.

My mom's been trying to clear out her house, aware that my siblings and I will inherit a tremendous burden if she doesn't do it herself. She gives me a stack of books each time I go. Last visit, she slipped a doozy into my hands, *The Thousand and One Nights*. Though the copy was clearly an old one, the colors of the cover were still brilliant, as if it hadn't been read much. Inside I found an inscription in my grandma Marcella's hand. "For Charles William

Hunt from Daddy and Mother, Eighth Birthday, March 3—1941."
My grandparents gave my young uncle this gift three weeks before
he died. A murderous sultan, a man whose jealous and suspicious
brother had convinced him to believe "all women to be naturally
treacherous," a man who has ordered his court to provide him
with a new wife every day; "In order to prevent disloyalty . . .
he should . . . have her strangled next morning . . . And thus,
every day, was a maid married and a wife murdered." What a tale
for children. Scheherazade, daughter of the grand vizier charged
with conducting these executions, wants to spare her father the
terrible task of killing the young wives. Scheherazade cannot
abide this abuse. So she tells her father a story to convince him
to allow her to marry the horrible sultan. Then brave Scheherazade tells a thousand broken stories, one per night. Storytelling
as survival, as living. With the promise of providing an ending
the following night, the sultan remains interested. Scheherazade's
stories not only keep her alive but also spare the one thousand
young women the sultan would have consumed and murdered
for each night of story. Many of Scheherazade's stories are not
collected in this book. My uncle's edition has only twenty-
five, leaving a reader to imagine 975 tales that may or may not
exist.

Knowing he'd soon be gone from her sight, my grandma gave
her son a book that ends and also doesn't end. The inscription
of his entire name, first, middle, and last, is like our attempts to
name the waves in the ocean. In this inscription my grandma asks
her son to hold his place, to not get lost in that great ocean, to not
become a droplet with no name. Or at least not until she too could
join him in that sea.

In the end, I realized there would be no end to clues. For

example, this morning, considering a note about *The Story of Ferdinand*, I learned that Munro Leaf, the book's author, also worked on the cartoon series *Private Snafu*, World War II–era adult animations that instructed by demonstrating the results of doing everything wrong. SNAFU, the military acronym for Situation Normal: All Fucked Up, and one my father used in chapter 3, a chapter I'd read just moments earlier. When these crisscrosses occur I do not think, Oh, coincidence. I think, Hi, Dad.

The Walt Whitman I read at his funeral is the part where Whitman explains the first law of thermodynamics. It has carried me through many deaths.

> *Return in peace to the ocean my love,*
> *I too am part of that ocean, my love, we are not so much*
>   *separated,*
> *Behold the great rondure, the cohesion of all, how perfect!*
> *But as for me, for you, the irresistible sea is to separate us,*
> *As for an hour carrying us diverse, yet cannot carry us diverse*
>   *forever;*
> *Be not impatient—a little space—know you I salute the air, the*
>   *ocean and the land,*
> *Every day at sundown for your dear sake my love.*

A little space, indeed. At this end that is not an end, while I wish for clarity, what I have instead is a bit of chaos. Here's what happened: I thought I was done writing this book. I returned to the tremendous stack of papers I had assembled over the years spent working on it. I wondered what I might be able to get rid of, to recycle. In the piles, I found a bunch of photos from middle school, notes from former boyfriends (Hi, Carlos!), letters from my grandmas, letters from my high school friend Lila when she was living in Egypt. I found my mortgage. I found a yellow legal pad belonging to my father with the word "evidence" printed across the top. No joke. It says "evidence." That's the brand name. I found my dad's journal from 1987 with a list of the books he'd read between January and July of that year, and then I found a copy of my dad's flying book with a new version of chapter 1, a different place to start.

Ed Park writes, "Thousands of sheets of paper, perhaps all of Walter Walter's hopeless writing whirling like birds as they blew away." I have no idea where these newfound copies of my dad's book came from. I bet I printed them off his computer soon after he died, when the software he used was still relatively up-to-date, when he still felt close enough to me that I didn't need to read his book, just wanted to have it near. I really don't remember where these parts of his book came from. They appeared from nowhere. Clearly, though, this isn't a fact even if it might be true.

I will not ask you to read this new chapter 1, or any more of his book, especially since what I found is mostly a revision. I know, we've already come all this way. A person gets tired. He's my dad, after all, and there are so many other stories you must get to in the short time we've been given with eyes, ears, and hands made for reading things.

Renee Gladman worries that if her book and title know each other, they will conspire. They might leave her out. "I wrote a book at a glass table and wouldn't tell it its name." I will tell you this about the newfound pages from my dad's book: The story changes some, but most important, my dad's book has a title.

With Gladman in mind, I am reluctant to tell you the name. Titles have always been hard for me, as they can feel like coffin nails, sealing in that which had once been alive. But we've come so far, I want to give you something. My dad called his book *The Garden of Infinity*. It's not a great title. Or maybe it is. Borgesian. Titles are hard. And part 1, the only part of his book that, to my knowledge, exists, he called "How to Fly and the Plot So Far." I like that title better. As Ursula K. Le Guin tells us, magic can consist in the naming of a thing. My dad was writing a how-to book. Instructions for those who wish to fly without wings.

In the newfound pages, he gives us advice. He says that if you want to fly you'll need:

> **A craft.** The craft is a human body, in his case, "non-unique in every way."
>
> **Builders.** Or parents. If you want to fly, you have to be born. He writes of being born to parents who know "nothing about secret codes or the language of dogs."
>
> **Landscape.** This section is the story of a treehouse in his backyard, of first feeling the sky, and the troop of Catholic brothers, bullies who moved in down the block and pointed out to my dad again and again that where once there'd been a brother, now he just had death.

So, to fly you need a body, you need to be born, you need to speak dog, you need the earth and the sky, and you need to not be fearful of your neighbors, even if they seem to be jerks. That's pretty good advice.

I found his chapter 1 after I thought I was done. Or, at the end, I found the beginning.

One last bit here, then, really, we will be done reading my dad's book. But I have to include this part, this start, so we can finish. He writes:

late April He died April 30. A strange time to die, just as the fruit trees begin to flower here where we live.

though not to me How did he know the birds weren't speaking to him?

Missy The name Amy has changed to Missy; perhaps he thought it a bad idea to name a dead character after a living daughter. I agree and in fact once had to make a similar substitution.

That is how this story begins for me. I remember that.
I walked outside and breathed the air. It was **late April**.
The jonquils were up, cheerfully bugeling a good morning. Cherry blossoms whispered a shy greeting. The birds
spoke, **though not to me**, of avian concerns. I walked
about—nothing vigorous—and then went back to my
door, stepped inside, entered the hall to the kitchen, and
every cell in my body cried out, "**Missy**, it's a beautiful
day." But I did not say a word. For Missy, I knew, was not
there. But to my unspoken exclamation, I heard a mut-
tered response above in the bedroom, indistinct through
wads of bedclothes, and my mind carried me to the coffee
pot to pour a cup, add the milk, and ascend the staircase
with this morning's offering to my love, my wife.

I am alone in the house and I cannot help but wonder
what it was that I was planning for all these years. That
morning when this story begins, I stood in the kitchen
and planned nothing. I knew nothing. But I felt Missy all
around me, heard the sound of her, and I puttered content-
edly in her presence, and it was not until I had showered
that the feeling drifted away into the golden sunshine.

The legal pad I found, "evidence," is filled with notes my dad
kept while writing *The Garden of Infinity*. In *The Art of Living*,
Thich Nhat Hanh writes, "It's not scientific to believe that after
our body decomposes we become nothing." I am, if anything, a
reader and a believer in science. My dad's cursive is hard to read,
but in the "evidence," there are bits on flying dreams and dead
aviators. There are notes on AA and silent-film actresses. And in
the middle of these notes, there's one he wrote to me. It reads,

MANDY—my nickname—WE WENT TO DINNER W/HERBS AT EMILY
SHAWS. HOME EARLY? DAD

In 1967 my parents celebrated their tiny wedding with a meal
at Emily Shaw's. This restaurant hasn't existed since 1989. The
building still stands, and a newer, fancier restaurant has moved
in. I know I should keep my mind on the living, but when I see
this note, it's all I can do to not drive down to Emily Shaw's and
search for a way to have dinner with my mom and dad in a dead
restaurant. It's only a mile from their house, so even if my dad
ends up drunk at the bar, chances are he'll make it home safe,
especially since he's already dead. Emily Shaw, also dead (since
1974), might pour the sherry, serve the Jellied Consommé, whatever that is, while Tallulah Bankhead (dead since 1968), a regular
at the bar, might sing by the piano. I want that. I'd like to be there.
But not as much as I want to be here, in this life right now, this
living.

Kelly Link's short story "Lull" is a haunting masterpiece I've
read close to forty times. I love to study this story. It's structured
with the ingenuity of ice crystals or calculus, a pattern so delicate and intricate it thrills me. And it's a heartbreaker, which is a
plus in my book. One short section of it has spurred a philosophy I think of as the Third Thing. In this scene the devil and the
cheerleader are in the closet at a party, playing Seven Minutes in
Heaven. Rather than kissing in the closet, the devil and the cheerleader tell each other stories.

"Well, what's the scariest thing?" says the cheerleader.
"You're the expert, right? Give me a little help here."
    "The scariest thing," the devil says. "Okay. I'll give you

two things. Three things. No, just two. The third one is a secret."

When I was a teenager my friend Patchen was murdered. It was inconceivable that he could be gone, as he was one of the most alive people I've ever met. Patchen had built a raft and was floating through Peru, down to the Amazon. He was shot by two Aguaruna men along the banks of the Marañón River. The men were drunk. Patchen had played the drums like Animal from the Muppets. He'd been raised in the woods by a single mom, Sandra. She's a naturalist and a wonderful woman. Woodchucks and chickadees lived in their house with them. They had a friend who was a moose. People took Patchen's death very badly, as he was someone who made community. He was only twenty-six. In the days and months that followed Patchen's death, I understood how a dead friend could make the living feel more alive, a real salvation and a responsibility to live life fully, as I live for Patchen now too.

At one memorial my friend Sally asked Sandra, "How did you make such a good son?" What formula had she followed? Sandra answered quickly. "There are three things you need to do," she said. "First, nurse your children until they are old enough to tell you they want to stop. Second, discipline them only with humor. And third—" But this all happened thirty years ago, back when I never even thought of being a mom, and so I'm afraid I have forgotten the third piece of advice Sandra gave. It haunts me now, especially since I am a mom who has significantly failed at practicing Sandra's other two pieces of advice for raising children. Maybe my brain won't let me remember the last bit of wisdom

because we need unknowns. We need blanks. That way, on occasion at least, I might be doing something right without even
knowing it.

At middle school dances of yore, children were advised to
"leave room for the Lord," space between their bodies, space for
the Third Thing. Or, as Whitman writes, "a little space." Not life,
not death, but a third thing, an in-between, something like a story,
something like a holy ghost.

My dad did not believe in God as God had been taught to
him. That god had taken his brother away at a young age. How
could that make any sense? But my dad did believe in clues and
patterns, like 2 Down, Japanese sash; or the symmetry of a maple leaf; or the railroad and its labyrinth of timetables and routes
crisscrossing the land. He believed in patterns like a, b, c, d, and
genetic codes and coincidences and joyful human absurdities like
"refrain" meaning both hold back and return again and again. He
believed in the joyful unknown, the third thing.

Some days, with clues scattered everywhere about me, I feel
the frustration of a nonreader who studies the strange shapes
someone else has called words. I struggle to see the patterns, to
decode some meaning, but instead find mostly a big jumble of attempted communications that make no sense. I listen to the birds
and hear their words without ever really understanding what it is
the birds are trying to say.

My daughter's seventh-grade science teacher, Ms. Schaffer-
Sermani, created a simple and inspiring project at the start of the
Covid-19 pandemic. She asked her students to watch their yards,
to watch even just a tiny section of their yards. She asked them to
consider the boundaries. What enters and exits the yard? She had
them think wholly, of an entire ecosystem in their own backyard.

She had her students consider smells and air flow, predators and pollinators, slugs, soil. I think about Ms. Schaffer-Sermani's experiment and observations. To my own considerations of our backyard, I add a thought for the people underground, the toil, their blood, the unseen bits of them in the air, thoughts of the millipede, how exhalations in the ocean might have made their way here. I think of Benoit Mandelbrot and some idea of the macro mirrored in the micro. In writing, reading, and imagining, I sometimes believe I can control things. Though I'm in control of nothing. Not even my own backyard, small as it may be. Clues come. Many of them make no sense. This week alone there are pink milkweed balls and large sprays of trefoil, the flower I call eggs and bacon. There's a barred owl making a nest. I tell myself a story where all these parts, people, bacteria belong, relate, connect. There are maggots in the garbage bucket. There was an oil spill in my backyard right before I moved in. Oil that once was what? That started where? I collect but I am too near to see the whole.

As I try to bring this book to a close, to put some sort of lid on it and know the shape of its final container, my impulse is to jam-pack every last indication and event inside. This morning I think, How does my dog fit in? Where can I put the story of the olive and the chipmunk Tricia told me yesterday? What about the way I serve friends Popeye's chicken and pretend my husband made it? How about the way I thought my beloved pen pal and bosom buddy, Makeal, was a boy for years? Where does that go? What about Michele and the Archangels? Ruby and the twin twins? How can I account for everything? A book that contains all because we are all connected. But then, such a book of everything, Einstein's last theory, a place where there is room for all the stories, must also include the idea of tremendous holes and vacuums and ghosts and deaths. Keep the absent present. That's the whole story, the holes. Stay broken, stay open. The last chapter I found, the first chapter of my dad's book, though more humble than the sacred space behind a mystical waterfall, will stay secret, unpublished here, a silent clue gone uncollected, the third thing in this how-to for those of us who wish to fly.

Blackwings

But about my dog. Pablo is named for another, long-dead dog who lived with my friend Lisl Steiner. My daughters are still playing in the yard, *See* Circulation Desk, right where they were way back at the start of this book. While they play, Pablo unearths a gruesome, delicious find. He approaches the girls with the head of a baby deer in his jaws. The girls scream. His delight is their horror. Maybe he's just writing love stories. He often brings me deer skulls, leaving them at my feet like hostess gifts. He deposits the baby deer head near the girls, mistranslating their screams as a command to surrender the precious find. My husband gets a shovel and uses it to move the head from our yard. I watch a morbid, medieval, curious parade form. The dead deer head leads the way, then the sturdy shovel, then my husband marching into the forest with three little girls, more alive than most of us, following directly behind, dancing, observing, beginning their own collection of clues as to where and how and why we go when we go.

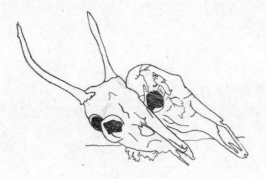

Where *is* that bird with all the answers? I don't know. I'm left with many questions. Especially this one. When we die and return to earth, will we be able to fly?

I saw a raptor this morning. After a night of freezing rain, its feathers were dark and disheveled. The bird had been through the wringer. I once worked as a secretary at a raptor center. There, I got to know many, many raptors. A baby kestrel once even took her rest on top of my computer monitor. But, against the bright gray sky, I could not identify this dark bird. It looked like a cartoon vampire. It looked like death.

Kaspar Hauser, the German youth raised in extreme isolation, was found in a square in Nuremberg in 1828. He was blinkered by the sun, unable to communicate or speak, the skin of his feet soft as a baby's. So many unknowns about his origins. I learned about Kaspar from Sebald. I teach Kaspar to my writing students. I say, "Let's think without words," an experiment that lasts a fraction of a second for us, lovers of language.

Yesterday two pileated woodpeckers meant a heartbeat, a

steadiness. The northern flicker, all things in balance. The oriole means the worst is over, and a large dragonfly that entered my house meant time for transformation. This wet bird, the dark raptor, was just trying to rest and dry out on a high branch, trying to mean nothing in these woods, and here I was, so stuffed with language, words spilled out of me, starting a narrative, wanting this bird to tell me a story. But that raptor was strong. Owl? No. Eagle? No. Vulture? No. Osprey? No. Sharp-shinned hawk? I don't know. It resisted. It didn't need language.

An editor from the city came to interview me. As she drove down my road a rafter of wild turkeys scooted across the street in front of her car. She was delighted by the birds and asked me, "Are those your turkeys?"

She'd connected turkeys and chickens. Many people raise backyard chickens in my town, and the turkeys she saw do indeed live in my backyard. But I didn't understand her question at first. I see these turkeys every day. I'd just never thought of them as mine. Do these turkeys belong to me? Do I belong to the dandelions? What is it to belong? Shipley remains silent on this word, though he does give me be. See fetus, and long. See lent. And "long" is so many things, so many tangled roots: loan, leave, slow, spring, seed, lentil, lenient, indulgent. "Belong" does not want to be tied down to one narrow definition. Are the turkeys mine? After a pause I answered, "Yes. They are my turkeys." And I am theirs.

I sit at the window to separate house finch from purple finch, trying to know the sparrows, as if knowing the name is knowing the bird. I split hairs and often arrive at the same thought: I'll just ask the bird what kind of bird it is. Then a quiet beat when I hear their answer. Then a further quiet beat because their answer isn't a word, isn't even an answer but something full of silence, a broken sense that feels like the bellowing hush of empty space the moment after we finish reading a book.

The Forest: A Bibliography

Akutagawa, Ryunosuke. "In a Grove."

Alcott, Louisa May. *Little Women.*

Alhazred, Abdul. *Necronomicon.*

Als, Hilton. "The Show-Woman," *The New Yorker.*

Andrews, V. C. *Flowers in the Attic.*

Anonymous. "Pretty Boy." (One Direction fan fiction)

Archimboldi, Benno von. *The Father.*

Attar, Farid ud-Din. *The Conference of the Birds.*

Aurora, The. Iowa State Agricultural College.

Baldwin, James. *The Fire Next Time.*

Baudelaire, Charles. *Les Fleurs du mal.*

Beckett, Samuel. *Worstward Ho.*

Bénet, Stephen Vincent. "Good Picker."

Bible, The.

Blanchfield, Brian. *Proxies: Essays Near Knowing.*

Book of Ether, The.

Borges, J. L. *Book of Imaginary Beings.*

Borges, J. L. *La biblioteca total.*

Borges, J. L. *Labyrinths.*

Boston Surgical and Medical Journal. "Cholera Infantum."

Brockhaus Enzyklopädie.

Brontë, Charlotte. *Jane Eyre.*

Brontë, Emily. *Wuthering Heights.*

Browne, Thomas. *Musaeum Clausum.*

Browne, Thomas. *Urn Burial.*

Butler, Octavia E. *Parable of the Sower.*

Butler, Octavia E. *Parable of the Talents.*

Calvino, Italo. *If on a winter's night a traveler.*

Cardiff, Janet. *Her Long Dark Hair.*

Carson, Anne. *Eros, the Bittersweet.*

Carson, Anne. *If, Then Winter.*

Cave, Nick. "Dear Cynthia."

Cave, Nick. Soundsuits.

Chandler, Raymond. "The Black-Eyed Blonde."

Chandler, Raymond. "The Man with the Shredded Ear."

Chaucer, Geoffrey. *The Canterbury Tales.*

Collins, Paul. "Solresol: The Universal Musical Language."

Crazy About One Direction. Directed by Daisy Asquith.

Davidson, Jeremy. *The Kept Private.*

Dawkins, Richard. *The God Delusion.*

DeVoe, Ronnie. Twitter feed.

Dewell, Ada Mills. *Poems.*

Doonan, Simon. *New York Observer.*

Ehrenreich, Barbara, and Deirdre English. *Witches, Midwives, and Nurses: A History of Women Healers.*

Elsaesser, Jessica, and Alaska McFadden. *Beginning.*

Elvira Madigan. Directed by Bo Widerberg.

Evenson, Brian. *The Open Curtain.*

Faulkner, William. *As I Lay Dying.*

Fleming, Ian. *Goldfinger.*

Flying Lotus. *You're Dead!*

Fox, Paula. *Desperate Characters.*

Free Solo. Directed by Elizabeth Chai Vasarhelyi and Jimmy Chin.

Garza, Cristina Rivera. *The Iliac Crest.*

Gay, Ross. "Joy Is Such a Human Madness."

Gladman, Renee.

Goldman, Andrew. "Richard Ford Is a Man Who Actually Listens."

Grahn, Judy. "A Woman Is Talking to Death."

Gray, Spalding. "Sex and Death to the Age 14."

Guyton, Tyree. *The Heidelberg Project.*

Haeger, Vera Elizabeth Mills. *The Mills Family: Twelve Generations Descended from Pilgrim Simon Mills I from Yorkshire, England 1630.*

Hammer, Karl E., *Miriam: The Disappearance of a New England Girl.*

Hartman, Saidiya. *Wayward Lives, Beautiful Experiments.*

Hawking, Stephen.

Henkes, Kevin. *Birds.*

Hinton, S. E. *The Outsiders.*

Homer. *The Iliad.*

hooks, bell. *Communion: The Female Search for Love.*

Hunt, Chuckie. *Funnies Book.*

Hunt, Marcella. *My Childhood.*

Hunt, Samantha. *The Dark Dark.*

Hunt, Samantha. *The Invention of Everything Else.*

Hunt, Samantha. *Mr. Splitfoot.*

Hunt, Samantha. *The Seas.*

Hunt, Walter. *The Garden of Infinity.*

Hunt, Walter. *The Land of Counterpane.*

Invisibilia. "Two Heartbeats a Minute."

Irving, Washington. "The Legend of Sleepy Hollow."

Jefferson Bee, The.

Jensen, Toni. *Carry: A Memoir of Survival on Stolen Land.*

Jones, Patricia Spears. *Swimming to America.*

Joyce, James. "The Dead."

July, Miranda. "Dear Samantha Hunt."

July, Miranda. *No One Belongs Here More Than You.*

Kaczynski, Theodore. *The Unabomber's Manifesto.*

Kawabata, Yasunari. "Canaries."

Keene, Adrienne. Twitter feed.

Keene, Carolyn. Nancy Drew series.

King, Stephen. *The Shining.*

Kinnell, Galway. *The Book of Nightmares.*

Klopstein, Aaron. "Cat Hairs in the Custard."
Klopstein, Aaron. "Twenty Inches of Monkey."
LaFontaine, Wanda. *Love's Tormenting Itch.*
LaFontaine, Wanda. *On the Aft Deck.*
Leaf, Munro. *The Story of Ferdinand.*
Le Guin, Ursula K. *The Wizard of Earthsea.*
L'Engle, Madeleine. *A Wrinkle in Time.*
Lewis, Sinclair. *Arrowschmidt.*
Link, Kelly. "Lull."
Lopez, Barry Holstun. *River Notes: The Dance of Herons.*
MacDonald, George. *The Golden Key.*
Marshall, Paule. *Brown Girl, Brownstones.*
Martin, Jacqueline Briggs, and Mary Azarian. *Snowflake Bentley.*
McHugh, Heather. *Broken English: Poetry and Partiality.*
McPhee, John. *In Suspect Terrain.*
Milletti, Christina. *Choke Box.*
Moonstruck. Directed by Norman Jewison.
Morrison, Toni. *Beloved.*
Morrison, Toni. *The Bluest Eye.*
Müller, Eva. *In the Future, We Are Dead.*
Munson, Portia. *Pink Project.*
Murakami, Haruki. *After the Quake.*
Murakami, Haruki. *Underground.*
Narcissister. *Marilyn.*
Nature.
New York Times, The.
Nhat Hanh, Thich. *The Art of Living.*
Noah, Trevor. *Afraid of the Dark.*
Noyes, Alfred. "The Highwaymen."
Okeowo, Alexis. "How Saidiya Hartman Retells the History of Black
    Life."
Old Farmer's Almanac, The.
Oliver, Mary. *Owls and Other Fantasies.*
One Thousand and One Nights, The.
Ovid. *Metamorphoses.*

Paris Match.

Park, Ed. "An Oral History of Atlantis."

Park, Ed. *Personal Days.*

Pitol, Sergio. *The Art of Flight.*

Poe, Edgar Allan. "Annabel Lee."

Poltergeist. Directed by Tobe Hooper.

Queneau, Raymond. *Cent mille milliards de poèmes.*

Reader's Digest.

Robison, Mary. *Why Did I Ever.*

Rulfo, Juan. *La Cordillera.*

Rulfo, Juan. *Pedro Páramo.*

Sagan, Carl. *Cosmos.*

Saint-Exupéry, Antoine de. *Wind, Sand and Stars.*

Salinger, J. D. "A Perfect Day for Bananafish."

Sante, Lucy. "The Mother Courage of Rock."

Sappho.

Saunders, George. "CivilWarLand in Bad Decline."

Schneemann, Carolee. *Interior Scroll.*

Seances. Directed by Guy Maddin.

Sebald, W. G. *The Emigrants.*

Sebald, W. G. *The Rings of Saturn.*

Sheldrake, Merlin. *Entangled Life: How Fungi Make Our Worlds, Change Our Minds & Shape Our Futures.*

Sheldrake, Rupert. *A New Science of Life.*

Shelley, Mary. *Frankenstein.*

Shepard, Lucius. *The Jaguar Hunter.*

Shepard, Lucius, and Robert Frazier. *Nantucket Slayrides.*

Shipley, Joseph T. *The Dictionary of Word Origins.*

Sillman, Amy. "Seating Arrangements."

Sís, Peter. *The Conference of the Birds.*

Skorpen, Liesel Moak. *We Were Tired of Living in a House.*

Smith, Ali. "Erosive."

Smith, Ali. "Universal Story."

Smith, Patti. *Just Kids.*

Solnit, Rebecca. *A Field Guide to Getting Lost.*

Song Dong. *Waste Not.*

Southey, Robert. "The Inchcape Rock."

Staples, William. "Whistling in Heaven."

Steinke, Darcey. *Flash Count Diary: Menopause and the Vindication of Natural Life.*

Sterne, Laurence. *The Life and Opinions of Tristram Shandy, Gentleman.*

Stevenson, Robert Louis. "The Land of Counterpane."

Stevenson, Robert Louis. *Treasure Island.*

Thoreau, Henry David. *Walden.*

Thurber, James. *The Secret Life of Walter Mitty.*

Tolstoy, Leo. *Anna Karenina.*

Torah, The.

Towada, Yoko. "Where Europe Begins."

Trout, Kilgore.

Truscott, Adrienne. *Asking for It: A One-Lady Rape About Comedy Starring Her Pussy and Little Else!*

van der Kolk, Bessel. *The Body Keeps the Score.*

Village Voice, The.

Wagner, Sally Roesch. *Sisters in Spirit: Haudenosaunee (Iroquois) Influence on Early American Feminists.*

Welch, Gillian. "I Dream a Highway."

White Diamond. Directed by Werner Herzog.

Whitman, Walt. "Out of the rolling ocean, the crowd."

Wilkerson, Isabel. *Caste: The Origins of Our Discontents.*

Williams, Kit. *Masquerade.*

Wilson, Emily. *Man Libs*, Babe.net.

Wollstonecraft, Mary. *A Vindication of the Rights of Women.*

Wood, James. "An Interview with W. G. Sebald."

Yale Record, The.

Zimmerman, Jess. "'This Goes All the Way to the Queen': The Puzzle Book That Drove England to Madness."

Acknowledgments

Thank you to my mom, my daughters, and my uncle Charles for adding artwork to this book. I'm grateful for permission from my family to include chapters from Walter Hunt's work.

Thank you to Pratt Institute, Bard College, St. Francis College, the Peter S. Reed Foundation, Jeannette Haien Ballard, MacDowell, the New York Foundation for the Arts, and the John Simon Guggenheim Foundation. Thank you to P. J. Mark, Jenna Johnson, Ian Bonaparte, Lianna Culp, Brian Gittis, Alex Merto, and Gretchen Achilles for your steady guidance, wisdom, and creativity. Thank you to Lauren Kern for help with "There Is Only One Direction." Thank you to Henry Freeland for help with "Queer Theorem." Thanks to all the Hunts, Nolans, and Hagans.

Earlier versions of some of these essays appeared in *New York Magazine*, *Literary Hub*, and *Lapham's Quarterly*.

A List of Illustrations